Burlesque
In a Nutshell

David,
Enjoy....
Dusty Sage

Dusty Sage

Burlesque

In a Nutshell

Girls, Gimmicks & Gags

by **Dusty Sage**

BearManor Media
2016

Contents

Dedication

THIS BOOK IS DEDICATED to everyone who ever graced a Burlesque stage and to all those who worked behind the scenes to breathe life into a Burlesque show.

The strippers, the chorus girls, the comics, the straight men and talking women, the light men, the stage managers and stage hands, the musicians, the wardrobe ladies and seamstresses, the choreographers and dance directors, the prop-men, scenery builders, painters and electricians, the fly men who pulled the ropes that raised the curtains, the Candy Butchers, the box-office attendants and ushers, and last but not least, the theatrical agents who kept the theaters booked with talent.

Special thanks to my friends Jennie Lee and Dixie Evans, and to all my close stripper friends from Exotic World; especially to Stacy Farrell, Jeanine France, Tanayo, Jeannie Anderson, Sheila Rae, and my partner in mischief-making and honorary member Barb Burrows. Extra special thanks to Electra and Mitzi Sinclair for letting me interview them over and over; for sharing their wonderful photos with me and never tiring of Burlesque talk.

Very big thanks to everyone I interviewed. Without them I wouldn't have this book. A special thank you to my close friend Charlie Arroyo, who became owner of Exotic World after his wife Jennie Lee, died. Charlie gave me carte blanche to research everything in The Exotic World Museum, and he patiently answered all my questions.

A standing ovation for my publisher Ben Ohmart for his faith in my book, and to my proofreader and dear friend, ex-Go-Go dancer and fellow animal rescuer Debb Brenton, for her help and encouragement in writing this book. She's the gal who glued this book together, one page at a time.

Heartfelt thanks to my dear friend Lynn Crowe for putting up with my constant chatter about this book; who's in it, and what they did and did not do. Thanks for the hankie when I got weepy. That goes double for my bosom buddies Ben Urish and Yvette Paris, who wrote and called long-distance monthly with well-appreciated encouragement and contributions.

My biggest thanks and probably the most important, go to my long-suffering husband Don, for pulling double-duty with our rescue and boosting my spirits when I thought I'd never finish writing this book.

All the proceeds from this book go to the funding of programs that assist in the prevention of animal abuse, and to help aid senior citizens in the cost of spaying and neutering their companion pets.

Foreword

by Ben Urish

NOT ALL THAT LONG AGO, books about burlesque, striptease, and strippers were relatively uncommon. Such is definitely not the case anymore. The neo-burlesque scene started in the mid-1990s, picked up steam in the early 2000s, and from then on there have been published socio-cultural investigations, historical overviews, coffee table picture books, neo-burlesque "how-to" studies, veritable encyclopedias of classic striptease, and a steady supply of biographies and autobiographies on strippers themselves. The volume you are reading now is a unique and welcome addition to that litany because it combines serious research, insightful interviews, rare photographs, and personal reminiscences.

In the mid-1980s, I was searching for comedians who had worked in Burlesque to interview them about their careers. After seeing a notice in a magazine, I contacted Jennie Lee at The Exotic World Burlesque Hall of Fame and Museum. Lee, a former Burlesque star and promotional business entrepreneur, asked me if I'd like to get in touch with retired strippers in addition to the retired comedians I had asked about, and I said yes. Through her I was introduced to another striptease star, Dixie Evans, who eventually took over running the museum after Jennie's death in 1990. Both women introduced me to many other Burlesque stars and I kept up correspondences and conducted telephone interviews with many of them.

In 2000, I was able to attend the event held annually at Exotic World to both raise money for, and awareness of the Museum, and I finally met many of the people in person that I had been dealing with long-distance. The event had grown out of Jennie's annual parties for members of the Strippers Union she had co-founded in the mid-1950s.

Working the Museum's gift counter was Dusty Sage. "You'll like her," Dixie told me, and knowing how much I admired Jennie Lee, she added, "She was friends with Jennie."

The gift counter was in one section of the Museum and Dusty was there with her friend Barb, energetically entertaining the event attendees with jokes and stories as they perused the materials that were for sale. Barb took some people to another part of the Museum and I introduced myself to Dusty. We chatted. I told her about my background and work, and said I'd like to interview her about her career. She laughed and told me she was interviewing Burlesque performers herself for her own project. I found Dusty and her witty sense of humor very appealing, and her stories fascinating.

Dusty was too young to be part of the classic era of Burlesque theaters, or even the Nightclub era that followed. But she was part of the "Topless Entertainment" revolution that broke in San Francisco and the West Coast in the mid-1960s and spread throughout the USA. She Go-Go danced, often fronting for regional and national bands in major clubs. ("Fronting" was dancing as part of the show in live musical performances, so named because dancers often worked between the musicians and the audience, i.e., "in front of" the musicians.)

The mid-to-late 1960s was also the time when many of the Nightclub era stripteasers decided to retire. Popular music and the larger entertainment scene had changed; some were hitting middle age, and the so-called "sexual revolution" made their style of performing seem passé or even archaic. Several stuck it out a while longer; some went into other aspects of show business, and most just moved on to something else. Jennie Lee herself ran a dance-bar at this time, and Dusty worked there, the site of their first meeting. Dusty met and worked with a lot of these classic Burlesque women at Jennie's establishment.

Jennie always wanted Burlesque dancers to be given the respect for their work and their artistic professionalism just as was afforded to other entertainers. By all accounts, Jennie had a rich sense of fun and loved to socialize, and it is no surprise that she and Dusty hit it off. By the mid-1980s, Dusty and Jennie were reacquainted and Dusty met (and in some cases, re-met) many of the now legendary strippers and heard their "war stories" with Jennie; notably at their annual Union Reunion parties that later evolved into the fundraisers I mentioned previously.

But back to what makes this book so special and unique. To begin with, Dusty has had a long and varied career and this is not her first foray into professional writing. For years she wrote a popular column for *Easyriders* magazine as well as modeling for them in ads, layouts and cover shoots. She developed a pithy, yet conversational style of writing that keeps the readers' attention with just the right details, and lets the subjects' personalities keep the focus.

Much more importantly, however, is that Dusty became an "accidental anthropologist." Anthropologists are supposed to try and be both insiders and outsiders of the people and cultures that they document. They must be insiders, to fully know and appreciate the people on their own terms; and outsiders, to be able to see the bigger picture with some objective clarity. Dusty's work here meets these criteria wonderfully.

Dusty's background as a striptease and topless entertainer made her something of an insider to her older subjects. She encountered similar people and situations in her career, and she knew what it was like to be on the stage nude or semi-nude. She generally knew what they were talking about. And yet, she was a product of a later age—she wasn't quite one of them, not exactly. She hadn't toured the Burlesque Theater Wheels or dealt with the famous booking agents. She danced, but the bands and the music, and the costuming were of a different sort. And so, she was simultaneously an insider and an outsider.

Dusty both participated and observed, as a good anthropologist is supposed to do. Her respect and admiration for her subjects is clear. She sets them up and gives them the spotlight one more time, getting out of their way and letting them speak for themselves. Her perspective in shaping their stories makes this a sterling addition to the publications on Striptease and Burlesque, old and new.

I stated that Jennie Lee wanted Burlesque performers to be given the same respect for their professional work as is given to other entertainers. In this volume, Dusty Sage does just that. Jennie would be proud of her friend.

~ Ben Urish

Ben Urish is a Culturologist specializing in popular culture studies. His article "Narrative Striptease in The Nightclub Era" was published in the Journal of American Culture *and he is the co-editor of the book* The Dynamics of Interconnections in Popular Culture(s).

Introduction

THIS BOOK IS NOT INTENDED to be just another History of Burlesque. It is about my friendships with the strippers of the 1930s, 1940s, and 1950s. It's about being a part of Exotic World and a member of The League of Exotic Dancers. Plus, over twenty years of research, boxes of letters, well over one thousand photos and candid shots and thirty-seven taped interviews with wonderful, remarkable, and unforgettable people, who made Burlesque the fascinating subject it is and will remain.

The concept of this book began when I renewed my acquaintance with Jennie Lee the "Bazoom Girl" and founder of The League of Exotic Dancers of America. I had been a dancer from 1964 until 1973, and worked for Jennie at her Sassy Lassy club in San Pedro, California. In 1987, I saw a newspaper article about Exotic World and realized she lived very close to me. I left a message on her machine. From that simple phone call, my world would be shared with sparkling, effervescent, and sometimes intoxicating conversations about pasties, G-strings, camaraderie, and what life was like for a stripper.

When Jennie called me back, the first words she spoke were: "I heard you were one of us." I wasn't quite sure what "one of us" meant. Since I've done a few things I won't admit to, I was apprehensive about answering. Jennie soon clarified her meaning. Afterwards, she remembered me and invited me to her upcoming Thirtieth Exotic Dancers League Reunion at her Exotic World Ranch in Helendale, California.

It was the thrill of a lifetime for me. Jennie asked me to bring a photo of myself, and something from my dancing days to donate to the Museum she was putting together. So I brought my favorite pair of florescent orange pasties in a little gold box. She took it, smiled and said, "What? No tassels?" Just like that, we bonded. It was Jennie's way of welcoming me into her circle of friends. God bless her bigger-than-life heart.

1

At the reunion I met Dixie Evans, Jeanine France, Stacy Farrell, Flame O'Neil, and Jeannie Anderson, who is one of Jennie's closest buddies. I would've eaten a bug to get these great gals to like me. Lucky for vegetarian me – I didn't have to.

Jennie and I got together for lunch and happenings at her ranch many times before cancer prevented her from doing the things she loved.

After I retired from dancing, I wrote a monthly column in *Easyriders* motorcycle magazine for twelve years. In the 1960s, Jennie Lee wrote a column for *Confidential Flash* called "Who's Who in Bur-Le-Q". It soon became apparent to both Jennie and me that with Jennie's help, I could write a book about strippers. She enjoyed showing me old photos of herself and other strippers. Jennie gave me many of the photos in this book. She turned me on to phone numbers of other strippers, which she felt would be helpful. Being part of a project, Jennie temporarily forgot her terrible illness. She was a joy to be around.

Sadly, Jennie passed away from cancer on March 2, 1990. Afterwards, Dixie Evans took over Exotic World for Jennie and Jennie's husband Charles Arroyo. She too, took me under her feathered boa wings.

In August of 1994, I received a letter from Jane Briggeman. Jane, along with her twelve-year-old cat Rosie, had moved from Wisconsin to rent a bungalow from Dixie and Charlie at Exotic World. Jane was taking Dixie to lunch for her birthday and wanted me to tag along. She had seen me with Dixie on one of the *Jenny Jones* TV shows and wanted to meet me.

During the lunch we discovered both Jane and I were researching Burlesque with the intention of writing about it. We became friends, sharing research data, and even flying together for in-person interviews.

Somewhere along the way, I stopped working on my book. There simply were not enough hours in the day. I worked part-time for the county resources looking after the elderly and handicapped. My nonprofit animal rescue consumed whatever energy and time I had left. I also worked with Hospice, caring for the companion animals that their owners were no longer able to manage. Sometimes I would have to find new homes for their pets. During my sabbatical from writing this book, my organization rescued and found forever homes for over two hundred dogs, cats, goats, horses, bunnies, and even desert tortoises.

You will be surprised to learn how many strippers are involved in animal rescue. These women may have big boobs, but beneath them beats an even bigger, compassionate heart. Although I no longer do rescue work, these ladies will forever be special to me.

Jane went on to form her own nonprofit in the form of The Golden Days of Burlesque Historical Society. She then wrote several absolutely wonderful books. Her book *Burlesque: Legendary Stars of the Stage* is not only informative, but a beautiful coffee table book. Jane's second title, *Burlesque: A Living History* is dynamite, as is the second edition of *Burlesque: Legendary Stars of the Stage*. Anyone who is an aficionado of Burlesque should read her books. They are real keepers.

Because of my earlier collaboration with Jane Briggeman, we have befriended and interviewed some of the same people. Therefore, you will be reading about a few of these people from two different perspectives. Mine is through a dancer/writer's point of view, and Jane's from a writers approach.

In August 2013, Dixie Evans passed away. This brought back a flood of memories, along with a flood of tears. I unpacked all her letters, re-reading them many times. Several of them made mention of the book I wanted to write. She wrote; *please finish it,* in several of her letters.

I started listening to my thirty-seven taped interviews, many with tears rolling down my face. So many of these girls are gone now, but their stories were waiting to be told. After digging through box after box of research, photos, and letters, I knew I had to finish my book.

For nearly twenty years I've been a part of Exotic World and its inhabitants. It really has been one hell of a journey! I treasure every moment I've shared with these gorgeous gals who opened up and befriended me. From the bottom of my heart, thank you, ladies, one and all!

Abraham Bennett Minsky (1880-1949). Photo courtesy of Authors Collection.

Michael William Minsky (1887-1932). Photo courtesy of Authors Collection.

Herbert Kay Minsky (1891-1956). Photo courtesy of Authors Collection.

Morton Minsky (1902-1987). Promo shot of Morton as Technical Advisor on the set for the 1968 film *The Night They Raided Minskys*. Photo courtesy of Authors Collection.

Chapter 1

Life Begins at Minsky's

THE NAME MINSKY is legendary in the history of Burlesque. Minsky's Theatres and their unique approach to Burlesque entertainment were revolutionary. The four Minsky brothers represented the Minsky Mystique, which was synonymous with the Burlesque theaters of America. The Minsky brothers were literally the first and last Dynasty in the history of Burlesque.

In 1912, Louis Minsky, the family patriarch, whose father was a Russian Jewish Rabbi, built a complex of two theaters on Houston Street in Manhattan's lower East Side. The street level theater was leased to the great Yiddish performers of that time, but the roof theater remained vacant. So Louis suggested that his two oldest sons, Abe and Billy, take it over and use it to show silent films. The theater was called The National Winter Garden and for a while, its business flourished. Then, the big movie circuits formed and independent operators like Abe and Billy couldn't compete with the larger companies. So the two Minsky brothers switched over to Vaudeville and in 1917, they presented their first Burlesque show. The public's response was one of immediate approval regarding the Minsky flair for showmanship and their ability to spot talent.

Abe was the playboy of the four brothers. In the 1920s, he traveled to Paris, France, to see how they ran the Follies Bergere and the Moulin Rouge. He brought back the concept of the Burlesque Runway. Although it was originally adapted to compensate for poor stage lighting, it proved to be enormously popular with audiences and eventually became a fixture in all of the early Burlesque theaters. In 1909, before his Burlesque venture, Abe ran a number of small storefront Nickelodeons, viewing short silent films that were in vogue between 1905 and 1915. The entry cost was a nickel, hence the name Nickelodeon. Eventually, these little movie houses became the precursor to larger, more lavish movie theaters.

Billy was the showman, and he likened himself to Broadway Impresarios Florenz Ziegfeld and George White. Naturally, the Minsky's couldn't compete with the lavish and dazzling productions put on by those seasoned producers. Still, Billy's lifestyle was one of flamboyance and extravagance. He wore a tuxedo to every Burlesque performance and showered gifts of jewelry, furs, and new automobiles on his wife Mary, the former Mary Kaufman. Billy once gifted Mary with a big, bright yellow Packard touring car. The car had been custom built for baseball's Babe Ruth, who had refused to accept it because it was too garish for his taste.

Billy had been a reporter on Ralph Pulitzer's *New York World*; he was aggressive and shrewd. To give an example of Billy's ingenuity: while working as a reporter, his assignment was finding access to the press-barred wealthy Vanderbilt's wedding. Billy devised a scheme to gain entry disguised as a florist's delivery boy. It was just one of Billy's many journalistic stunts.

A few years later, after graduating from New York's Columbia University of Law, Herbert joined in the Minsky enterprise. Herbert was mild-mannered and aesthetic with a love for Opera. He was the quiet but deliberate legal consultant for the business. One gets a sense of Herbert's influence on the Minsky Theatres in the smooth voices of their "Singing Emcees." Dexter Maitland, Paul West, Connie Ryan, and Herbert's favorite singer Robert Alda, serenaded the lovely chorines as they paraded back and forth across the stage, with songs like "A Pretty Girl Is Like A Melody."

Singing Emcee on an elaborate stage with a line of chorus girls (circa 1938).
Photo courtesy of Authors Collection.

Morton, the youngest, had also graduated from Columbia University, and threw his knowledge for running a business into the Minsky mix. Morton had a gift for writing clever advertisements, which piqued the public's curiosity and made them want a peek or two for themselves. He ran a series of Minsky publicity ads in *The New Yorker* magazine that showed a certain style of sophistication, which brought societies intelligentsia in for a racy romp, while rubbing elbows with the working class; and they loved it.

Frequent Minsky attendees were Writer and Actor Robert Benchley, with his monogrammed flask full of bath tub gin; Financer Otto Kahn, Critic Edmund Wilson, Publisher Conde Nast, Artist Reginald Marsh, and a bevy of New York Professors who regularly donned their top hats and tails for a night of comedy and cuties.

In the 1900s, daring darlings displayed their charms demurely with a wiggle and a wink, while wearing enough clothes to ward off a winter's storm. Later on, around 1926, the bras and britches began to fall like leaves in an autumn wind. Flo Ziegfeld, George White, and Earl Carroll began showing artfully staged and scantily costumed chorines who were bare-breasted and posing on pedestals. Minsky tried showing the same type of undress in his shows, but with movement and lots of it. After all, it was the roaring twenties; why not roar? That's when, along with the raucous, ribald jokes of the corny comics, the city's political powers began a witch-hunt of censorship and police raids. Newspaper critics and lawyers pointed out, factually, that as far back as November 1, 1896, *National Geographic* was showing bare-breasted natives and men without loincloths. In the end, however, the public outcry was, "Not on our stages!" Lewdness and liquor be damned.

During the 1920s to 1933, Prohibition was enforced. It took some of the fun out of life and was soon replaced by bootleg booze and naughty-bawdy Burlesque. The radio blared out the lyrics to a popular song of that period called "Ain't We Got Fun," which states in part, "*Not much money, oh, but Honey, ain't we got fun. Times are bum and getting bummer. The rich get rich and the poor get poorer.*" The song summed up the general publics' mood, which worsened in 1929 under the shadow of the Wall-Street crash. Everyone wanted to let their hair down and forget their financial woes, which allowed Minsky's cheap and cheeky entertainment to prosper in the 1920s and 1930s.

In 1931, the Minsky brothers leased The Republic Theatre on Forty-Second Street in New York, right across the street from The New Amster-

National Winter Garden season pass and courtesy pass signed by Herbert Kay Minsky. Photo courtesy of Authors Collection.

Billy Minsky's Republic Theatre (1931). Photo courtesy of Authors Collection.

dam Theatre where Flo Ziegfeld was producing his Follies. Soon after, Minsky's became known as The Poor Mans Follies, where you could "Pay Less to See More." In 1932, there was Billy Minsky's Brooklyn Burlesque Theatre on Flatbush Avenue near Fulton Street. In 1933, Minsky's Park Burlesque Theatre opened in Boston on Washington Street near Boylston. By then, Baltimore, Maryland was enjoying Minsky's Palace Burlesque Theatre, and Miami Beach, Florida's Million Dollar Pier boasted Minsky's Burlesque Music Hall. Minsky also owned The Avenue Theatre in Detroit, Michigan, which was always a sell-out, as was their Adams Theatre in Newark, New Jersey.

The Minsky's later opened theaters in Philadelphia and Pittsburgh, Pennsylvania. Altogether, the Minsky name was associated with eighteen Burlesque theaters during their reign.

The last important Minsky Burlesque theatre was Minsky's Oriental located on Broadway at Fifty-Second Street. It opened December 26, 1936, with Gypsy Rose Lee christening the Box Office with a bottle of Champagne. Phil Silvers was the house comic with Julie Bryant, an ex-Ziegfeld Follies girl as the Star Stripper. *The New York Times* Theater Critic Brooks Atkinson captioned his revue of the opening show with "Minsky The Magnificent."

The lovely Julia Bryant. Photo courtesy of Authors Collection.

Program for Billy Minsky's Brooklyn Burlesque (September 25, 1932). Photo courtesy of Authors Collection.

Inside of Brooklyn Burlesque Program (1932). Photo courtesy of Authors Collection.

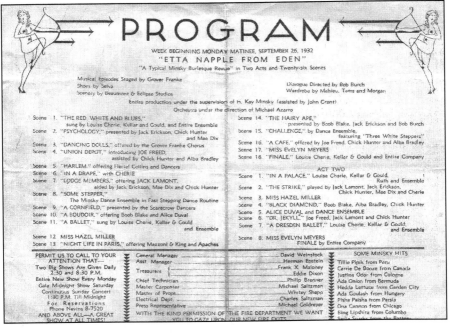

Program for Minsky's Park Burlesque (1935). Photo courtesy of Authors Collection.

Inside of Park Program. Photo courtesy of Authors Collection.

PARK THEATRE

PRESENTS

A SUPREME CIRCUIT TRAVELING SHOW

"TEMPTATIONS OF 1935"

A New Burlesque Revue in 2 Acts and 30 Scenes
Devised and Staged by PAUL MOROKOFF
Technical Director, PHIL BRENNER   Dialogue Staged by MELVIN HARMON
Costumes Designed and Executed by LUCILLE WEBSTER

ACT I

Scene 1—"Cherie"—Opening
        Aileen Melbourne, Lew Ross and the Tempters
Scene 2—Late Again
        Maxie Furman, Mervin Harmon, Alice Donaldson,
        Betty Rowland
Scene 3—Going High Hat with Mary Ellis and her Baby Dolls
Scene 4—The Auburn Flash .... Betty Rowland
Scene 5—Your Favorite Vegetable ...... Benny "Wop" Moore,
        Mary Ellis, Alice Donaldson, Betty Rowland and Jess
        Mack
Scene 6—A study in Silver Rhythm ...... Sylvia (the dancer)
        Assisted by Aileen Melbourne, Lew Ross and the
        Tempters
Scene 7—Personality Plus .... Mary Ellis
Scene 8—Cobbler and Son .... Frank O'Neill and Jess Mack
Scene 9—Moments with the Petite Rose La Rose
Scene 10—The Peppy Twelve Morokoff Steppers

PARAMOUNT GRILL

Just Around the Corner

POPULAR ENTERTAINMENT

Scene 11—Restful and Quiet .... Maxine Furman,
        Mervin Harmon, Alice Donaldson, Aileen Melbourne,
        Betty Rowland, Mary Ellis, Lew Ross, Frank O'Neill
        and Harry Rose
Scene 12—Lady of the Cellophane
        Aileen Melbourne, Betty Rowland, Lew Ross and the
        Cellophanettes
Scene 13—Flash—Flash—Dot and Dash .... Ideal Steppers
Scene 14—Sweet and Gorgeous Jean Lee in a Specialty
Scene 15—Two Pals .... Benny Moore and Harry Rose
Scene 16—Tempting Tempters .... The Morokoff Unit
Scene 17—Regrets with Pleasure
        Maxine Furman, Mervin Harmon, Alice Donaldson
Scene 18—That Bundle of Loveliness .... Louise Stewart
Scene 19—Song of the Flame—A Fantasy Modernique with 60
        Tempters

INTERMISSION
A Breathing Space to prepare you for our Great Second Act

ACT II

Scene 1—The Isle of Bali .... Sylvia and her Bali Eye-Fulls
Scene 2—Delightful and Glamorous Jean Lee
Scene 3—Hoke Discipline
        Benny Moore, Mervin Harmon, Harry Rose and Lew Ross
Scene 4—Speed & Ginger ... Betty Rowland and Morokoff Unit
Scene 5—Again we present Rose La Rose ....
Scene 6—Washboard .... Four Serenaders
Scene 7—Where's That Girl
        Maxie Furman, Mervin Harmon, Mary Ellis, Alice
        Donaldson
Scene 8—Flashes of Melody
        Aileen Melbourne, Lew Ross and Morokoff Belles
Scene 9—A Bit of Nonsense
        Benny Moore, Harry Rose, Frank O'Neill
Scene 10—For Your Pleasure .... Louise Stewart
Scene 11—Passing on Parade ...... All Tempters—Grand Finale

Presenting

That Royal Family of Fine Liquors

Crested   LORD JEFFERY   Brands

DISTILLERS COMPANY, INC.
Phone Capitol 5175-76

Cover for Minsky's Burlesque Music Hall joke book (1936). Photo courtesy of Authors Collection.

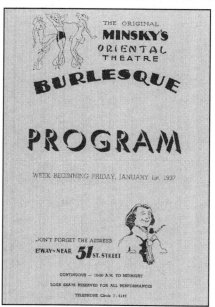

First Program for Minsky's Oriental Theatre (January 1, 1937). Photo courtesy of Authors Collection.

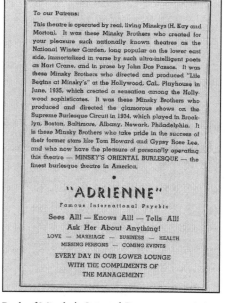

Back of Minsky's Oriental Program containing a message from Herbert and Morton Minsky, the brothers who ran the Theatre (1937). Photo courtesy of Authors Collection.

After Billy died in 1932, some of the sparkle left the shows. There were minor legal problems and threats of raids that often plagued the Minsky's, but none that legal-eagle Herbert Minsky couldn't handle. Then, the great success of The Oriental Theatre became short-lived after power hungry, puritanical, 5' tall New York Mayor Fiorello La Guardia decided to censor and eradicate all the Burlesque houses in New York. By the end of 1936, La Guardia and his cohorts had begun their many bans on Burlesque.

Raid on Minsky's Oriental Theatre in late 1937. Detective, warning Paris Stripper Mimi LaRue not to perform her risqué Peacock Dance, or face jail. Photo courtesy of Authors collection.

Wire photo of Herbert, far left, and Morton with his hand on Herbert's shoulder, at the Washington D.C. meeting (February 26, 1937). Photo courtesy of Authors Collection.

On February 26, 1937, Herbert and Morton Minsky attended a meeting in Washington D.C. with the House Immigration Committee on the "Art of Striptease." They met with Representatives Samuel Dickstein, J. Will Taylor, and John H. Kerr. Herbert Minsky declared, "The shapely stripper must be taught by specialists," adding, "Burlesque is as American as apple pie."

In 1932, after Billy died, Abe split with Herbert and Morton. He ran several Burlesque theaters on his own, including The New Gotham.

On April 30, 1937, the local Police Department was alerted that a stripper at Minsky's New Gotham Theatre in New York's Harlem was seen dancing without a G-String. That evening a raid ensued, resulting in several arrests. The Manager and girls were hauled off in paddy wagons and forced to appear in court the following day.

When I interviewed Joey Fay he said, "In my opinion, Abe's wife Molly was partly responsible for shutting down Minsky's because she kept telling the girls to take more off.

Mayor La Guardia and License Commissioner Paul Moss joined forces, and Burlesque Houses were refused license renewals except un-

Minsky's, shut down and guarded by a police officer. Photo courtesy of Authors Collection.

der certain conditions of impossible censorship. Furthermore, the use of the term Burlesque, and the name Minsky were forbidden on Marquees in the State of New York. Most of the Burly Biz moved across the Hudson River to New Jersey. It was the beginning of the end for Minsky's Burlesque.

Around 1941, Herbert Minsky solved their legal predicament by declaring bankruptcy on all of his Burlesque concerns in New York.

One of Minsky's Theatres in 1937. Photo courtesy of Authors Collection.

The Chicago Rialto. Photo courtesy of Authors Collection.

By 1939, Harold Minsky, Abe's adopted son, was running several of Minsky's Theatres outside of New York. Harold, who was born March 15, 1915, was working in several of the Burlesque box offices by age sixteen, and by age nineteen, he already knew everything about the Burly Biz. Harold was the last Minsky to participate in the Minsky Empire. In the 1940's, Harold Minsky fought to retain a license for Chicago's Rialto Theatre and a Burlesque house located on State Street, which he ran until the late 1950s. It wasn't long, though, before Las Vegas lured him with bright-lights, big-spenders, showgirls, and spectacular revues. After much success in Las Vegas, Harold Minsky passed away on December 25, 1977, in Las Vegas, Nevada, at the young age of sixty-two.

Chapter 2

The Original Electra

IN MARCH OF 1995, author Jane Briggeman and I flew from Ontario Airport in Southern California, to Reno, Nevada. We were off to interview the Electric Light Queen and the Man on the Flying Trapeze. At the airport, we were greeted by a seventy-five-year-old diminutive, Burlesque diva. Her slender, eighty-five-year-old husband Al Grey accompanied her. They just blew my socks off the first time I saw them! Electra was my first interview with a real live Burlesque Queen and one of my most memorable.

Jane and I took them to one of the clubs in Reno for a buffet luncheon. We could barely eat we were so excited. It didn't seem to affect Electra or Al's appetite; they both had seconds. Electra took center stage and we were her captive audience.

Al was, among many other things, a Caricature Artist and Photographer. On his dinner napkin he drew the cutest sketch of me as a stripper. I still have it. Electra told us about the local radio show she was on; reminding us the show had no knowledge of her Burlesque background. She used her middle name Goldie, and Al's last name. She mugged to a pretend camera for us, doing her witty version of a Mae West character responding to the local news.

Electra had bleached her hair blonde and had been doing Mae West impersonations off-and-on for about thirty years. She did shows for the Moose Lodge, V.F.W., and various grand openings. She also performed at birthday parties for the older set and some local T.V. shows.

Afterwards, Al (whose real name is Alfred Orlando Grey) drove us to their mobile home. He seemed so small, I wasn't sure he could see over the steering wheel! Yet, for a man his age he still had perfect posture. This was the result of all his years of entertaining atop a pole performing acrobatics, and being an aerialist in carnivals. He started out in his early twenties working in conventions, theaters, and carnivals. He even worked in the famous World of Mirth Carnival alongside a young Dixie Evans. Often times, he worked with a female partner who he held over his head while balancing on a barrel that rolled beneath him.

Jane and I took turns interviewing both Electra and Al, and looking at their albums. It was such an interesting evening for both of us. During my interview with Electra, she mentioned that they just don't put on big theatrical extravaganzas much anymore; remarking that the last time she saw one was *Splash,* which was still playing in Reno. My response was: "Would you two like to go see it again tonight? I've got credit cards; the sky's the limit!" Both Electra and Al were up for any adventure and quickly made us all reservations. What fun, taking those two stars to see *Splash.* To me, the real stars were in the audience and we were sitting next to them.

After we got back from the show it was late, and we were all ready to call it a day. Electra pulled open the convertible sofa bed in her living room for Jane and me to spend the night. We weren't alone; we had five of Electra's six cats to chaperone and climb all over us. Who could sleep anyway, after such an exciting day? I know Jane didn't mention my name when she wrote about this in her book, *Burlesque: Legendary Stars of the Stage,* but that's all right. I too, have forgotten people I've slept with.

Electra was born Electra Goldie LaValle in 1921 in Seattle, Washington, where seven years earlier Rose Louise Hovick, who later became Gypsy Rose Lee, was born. Electra's parents were Margaret Patterson, a French gown maker, and oilman William LaValle. Her mother's sister Mimi was already a Specialty Dancer in Vaudeville when Electra was born.

Electra's aunt Mimi was responsible for little Electra's tap and modern dance lessons at age three. By age four, Electra's mother took her to The Follies Theatre to deliver Aunt Mimi's hand-sewn gown. While waiting in the wings watching Aunt Mimi perform, little Electra ran onto the stage. She began to wiggle, shake, and shimmy, imitating her aunt Mimi. The crowd went wild! The little future star began to twinkle to the sound of "Encore! Encore!" The Manager hired Electra on the spot. He doubled Aunt Mimi's salary and Electra became part of her act.

At age four, Electra LaValle began her career in show biz. Soon she was dancing and singing, "I Wish That I Could Shimmy Like My Sister Kate." She took elocution, singing, and piano lessons, and performed in theater skits, singing and dancing her way across the states. Sometimes Electra merely did what was then called "cardboard" work. That meant she was simply part of the background in an act. Sometimes her job was singing while accompanying herself on the piano. Other times she recited lengthy, humorous poems.

Electra's father worked for the newly formed Texaco Oil Co., setting up new accounts across the United States and in Europe. Sometimes

The "Original Fan Dancer" Faith Bacon in her prime. P

he was absent nine and ten months of the year. By the time Electra was eleven, her aunt Mimi had met and married a titled man named Sir Roger Siècle. She quit the biz. So Electra's mother traveled wherever Electra's agent sent them. Frequently they would have several options at one time. Electra told me that her mother would often flip a coin to decide which way to go. Occasionally, they worked in places referred to as *gin joints* with just a curtain for a dressing room. Electra's mother Margaret earned extra money making costumes for the entertainers in Electra's troupes.

In 1934, Electra worked in the Streets of Paris Pavilion at The Chicago World's Fair. She met Sally Rand for the first time. Sally and Electra would remain friends until Sally's death in 1979.

Sally had perfected her famous Fan Dance, but she wanted to give her career the needed boost that would catapult her to fame and recognition. Her grand scheme was to do a mock Lady Godiva on a white horse. The day before the official opening, Sally rode through the Midway and onto the stage riding sidesaddle. She was almost as naked as the horse beneath her. Only her long blond wig and a very thin body suit covered her torso. The effect was spectacular! She was greeted with thunderous applause. The next day she was front-page news, including her arrest for obscenity. She performed her now infamous Fan Dance for the duration of The Chicago World's Fair. Her salary went from $75.00 per week to $1,000 per week. Sally was one of the biggest draws at The World's Fair.

Faith Bacon was the original Fan Dancer in the 1920s; however, there was a running dispute between Faith and Sally as to who actually introduced the Fan Dance first. Faith's career waned as Sally became more famous. Unable to handle the loss of stardom, Faith eventually took her own life by jumping out of a two-story window.

Electra told me she did "statue work" in theaters by standing nude on a pedestal. Sometimes it was called a "posing show" and was often done in carnivals. Because of its art form, it was deemed acceptable. The curtain would come down, the girls would change pose, and up went the curtain again. Electra told me, "You've got to have a good bladder, because you can't even raise your hand to go potty. You must remain perfectly still for hours at a time." Actually, it was a clever way of showing nudity. Flo field and George White Scandals did it, as did many other Broadway in the early 1900s to early 1930s.

1936, Electra and her mother were living in Albuquerque, and Electra joined the Cushman's Revue, which was con- man's Ziegfeld Follies of that time. She was in the chorus line with seven other lovely girls. She danced in the 1936 *March of Rhythm* at The Paramount Theatre in Chicago.

Wilbur Cushman and his wife Hazel owned the renowned School of Dance and Screen in Albuquerque. They had been established Vaudevillians in earlier years. Wilbur's claim to fame was acting with the Duncan sisters who played Topsy and Little Eva in a 1924 theatrical performance of *Uncle Tom's Cabin*. In the 1940s, the Cushman's moved to Hollywood where they directed and choreographed dancers for different movie productions. Electra was one of the dancers in several movies.

Julie Valdez, Miss America of 1933, was one of the dancing teachers at Cushman's school. Vivian Vance of the *I Love Lucy* show was in some of Cushman's Revues. It was there Vivian made a name for herself, singing her version of Fanny Brice's

Poser in fantastic costume (1930s). Photo courtesy of Authors Collection.

"My Man" and other torch songs. The Choreographer Pan Hermes and his sister Vasso, practiced in Cushman's studio. Pan was a self-taught dancer who went on to choreograph most of Fred Astaire's movies.

Electra toured with Cushman's Revue for a couple of years. It was legitimate theater with comics, novelty acts, and an orchestra. Electra's mother helped make the eight-girl Revue's costumes. In one such show, Electra's mother, with the help of the theater's electrician, hooked up flashlight bulbs to the girls' shoes. Little batteries were taped onto the back of the shoes. When the theater lights were dimmed, the shoes appeared to be dancing by themselves. It was a big hit. Both mother and daughter loved working for Mr. Cushman. Electra was quite proud of being in his different Revues.

In December of 1938, Electra received a letter from her agent for a lengthy booking starting in February the following year. The Golden Gate International Exposition would run for two years. Would she be interested in working in one of the Treasure Island Pavilions?

Electra took the offer and they turned out to be two of her most artistic years. She became "Queen of Illusionists." She was set to work in the

House of Illumination concession, which was located near Sally Rand's Nude Ranch. Both were on the Treasure Island section of the Expo. Electra arrived in San Francisco a couple of weeks early to prepare for her Illusions Act. The workers were still installing the twenty to thirty large mirrors for the grand opening of the House of Illusions. Her friend Sally Rand contacted her about working in her Nude Ranch concession. Since Electra was waiting to dance her Illusions Act, she would be happy to work for a couple of weeks with Sally.

The first day, Electra was handed her costume, which consisted of a tiny flesh-colored top and bottom, wide belt and holster, a ten-gallon cowboy hat, western neckerchief, and cowboy boots. There were forty other girls in the same outfits. All the girls were to parade down the middle of the street in front of Sally's Nude Ranch. Some, like Electra, were riding horses. According to Electra, "It was hell on the hinny!"

For the next three weeks, Electra worked for Sally behind a huge plate glass enclosure that cost $45, OOO to install. The gals were all wearing the same outfits, twirling lariats and lying around on blankets playing cards, shooting bows and arrows, and acting like they were living on a dude ranch in the nude. Holly Knox has written about Sally Rand's life in her interesting book, *Sally Rand: From Film to Fans*. I recommend it highly.

Archery at the Nude Ranch. Photo courtesy of Authors Collection.

Sally Rand and her rodeo husband Turk at her Nude Ranch.
Photo courtesy of Authors Collection.

For thirty weeks, Electra worked at The House of Illumination performing her Oriental Dance routine. It took her two hours to make herself look Asian, including six-inch fake fingernails. Her mother designed a fantastic Oriental costume. The five mirrors she danced in front of were placed in a half-moon shape and lights bounced off of them, giving an illusion of five dancers instead of one.

Electra in her Oriental costume. Photo courtesy of Electra.

During her time at The Expo, Electra became friendly with some of the swimmers in Billy Rose's featured Aquacade. Johnny Weissmuller was one, and a very young Esther Williams was another. Johnny was one of the world's fastest swimmers in the 1920s. At age nine he contracted Polio, so his doctor suggested he take up swimming to fight off the disease. His love of swimming stuck, and he went on to win five Olympic gold medals and one bronze. Johnny earned fame playing *Tarzan of the Jungle*

Electra's publicity photo used at the House of Illumination. Photo courtesy of Electra.

Electra's mock Parrot Dance. Photo courtesy of Electra.

in many movies. Esther was National Swimming Champion before performing in a series of Aqua-musicals in movies, where she became a star.

Electra was easy to be around. She had a quick wit, was friendly and fun. Throughout her entire life she loved people, especially show biz people. She made many life-long friends in the Burlesque community and considered them part of her family. While stripping in San Francisco, Electra worked with Georgia Sothern's younger sister Jewel. Electra was shocked when in 1948, out of the blue; the news came of Jewel's death from cancer at age thirty-four. Jewel had been one of Electra's close friends and she had long admired her dancing skills.

After the San Francisco Exposition ended in late 1940, Electra stayed in San Francisco for several more years. There were plenty of nightclubs, and plenty of offers came to her. Spring of 1941 found Electra working at San Francisco's Streets of Paris Nightclub. Besides doing her Specialty strips, she was the perfect foil to M.C. and Comedian Don Santo's antics. She worked in several of his routines as a Straight Woman.

In her earlier theater days, Electra had the good fortune to work with Gypsy Rose Lee and the ever-popular Comic Rags Ragland. Rags, who

Gorgeous Gypsy. Photo courtesy of Authors Collection.

had a knack for fracturing the English language, chose Electra as his Talking Woman instead of Gypsy, mainly because of Electra's small stature. This caused a long running rift between Gypsy and Electra; but because both Gypsy and Electra were from Seattle, Washington, Electra made a joke about it calling it "The Battle from Seattle!"

Electra was still working in San Francisco and Rags was still making people laugh, but now it was on the big screen. They had gotten together a few times to yak it up about their old Burlesque days and about Rag's ex-girlfriend Maxine De Shon. Electra had known Maxine before Maxine and Rags had been a couple. It saddened Electra when the tall and lanky Rags died so young, and at the height of his career.

Rags started out as a truck driver and later became a boxer; however, his real talent was comedy. He was a natural comedian who became Minsky's House Comic for years. He eventually went from Burlesque to Hollywood films and renewed popularity. He was beloved not only by his peers in comedy, but everyone connected to the theaters he worked in. Rags befriended most of the strippers and had an especially close friendship with Strip-Queen Georgia Sothern. He had been married to Showgirl-turned-Stripper Maxine De Shon. Sadly, Rags died in August 1946, at age forty-nine in Los Angeles, California.

Maxine De Shon. Photo courtesy of Authors Collection.

Electra, third from left at City Hall. Photo courtesy of Authors Collection.

Photo sleeve with info from City Hall. Photo courtesy of Authors Collection.

Electra worked at the many clubs in the San Francisco Bay area until the end of January 1943. At that time, she and three other strippers were arrested for lewd conduct. All four spent the night in jail. Next morning, they were fined and released from City Hall. This was a wake up call; San Francisco was getting far too bawdy! The girls were being busted without any real provocation. Electra finished her contract and left California.

Electra had made a name for herself with her Electric Light Act and most people thought she was using a stage name. She wore costumes made of Cellophane with strips hanging from a lightweight bow shaped like a half-moon. Tiny flashlight batteries were embedded in the bow. When the lights were lowered, it gave the most striking effect as she did her dance moves around the stage. Sometimes her electric lights covered her whole body. She regulated them with a switch, hidden in her costume or in her glove. She did variations of her Electric Light Act for over five years in many, many states. Her Electric Light Act was so famous; it is depicted in the musical *Gypsy*.

In 1950, Electra married John Ludwig, a good-looking Naval Officer. She told me it was her biggest mistake. They were married for thirteen years. She continued to entertain and was on the road much of the time. In 1963, Ludwig divorced her on the grounds of willful absence. Electra was relieved.

She took culinary lessons while working in Michigan. Her aunt Mimi bought her mother a restaurant named The Galley, in Rhode Island. It was right on the ocean's edge. Electra's mother Margaret was a widow by then, and Electra was an only child who was happiest near her mother. They both enjoyed cooking and greeting the customers. It was there that Electra lost most of her scrapbooks, her gowns, her costumes, her music, and even her life-sized cardboard image that was used to publicize her in theater lobbies. She was heartbroken over the loss of these pictures of herself with Burlesque and other not-so-famous friends. All of it had been stored in their small apartment attached to the restaurant. A hurricane took almost everything. She was devastated!

They sold the business, moved back to San Francisco, and bought three small neighborhood bars nearby in Modesto, Oakland, and Sacramento. Electra also had a children's dance school in Modesto and gave lessons. She met Al Grey at her bar in Modesto. They hit it off and were inseparable. Electra's mother passed away in June of 1989.

Electra and Al married September 7, 1990, in Reno, Nevada, and Electra sold all her bars. They bought themselves a mobile home, and for

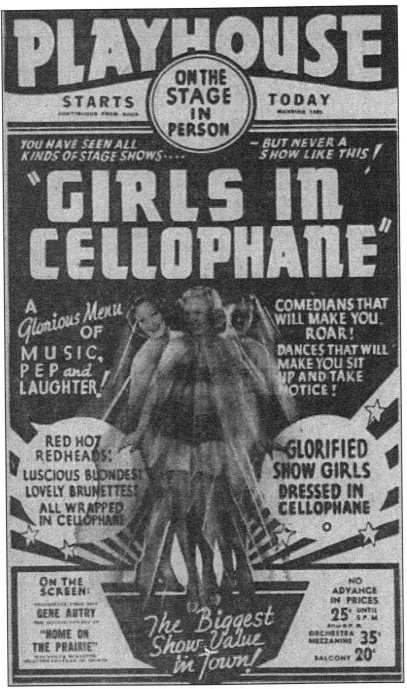

Club ad for girls in Cellophane in the 1940s. Photo courtesy of Authors Collection.

nine years they lived happily ever after. She always told me that Al was the love of her life. She said he was so much fun and could relate to her life in Burlesque. He loved her sense of humor and she loved his. They both loved animals. After I met them, they wrote to tell me they had rescued a small terrier dog. Al was ecstatic. He had always had a terrier that he would train for some of his acts.

We kept in touch until Electra passed away. Al sent me a card saying "We lost Goldie April 3, 1999." He always called her by her middle name. I was very upset, too.

I had just bought Electra a two-pound box of See's candy and I had it ready to send for her upcoming birthday. Every year since I'd met Electra, I had sent her a birthday gift of See's candy, and some mixed nuts for Al. The mixed nuts was an inside joke between Al and myself. Electra would always write to thank me and add, "Ya' got class, kid."

About six months after Electra passed away, I asked Al for a copy of her Death Certificate to verify some research. It stated that she died of heart problems complicated by her diabetes. I never knew she had diabetes or I would never have sent her candy. Then I remembered Electra saying, "I only allow myself one piece a day, and make it last a long time."

Al joined Electra March 8, 2001. He was ninety years young. Long before his passing, I helped him make arrangements with some rescue friends of mine near Reno. They found good homes for Electra's cats and Al's beloved terrier. Neither Electra nor Al ever had any children, except

Electra and Author (1995). Photo courtesy of Al Grey.

Electra in 1948. Photo courtesy of Authors Collection.

their furry ones. I still think of them whenever I see a box of See's candy or a can of mixed nuts.

Electra and I exchanged letters and sent each other small gifts over the years. I sent her some jewelry once. She wrote that I was spoiling her and sent me her sarong from one of her acts. I never did tell her it only fit on one leg. She had been such a little thing. It happens to be one of my favorite treasures. Another time, Electra and Al had to fly to Modesto, California, for Al's doctor's appointment and Electra sent me her house key. They were giving me their home in case the plane crashed. They wanted to be sure their pets would be taken care of. Of course, I returned their key after their safe return home.

I miss the many fun phone calls and the wee cards with Al's scribbled drawings of me. Their friendship was priceless.

Chapter 3

Mitzi

My friend Sheri Champagne introduced me to Mitzi over the phone in 1990.

Both gals were living in Florida and working for the same agency. Mitzi was seventy-three and Sheri Champagne was in her late fifties. They both did novelty acts for Captain Strip Telegrams, an agency who hired out older strippers for senior parties. I had heard so many interesting stories about Mitzi's life; I couldn't wait to interview her.

Mitzi was the easiest interview I've ever done. She knew just about everything involving Vaudeville and Burlesque. What's more, she loved talking about it and she remembered nearly every little detail of her long career. We talked for hours at a time and she would always say, "Call me again, soon." In-between calls, Mitzi would take notes to remind her of something interesting that happened at this or that club. She'd always say, "O.k. I have my cigarettes, my glass of wine, and I'm ready." Then she would laugh. She was so damned cute, even over the phone.

Mitzi voluntarily offered to put me in touch with her many retired stripper friends living near her in Florida. She even went to the trouble of calling some of them and clearing the way for me. Two times she actually set up the appointments. A few of the dancers Mitzi turned me on to were: Lois de' Fee The Amazon, who married a midget for publicity; Rita Atlanta, the girl who twirled in a tall champagne glass full of bubbles; dancer Diane De Lys, who was famous for her stunning interpretation of The Devil and the Virgin Act; and Evelyn West, the "Hubba Hubba" girl. As if that wasn't enough, Mitzi sent me a large package of wonderful pictures representing different periods in her career. Her generosity was over the top, to say the least.

Mitzi started her show biz career in Vaudeville at the age of three. While most kids her age were still hanging onto their mother's skirt-tails,

Mickey and Elsie McGarry working with the Mason Dixon Dancers in 1919.
Photo courtesy of Mitzi.

Mitzi was singing and dancing in her own little act. She was called "Baby Darling" and sang "Ma, He's Making Eyes at Me" to one of the band's musicians, who rolled his eyes and looked embarrassed. Her mother made Mitzi little costumes out of leftover material from her own. This was the beginning of more than seventy years as an entertainer.

Mitzi was born Florence Catherine McGarry on October 26, 1917, in Chicago, Illinois. Her father nicknamed her Mitzi. She was the only child of Michael James McGarry and Mary Elsie Lindeman, who together did a song-and-dance act on the Vaudeville circuit. Her mother's parents were born in Germany and her father's parents came over from Ireland. Mitzi was blessed with the luck of the Irish.

As a child, Mitzi grew up among many other dancers and singers. She loved the trained animal acts, the acrobats, the magicians, the jugglers, and she laughed at the comics in baggy pants riding on unicycles.

One of the first rules Mitzi learned about theater life was never to touch anything belonging to anyone else's act; especially the magicians, who warned the children, "If anyone touches my magic tools, I'll wave my magic wand and make them disappear!"

Mitzi didn't think her life was any different from any other child's life. All the children she grew up with were from show biz families, and most of them were part of their parents' act. The games they played were more about learning how to perform and take bows. Everything was about show biz.

Before Mitzi was old enough for public school, she had a private tutor and traveled by train with her parents and the Mason Dixon Dancers. The Mason Dixon Dancers consisted of three married couples, and featured Mitzi's parents Mickey and Elsie. The group danced on several flights of portable stairs. The routine was similar to Bill "Bojangles" Robinson's routine, the one he did with Shirley Temple in the movie *The Little Colonel.*

Mitzi's father won the title of Champion Soft-Shoe Dancer and a Gold Medal for Fastest Tap Dancer in America. Her three uncles Patrick, Andrew, and Ambrose McGarry were also dancers who did daring acrobatics as part of their number. Sometimes, little Mitzi danced and did small tumbling routines in her uncle's act. Mitzi told me, of all the acts, she always loved the acrobats best.

By the time Mitzi was four, she was working in the famous Gus Edwards Kiddie Revue. She played a bride dressed in a wedding gown along side a small boy dressed as her groom. The little groom would give her flowers, and Mitzi would smile and wink. The two of them would flirt while another child, who was dressed as a minister, performed the wedding ceremony. Mitzi remembered playing the role of a kidnapped child in one of Gus Edwards's skits. It was a melodrama with the typical mustached villain wearing a black top hat and cape. The audience would boo and hiss the villain, who would sneer and hiss back. In the end, little Mitzi would be rescued to resounding applause. Afterwards, the whole cast would take their bows to even more applause. These were some of Mitzi's fondest childhood memories.

German born Gus Edwards started out at age twelve singing in Burlesque houses, saloons, and Vaudeville variety shows. By the time he was eighteen, he was hanging out in New York's Tin Pan Alley playing the piano, co-writing, and hawking his own sheet music. Among the more popular songs Gus penned was "School Days," which later became his theme song.

At nineteen, Gus was part of a group known as The Newsboy Quintet who entertained the soldiers at training camps on Long Island, New York. In 1905, Gus met his future wife Lillian Boulanger, who became his lifetime theatrical partner. Gus started producing his signature Kiddie Revues that were centered on girls and boys in school. His wife Lillian played chaperone to the many girls and boys in his shows. He also wrote music and skits for revues that displayed talented teenagers. One such skit was the Postal Telegraph Boys, which included a young Groucho Marx. Other future stars in Gus Edwards shows were Eddie Cantor, George Jessel, Walter Winchell, Phil Silvers, dancers Ray Bolger and Eleanor Powell, and Actor/Comic Bert Wheeler. Gus Edwards died in Los Angeles in 1945.

When Mitzi was old enough for public school she stayed with her aunt and uncle in Toledo, Ohio. The rest of the year she toured with her parents, going from town to town and show to show. After the performances, some of the theaters would show movies as part of the "bill." Mitzi told me the performers children would always sit in the audience for a free movie. This also doubled as a baby sitter for the parents. She went on to say that sometimes she watched the same movie twenty times during her parents booking. She learned all the actors' lines by heart.

The Wall Street Crash of 1929 took its toll on Vaudeville. Theater doors were closed to all but a few Vaudevillians. Its low-cost entertainment was replaced by Hollywood's movie making machines pumping out cheap entertainment. The masses couldn't get enough of the "flickers," especially now with the arrival of the "talkies."

Just like hundreds of other Vaudevillians, Mitzi's parents couldn't find work. They moved back to Toledo, Ohio, where they started a small dancing school in their rented home. Mitzi was only thirteen, but she gave dancing lessons alongside her parents Mickey and Elsie. It was mostly neighborhood children whose struggling parents managed to save enough change for lessons. It seemed like every parent thought their tap dancing darling was headed down Hollywood's yellow brick road; in which case the weekly lessons were considered an investment. This kept the school doors open during The Depression.

Mitzi, accompanied by some of her dance students, put on small revues for hospitals and veterans clubs. It gave them experience working in

Mitzi, a seventeen-year-old dance teacher at her father's dance school.
Photo courtesy of Mitzi.

the public and put a few pennies in her pocket. After the repeal of Prohibition in 1933, small clubs in need of entertainers began to open everywhere. At 17, Mitzi tapped her way into some of the local clubs saying she was nineteen and small for her age.

Sometime in early 1937, Mickey McGarry contracted tuberculosis and could no longer give dance lessons. Mitzi was nineteen and had already earned three different dancing degrees. She gave most of the dance lessons while Elsie tended to Mickey's needs. The luck of the Irish ran out for Mickey in the spring of 1939. He was only forty-seven years young.

The 1940 census lists both Mitzi and Elsie as Dance Instructors. Along with giving dance lessons, Mitzi was still performing in local clubs. Her act was a Fan Dance and she became one of the many Sally Rand imitators. The only difference was the flesh colored body suit she wore beneath her fans. Since Sally Rand's Fan Dance had caught the public's attention and curiosity, all the clubs wanted Fan Dancers. Mitzi did this act locally for over a year.

Around this time, Mitzi met Harold Albert Micken, a local fellow her age whose family owned a market in nearby Toledo. It was a whirlwind romance and wedding that was short lived. Harold thought Mitzi would become a housewife, give up dancing, and work in the family market. It was too boring for a gal who was bottle-fed on show biz. Now she was fed-up with Harold. Without so much as a goodbye, Mitzi packed her costumes and grabbed a train heading for Chicago, Illinois. Mr. Micken was history.

Mitzi took a job as a hatcheck and cigarette girl at Colisimo's restaurant in Chicago. In the twenties, it had been a well-known watering hole for gangsters. A gangster named Big Jim Colisimo once owned it. He was gunned down in the doorway of his own establishment. Many famous people frequently dined or hung out at the bar in the 1930s and 1940s. Mitzi liked the work but wanted to pursue her dancing career.

In Chicago, Mitzi hooked up with Theatrical Agent Milton Schuster who specialized in booking exotics and strippers. He immediately saw her potential in becoming a headliner. Not only was she adorable, she was also a trained dancer who had personality plus. Mr. Schuster fronted the money for Mitzi's publicity photos, which she repaid after her first booking.

Mitzi reworked the many costumes she had used in her earlier Specialty routines, including her cute Can-Can outfit. Now they had to open gracefully, while stripping down to pasties and a G-string. She worked out newer, more flirtatious movements. She hinted at being sexy but was never really risqué. Sugar and spice, naughty but nice, that was Mitzi's style throughout her career.

In order to gain experience as a stripper, Schuster booked Mitzi into a club called The Avenue in Detroit, Michigan. One week later she had a contract as a co-feature. She stayed at The Avenue for several more weeks. Afterwards, Schuster booked her into another Detroit theater called The Gayety. Now performing as a feature, Mitzi was gaining popularity as a first-class stripper.

Mitzi's career was full speed ahead and her divorce was almost final, but she missed her mother; so she talked Schuster into booking her back home in Ohio. She worked the Ohio circuit until early 1942, when Schuster booked her into The Rialto Theatre in Chicago. Mitzi hit the big time at the Rialto and became a Headliner. She changed her routines and costumes every week. She created her own signature acts and was featured at The Rialto off-and-on for four years. The Rialto's Producer Paul Morokoff hired Mitzi for fourteen weeks at a time.

Mitzi's favorite act was the Li'l Abner and Daisy Mae routine created by Producer/Choreographer Paul Morokoff. This was an unusual Half-and-Half Act where one side of her costume was Li'l Abner and the other side was Daisy Mae. She also wore the Daisy Mae costume by itself, complicat-

Mitzi as Li'l Abner and Daisy Mae. Photo courtesy of Mitzi.

Mitzi as Daisy Mae alone. Photo courtesy of Mitzi.

ing the routine with a series of quick changes. The act began with Daisy Mae running around on the stage looking and calling for Li'l Abner. A spotlight would follow her and after a couple of minutes, Daisy would run behind the curtain. The spotlight would pan the audience searching for Li'l Abner while Mitzi changed into her dual costume. Then, a voice from behind the curtain would say "Here I am Daisy Mae," and the spotlight would rest on the two sitting on a bench. Mitzi would pretend Daisy and Abner were hugging for a while longer; afterward, she would end up behind the curtain again. Next, Mitzi would shed the Abner part of the costume leaving her as Daisy Mae, and return to do her strip number. It took perfect timing to pull off this routine, but the reward was often a standing ovation.

Mitzi was quite agile and sometimes she ended her routines by doing the splits. Throughout her entire life, Mitzi weighed the same as she did at age seventeen.

In 1943, Cupid came calling again. Mitzi married between the matinee and the midnight show. There was no time for a honeymoon and the most her hubby saw of Mitzi was from a seat in the front row. While Mitzi danced, her husband drank, and three months later Mitzi was a widow. He was killed instantly in a car accident.

As they say, the show must go on. Sometime in late 1944, Mitzi made her way to Hollywood, California, where she worked for Nils Granlund at The Florentine Gardens. The Florentine Gardens was a place where gorgeous and talented young show girls came to make a name for themselves, and where, a few years earlier, Nils discovered a young dancer named Yvonne DeCarlo who later became a movie star. He also discovered Lili St. Cyr and her two half-sisters, Dardy Orlando and Barbara Moffett. Gwen Verdon started out in the chorus line at The Florentine Gardens and in 1942, the movie *Rhythm Parade* was set in The Florentine Gardens.

The Florentine Gardens was not a strip club; it was more on the order of Ken Murray's Blackouts. The Blackouts played for years at the nearby El Capitan Theatre in Hollywood. Before Blackouts, Ken Murray worked for many years in Vaudeville and Burlesque. His show featuring Marie Wilson was a racy variety show with drop-dead lookers in the chorus line who could actually dance. Although it was more like Burlesque than a Ziegfeld show, it had a nightly audience that was a veritable Who's Who in show biz.

While in Los Angeles, Mitzi stripped at the Burbank Theatre with Betty Rowland, also known as "The Ball of Fire." She met The Amazon Yolanda and worked with Comics Slats Taylor, Harry Arnie, and Sliding Billy Watson, who was her favorite. She stripped at the nearby Follies Theatre for two weeks, where she met Evelyn West and Inez Claire. Inez was married to Comic Billy (Bumps) Mack. Mitzi also worked with Comic Billy (Zoot) Reed. Then it was back to Chicago for a return engagement at the Rialto Theatre followed by yet another tour of the Burlesque Circuit, also known as the Burlesque Wheel.

In 1947, Mitzi's old friend Paul Morokoff was hired by the Cavalcade of Amusements to produce their next revue, and Paul hired Mitzi as his feature. It was her first venture into the realm of Carnival Biz. Mitzi loved the people and the atmosphere. It reminded her of her childhood while

Mitzi and Helen Lovett on Burbank Theatre Marquee. Photo courtesy of Mitzi.

Helen Lovett. Photo
courtesy of Mitzi.

Mitzi in Can-Can costume entertains a group of service men at the
Hollywood Canteen in 1943. Photo courtesy of Mitzi.

traveling in Vaudeville. She eventually spent over twenty years amid the
Carnies, the sideshows, the big top, the girlie shows, and all the rest of the
ballyhoo.

In 1949, Mitzi was finally lucky in love. While working in a Girlie Revue for the Royal Carnival, Mitzi met Roland Dean Parker. He was a "jack
of all trades" who performed various jobs around the Carnival. Mitzi and
Roland shared a love for carnival life and each had grandparents who
came from Ireland. The luck of the Irish was back in Mitzi's life.

While touring the many carnivals in which they traveled, Roland
often worked as a Candy Butcher in the same audience Mitzi danced.
Candy Butchers work the aisles in-between the acts and during intermis-
sions. They hock small boxes of candy (chocolate-covered cherries were

Mitzi second from left performing in a Carnival Burlesque show. Photo courtesy of Mitzi.

Carnival crew, Mitzi, and husband Roland Parker holding a sledgehammer.
Photo courtesy of Mitzi.

the favorite crowd pleaser) with promises of a prize in every box. Someone was sure to win a gold watch, **IF** he was lucky.

Apparently watching strippers gives you a sweet tooth. I always thought a bottle of beer would go better with Burlesque, but then, what do I know; I was never in the audience.

These Candy Butchers were shameless shamans working the crowds with the magic of a medicine showman. They sold pictures of strippers and caught the crowd's attention with humorous one-liners. Working on commission, each Candy Butcher had their own style of salesmanship. Some of the better-known Candy Butchers became legends in the world of Burlesque and carnival girlie shows.

In the next fifteen years, Mitzi and Roland toured with different carnivals in the United States and in Canada. During this time, Mitzi sometimes worked under the name Mitzi Millions. The couple had their own girlie revues, which Mitzi managed, and for several years they were part-owners of four Burlesque theaters. In 1960, Mitzi sold her interest in all but The Folly in Kansas City, Missouri, which she retained a few years longer.

A Candy Butcher's candy box.
Photo courtesy of Authors Collection.

Mitzi and Roland enjoying an evening out. Photo courtesy of Mitzi.

In The Folly's glory days, only the best Burlesque beauties flirted and frolicked in the footlights. Only the Top Bananas fractured our funny bones with bawdy Burlesque skits that left us begging for more. Gypsy Rose Lee charmed them at The Folly. A very young Jennie Lee started out at The Folly with her "Forty-Four and Plenty More!"

Mitzi helped manage The Folly and she hired most of the strip acts. She hired her friend Evelyn West quite often; not out of friendship but because of Evelyn's huge popularity. Evelyn had a gorgeous face and figure. Her breasts were insured for $50,000 with Lloyds of London, adding the nickname Evelyn "Treasure Chest" West to her well-known "Hubba Hubba" girl title.

Evelyn, whose real name is Patricia McQunnlin, was more of a sexy walker than a dancer. She would come out fully dressed, including a fur coat and handbag. She did a little routine about her shopping trip and would talk about the skimpy unmentionables she bought, while pulling them out of her handbag and smiling sweetly. She would flirt with the audience, saying: "I know you're looking at my shoes," while she teasingly removed most of her clothes. Or she'd say: "I can't take it all off, I might catch cold!" She had an irresistible charm. Sometimes her husband would be in the audience acting like a heckler. They would interact with cute and clever banter making the audience laugh.

Evelyn cavorted on the Carnival Midway in 1950, proving she was a versatile performer who could adapt to any audience. She had a night-club act where she did a delightful parody of herself dating a wealthy man-about-town. For this act she used a Dummy named Esky. Starting in 1934, Esky was the little caricature logo seen on the cover of every

Evelyn West and her Dummy Esky. Photo cour...

ESQUIRE magazine. He was the archetype of the older, sophisticated and rich but risqué Playboy of the 1930s, 1940s, and 1950s. There is a similar logo on the old Monopoly game.

Mitzi told me that in the early 1950s, theaters started showing strip-tease film shorts either between the shows or sometimes during intermission. Mitzi said The Folly showed nudist colony films. *Sounds to me like a lot of healthy ladies having fun in the sun while the audience worked up a sweat.*

In 1967, due to Mitzi's mother Elsie's health, she moved in with Mitzi and Roland. This caused some friction in their relationship and their marriage only lasted until June 1969. They parted amicably and remained friends, talking over the phone almost nightly. Elsie died May 23, 1970, at Mitzi's Florida home.

I asked Mitzi what type of music she liked to dance to. Surprisingly, she told me her two favorites were from the early 1930s. One was "Dinner Music for a Tribe of Hungry Cannibals," which has the beat of jungle drums in the background. The other was "Chant of the Weed." *I listened to it, but I didn't inhale.*

In May of 1976, Mitzi took her last trip down the aisle and married Arthur Martin Sinclair, a retired Military man. I asked her how long that marriage lasted. She told me not long. She went on to say she never had good luck with men who weren't in the Biz.

Mitzi was in the movie *Lenny*. She played a stripper who helped manage the club and the other strippers. She was also in the movie *The Night They Raided Minsky's* and had photos of herself with Lauren Bacall and Laurens husband Jason Robards, who starred in the film.

In 1990, Mitzi and Sheri Champagne were both on the *Maria Lange* television talk show in Florida; the theme was older strippers.

Mitzi and Sheri traveled from Florida to Helendale, California, to perform in the 1991 Diamonds in the Desert Miss Exotic World Pageant. ⁀i performed her classic bump-and-spin strip routine to a recorded *Stripper*. She did an excellent rendition of a vintage Burlesque ⁀rm. She wore a big floppy fur-trimmed hat, a flowing ⁀when she was spinning, and long gloves, which ⁀ing them aside and never missing a bump. ⁀l a mean feathered boa and knocked ⁀. Sheri always wore a sparkling cham-⁀t was her trademark.. ⁀l one of her novelty acts. She danced ⁀someone in the band handed her a

esy of Evelyn V

telephone. Mitzi would act like she was dialing a number, hesitate while it supposedly rang and say, "Hi, it's Mitzi, remember me?" Then someone behind the band would say, "Who is this?" Mitzi would repeat her name and say, "Don't you remember me? You took me out to that fancy night club last month and told me I was a good sport." She would then say, "Yes you did, and now I'm pregnant!" Mitzi would act like she was listening to someone on the phone, stamp her foot and say, "You better marry me or I'll kill myself!" The voice behind the band would say, "Oh, you really are a good sport!"

Afterwards, Mitzi went into her jazzy dance routine and stripped down to a little top and bottom. The audience stood up and cheered. Mitzi may have been seventy-three, but she looked and danced like someone thirty years younger, and she did it with class!

Mitzi doing her Telephone Skit at Exotic World in Helendale, California. (1991). Photo courtesy of Authors Collection.

Mitzi performing a jazz routine. Photo courtesy of Authors Collection.

Later that year Mitzi, along with Sheri Champagne, Gina Bon Bon, Sadie Burnett, Dixie Evans, and I, did the *Montel Williams* television show in Los Angeles. The theme was older strippers who still strip for a living. I must confess Mitzi, Sheri, and Gina Bon Bon were the prize performers. The show was a big put on since none of us were actually stripping for a living. Dixie got us on the show so she could plug Exotic World and she did too. We girls had a lot of laughs over the whole thing!

A few months later, Mitzi and Dixie Evans did something similar on the *Joan Rivers* television show.

During this time span there was an explosion of interest in Burlesque on TV talk shows. Most of it was due to the movie *Blaze*, which came out December 1989. It was based on the life of flamboyant, sexy Stripper Blaze Starr and her relationship with the eccentric Huey Long, Governor of Louisiana. This movie resurrected the public's interest in Burlesque entertainment.

Almost all the stripper photos used in the background scenes in *Blaze* were loaned out from Jennie Lee and her Exotic World Museum. They had been returned to the Museum and were still packed in boxes in March 1990, when Jennie lost her battle with breast cancer.

Mitzi flew from Florida to perform at four more Exotic World Pageants. She was always a hit and was always approachable to members of the media. Many of the journalists traveled long distances to the Pageant, a few coming from as far as England and Germany. Mitzi was much appreciated for her cheerful, informative interviews.

Mitzi befriended Robert "Rubberlegs" Tanenbaum, a dancer who served as Emcee at the Exotic World Pageants. Rubberlegs had also worked in carnivals and ran his own girlie show.

Mitzi stayed with Rubberlegs at his home in Las Vegas, Nevada, while attending the 2000 Reunion of The Golden Days of Burlesque Society. She was thrilled to be among her peers, and in particular Val Valentine, whose

Val De Val, one of Mitzi's close pals. Photo courtesy of Mitzi.

mother was Mitzi's oldest and best friend. Val had been Mitzi's protégé.

Around 2000, Mitzi had a stroke. She lived through it but it complicated her capacity to maintain her independence. Rubberlegs willingly helped out while she stayed with him and his cats.

Sometime in 2003, Rubberlegs took Mitzi to The Exotic World Ranch where Dixie Evans looked after her. Mitzi was still able to converse with visitors at the Museum and enjoyed all the attention.

I went to visit Mitzi on many occasions. Sometimes we would go out to lunch or I would take her to have her hair done. She loved having her hair done. She called me once to say she was out of cigarettes and would I please bring her some? Exotic World was an hour's ride from my place but I took her a carton of smokes. She told me she found her cigarettes after she called and sheepishly asked, "Can we go have a bite to eat?" Now who could resist Mitzi? Not me.

In early 2004, while still living at Exotic World, Mitzi suffered a series of mini-strokes. On April 29, 2004, the final curtain fell for one of

Irma The Body, another friend of Mitzi's. Photo courtesy of Mitzi.

One last Mitzi. Photo courtesy of Mitzi.

Burlesque's best. She was eighty-six years young. Because of her looks and talent, Mitzi was a favorite with other strippers. She made life-long friendships because she refused to be a part of petty back-stage gossip and cutthroat competition.

Chapter 4

Three Special Stars

SHERI CHAMPAGNE

Sheri Champagne was known as "The Girl That Goes to Your Head." She was born Clara Green in Up-State New York in the late 1930s. She spent her first eight years in Brooklyn and was then sent to live with relatives in Massachusetts. She was the youngest of four boys and three girls. She dropped out of school in the sixth grade and went to live with her married brother in Virginia. Then, at age fifteen, Sheri ran off and got married. By age sixteen, she was abandoned in New York with a nine-month-old baby and only a sixth grade education; she had to grow-up fast.

While Sheri's sympathetic landlady babysat, Sheri searched the want ads and pounded the pavement looking for work. After a month of try-outs and turndowns, she was ready to throw in the towel, yet she knew she couldn't because she had a child to take care of. A friend dropped by and found Sheri sobbing on her front room floor. He convinced her she needed to forget her troubles for at least one night. He'd be glad to take her out. He said, "Make yourself look older; we're going to a nightclub. Pick ya' up tomorrow night."

Sheri had no idea that night would change her life. She piled on her makeup, put up her raven-black hair, pinched herself into a push-up bra, wiggled into a too-tight black dress, and stepped into a pair of stiletto heels. She looked twenty-one.

Sheri was surprised to find her date had taken her to a strip joint in a seedy part of town. It was strangely exciting to her as she watched the girls perform. Sheri had always loved to dance. When she was small, she used to wear a little green skirt and do the hula in her backyard. Her brothers and sisters would clap and encourage her to dance more. Sheri loved the attention.

While sitting in the front row watching an over-aged, over-ripe stripper dance, there was a heckler in the audience. The older stripper thought it was Sheri. She looked straight at Sheri and said, "If you can do any better, get up here!" Well, the wheels started turning in Sheri's head and she stood up and said, "Show me what to do and I'll do it."

The Manager was watching and saw that it piqued the interest of the audience. He started thinking; *this is good for business.* He took Sheri backstage telling the other strippers to get her into a costume and show her a couple of moves. That night Sheri did her first strip. It was sort of ragged, her knees were wobbly, and she almost fell several times from her stiletto heels. She must have done something right because the audience went wild! She was hired on the spot. Best of all, she'd be doing something she always loved to do, dance! Goes to show you 'gutsy' wins, and Sheri had enough guts for two people.

Sheri became a stripper at the Metronome Club. It was the start of a sixteen-year-old kid's career. She lied about her age and had her birth certificate doctored. Some of the girls at the club loaned her their older costumes to use until she could make her own. At first, Sheri danced under the name Taboo since it was her favorite perfume. She later changed her stage name to Sheri Champagne, her favorite drink.

A few weeks later she got a job at the Del Rio Club. It was there that Burlesque Producer Jack Montgomery, an Agent for Milton Schus-

Sheri's publicity photo. Photo courtesy of Sheri Champagne.

ter's Chicago theatrical agency, discovered Sheri. Montgomery's brother Howard was the L.A. Follies chorus line Dance Director, and had been for many years. The Agency sent her to Baltimore, Buffalo, Boston and everything in between. Sheri told me she was booked into the Shriner's conventions, V.F.W., American Legions, and Polish American Vets. *Wow, everything except Jewish circumcision rites!*

While dancing as a Headliner in Rhode Island, Sheri became engaged to, but never married Albert Perry, the Mayor of Providence. He took her to some of the Kennedy clambakes at Cape Cod. She met many celebrities at the Kennedys and had her picture taken with Bobby Kennedy. She was friends with Norm Crosby, and she worked with Frank Fontaine who played "Crazy Guggenheim" on the *Jackie Gleason* television shows. For a while, ex-Burlesque Comic-turned-Agent Jess Mack, managed Sheri. He was considered one of the best in the Biz.

In 1965 Sheri went topless; she hated it. She danced topless at the well-known Gilded Cage in Boston, Massachusetts, for a very long run. She liked to boast, "I was never banned in Boston!"

Sheri married one more time and had three more children. She divorced, was single for over twenty years and never remarried. In 1972, while living in Florida, she was picking her son up from school and was hit by a car going eighty miles an hour. She was pronounced dead at the scene. Lucky for Sheri, she was rushed to a nearby hospital where she was revived via a needle in her heart. She was later told she would never walk again, let alone dance. It took years of therapy and plenty of will power to re-train herself to walk, but walk she did; dance again she did, yet she never managed to completely lose all the weight she gained while confined to a wheel chair.

After doing Strip Telegrams with Mitzi in Florida for a couple of years, Sheri, along with her poodle Murphy, moved to Exotic World to help out Dixie Evans with the Pageants. She was one of the Emcees during her very first year at Exotic World. The only problem was, Sheri was sort of brassy with the younger strippers. I recall one poor little dancer on the stage doing some floor work. She had her legs in the air and from the knees down they were spinning like a windmill. It was fascinating to watch, as I had never seen anyone do that move before. Suddenly, Sheri grabbed the mike and hollered, "No spread eagle!" Luckily for the audience, the girl ignored Sheri and finished her routine.

Sheri and Dixie Evans did several TV shows together. They were on *The Sally Raphael Show*, *The Donahue* and *The Montel Williams* television shows.

Dressing room for Jenny Jones guest stars, left to right; Sherry, the show's two producers, and Miss Tanguray. Photo courtesy of Authors Collection.

Publicity photo of Miss Tanguray early in her career. Photo courtesy of Authors Collection.

Sheri was also on *The Jenny Jones Show* in Chicago with Dixie and me.

Sheri had a gorgeous red-orange sequined gown that I admired. She insisted that I wear it on the *Jenny Jones Show*. The dress needed some alterations in order to fit me. I told Sheri it might ruin her gown, but she said, "Who cares? You like it, wear it."

Sheri and I became close friends and she bought a small home in Apple Valley, California, near me. We used to hang out and get crazy sometimes. She liked to cook and often had my husband and me as her dinner guests. She made me the best vegetarian Thanksgiving meal I've ever eaten and she wasn't even a vegetarian. If she liked you and you didn't compete with her, she could be very giving of herself. Otherwise, Sheri wouldn't give you the time of day.

Sheri had one of those husky smoker's voices combined with a sassy Brooklyn accent. She had street smarts and was very competitive. When confronted, Sheri was someone to be reckoned with. She had learned life in the school of hard knocks and it toughened her up.

In early 1993, Sheri discovered she had cancer. She sold her home to a neighbor for half of what it cost her. She packed one suitcase full of clothes, boxed up her costumes and memorabilia, and drove back to Florida. She left everything else except her precious poodle Murphy. Sheri wanted to be with Al, her ex-lover in Florida. She knew he would stand by her to the end, and he did.

Sheri kept in touch with Dixie and me. She never complained about her pain. It was always chitchat about her dancing days, or the fun we had flying to Chicago, or how she missed us girls; and she always wanted to know what was going on at Exotic World. Once, she told me she was drinking Champagne; it was the only thing she could keep down, and then she sort of laughed at the irony of the whole thing.

Sheri called me the end of October 1993. By chance, Dixie Evans and Barb Burrows just happened to be at my home. Barb is an honorary member of Exotic World and one of Sheri's friends. At the time, we were making costumes for a revue we were getting ready to do at Indio's General Patton Museum. Sheri wanted so badly to dance in the show. We let her know what an asset she'd be to the revue. We took turns talking to Sheri about what costume looked the best on her and how we could help fix her hair. Sheri said her music would be "Hey, Big Spender," one she used to dance to. We kept everything upbeat. After we hung up, we all had a good cry. It was the last time any of us got the chance to speak to Sheri again. In a few months she was gone.

Sheri performing at Exotic World. Photo courtesy of Authors Collection.

The following year, with Sheri's ashes in a golden urn, Al drove from Florida to California. He brought Sheri's photos on a large memorial plaque along with her beautiful gowns, to put in The Exotic World Museum. Sheri had stipulated in her Will that she wanted to be put on display at Exotic World. Dixie promised Al that Sheri would always be on exhibit and she was, while the Museum was at Helendale, California.

Also according to her Will, Sheri chose the Exotic World Pageant as the day to place her ashes in the Museum. She knew the press would give her full coverage and she got it. Dixie was touched by Sheri's gesture and would always point her out and talk a bit about her career to visitors and the press. Sheri was always part of the tour.

GLORIA PALL

Besides stripping for Elvis Presley in the 1957 movie *Jailhouse Rock*, Gloria worked as a Straight Woman for Comic George "Beetle Puss" Lewis in several strip shorts that were filmed at the Follies Burlesque Theatre in Los Angeles.

Gloria was 5' 9" tall in her stocking feet; with heels she was six feet. Her height and snappy Brooklyn accent were the perfect foil for Beetle Puss, who was short and had to look up at Gloria. This combination was a great setup for all their Burlesque skits.

Although Gloria never had a career as a stripper, she was in the 1954 movie *The French Line* and the 1955 movie *Sinbad;* both with the famous Stripper Lili St. Cyr. Gloria played Stripper Sugar Torch in the 1961 movie *The Crimson Kimono.* Her scenes were filmed at The Follies Theatre in Los Angeles, California.

While working as a showgirl in Las Vegas, Gloria played Straight Woman to Burlesque Comic Hank Henry, who had been Robert Alda's partner in his earlier years of working in Burlesque. She later played Straight Woman to Comic Mousie Garner of the *Three Stooges.* Mousie and Gloria kept their friendship until Mousie's death in 2004.

Gloria was born Gloria Pallatz July 15, 1927, in Brooklyn, New York. Her father Jack Pallatz was Polish and her mother Pauline Cohen was Russian. While still in her teens, Gloria knew she wanted to be a model and a movie star. She worked as an airplane mechanic during World War

I just recently obtained this photo, so you all could see who the legs are attached to.

"JAILHOUSE ROCK"
An Avon Production - An M-G-M Release

Gloria, stripping in *Jailhouse Rock* while Elvis watches. Photo courtesy of Gloria Pall.

LEGS BY GLORIA PALL   Judy Tyler, Elvis Presley

*to Dusty
Just
teaching
Elvis a
few bumps
+ grinds
Love -
Gloria
Pall
"Jailhouse
Rock.
1957"*

Elvis looking through Gloria's legs in *Jailhouse Rock*. Photo courtesy of Gloria Pall.

II, but all that changed in 1947 when she was voted "Miss Flatbush" in Brooklyn, New York. Gloria bought herself a nose job to improve her already gorgeous face, and she headed for Hollywood. She was on her way.

In Hollywood, Gloria instinctively knew all the right nightclubs to be seen in and how to showcase herself to her best advantage. She entered a contest and was named "Miss Cleavage of 1952." Her first big appearance on the Hollywood scene was in the summer of 1952, at a party given for Marilyn Monroe in the home of Musician Ray Anthony. Gloria managed to upstage Marilyn by wearing the lowest cut dress on the Sunset Strip. It wasn't just low; it was slashed open down the front to her waist. Photographers grouped around her like bees on honey. Overnight Gloria became the most photographed newcomer in Tinsel Town. It wasn't long before she was noticed by dozens of photographers for men's magazines. Reporters wanted to know who the new sex kitten was. Gloria was quickly moving up Hollywood's stairway to the stars.

On her way up, Gloria graced the cover of as many as ten popular gentlemen's magazines including *Man, Gala,* and *Pic.* In-between photo sessions, Gloria modeled for car shows to keep herself in the public's eye. She got a big break as an Earl Carroll Showgirl in one of Earl Carroll's extravagant revues. She played bit parts in over fourteen movies, and was on twenty-two live television shows and sixteen filmed television shows. She was also a Showgirl for eight different Las Vegas nightclubs. She toured with U.S.O. shows and she worked as an Emcee while doing skits with Spike Jones on Spike's road show.

Gloria helped create, and starred in her own late night television show. The show was called *Voluptua and the Love Movies* and aired in De-

Gloria on cover of *Man* magazine (1952). Photo courtesy of Gloria Pall.

cember of 1954. Gloria hosted the program, which showed old Romantic B movies on late Wednesday nights on Channel 7 in Los Angeles. Gloria would vamp it and camp it while wearing sexy pajama tops or filmy nightgowns. Her come-on for the shows opening would be, "Welcome to my boudoir," spoken in a breathy whisper while lying on a satin couch. Sometimes Gloria would lie on a bear rug that would growl and roll its eyes. She wore a heart-shaped beauty mark on her face and her golden, jeweled, and mink-trimmed telephone rang "*Voluptua, Voluptua, Voluptua.*" Gloria would invite her male audience to take off their coat and tie, kick off their shoes, and get comfortable with her. At the close of the show, she would bid her audience goodnight by blowing kisses into the cameras lens. Gloria was burning up the screen, but she was too hot for suburban housewives to handle; they called her "Corruptua."

Gloria's show was canceled after seven weeks. It was considered too risqué for television and was drummed off the air by church groups, P.T.A. members, and irate housewives in fear of losing their husbands or corrupting their children.

I actually remember seeing her show, and by today's standards the sexy image of the show seems somewhat farcical.

Eight months earlier, on the very same station, the original *Vampira* had aired and was played by the sexy model Maila Nurmi. *Vampira* was a huge success and ran for fifty episodes. Glorias spooky spoof showed its fair amount of cleavage too, but the public wasn't buying *Voluptura's* bedroom scenarios. *By the way, Gloria and Maila Nurmi (a.k.a. Vampria) remained close friends until Nurmi's death.*

Allow me to take a moment to mention and memorialize Gloria's campy, vampy friend, Maila Nurmi. She was born in Finland in December 1921. She was a showgirl at The Florentine Gardens in Hollywood and a popular model seen often in men's magazines. Her facial features were striking, her body was slinky and sensuous, and she had a 17" waist. Her stint in *Vampira* made her a cult-figure, but it also typecast her throughout her life. *Vampira* was based on Cartoonist Charles Adams character Morticia, and opened the door for Maila to have more roles in horror features. One in particular was Ed Wood's movie *Plan 9 From Outer Space*, starring Bela Lugosi.

A couple of her companions were James Dean and Marlon Brando. Maila and James Dean used to hang out at Goggies Coffee Shop on Sunset Blvd. in Hollywood. They were both involved in the beatnik culture.

Maila was nominated in 1955 as "Outstanding Female Personality of the Year." Years later, she had her own antique shop in Hollywood where she

Maila as *Vampira*, voting for "Night-Mayor" of Hollywood (1954).
Photo courtesy of Authors Collection.

marketed her own line of clothing and jewelry. During this time, a woman in a beauty shop in Hollywood attacked her. The woman used a cigarette lighter and burned Maila's hair so badly she had to have her head shaved.

Maila was very much a cat person and had her arms badly burned trying to save her tabby when a fire broke out in her apartment. They both owed their lives to Maila's little dog Ratfink, who barked until Maila woke-up.

On January 10, 2008, Maila passed away of natural causes while sleeping. When she was found, her beloved tabby cat was lying next to her, having died of natural causes, too. *Spooky!* Fortunately, a friend adopted her little dog Ratfink.

Maila Nurmi's headstone with her etched likeness as *Vampira* (Hollywood Forever Cemetery in Los Angeles, California). Photo courtesy of Authors Collection.

Until Gloria's death four years later, when anyone mentioned her *Voluptua* show, Gloria became noticeably sad. She had always connected her show with Maila's *Vampira* show.

Gloria married Actor/Writer Robert Eaton in 1957. She caught him cheating on her and they divorced in 1958. Eaton went on to be one of Lana Turner's seven husbands. In 1965, Gloria married Allen Kane, owner of a Ford Dealership in Hollywood. The marriage lasted until 1983 and produced a son.

In the 1970s, Gloria had her own real estate firm that sold homes in Beverly Hills and West Los Angeles. The outside of her office, which was located on the Sunset Strip, was painted lavender. Everything inside was lavender, including her typewriters and desk. She dressed in lavender and purple clothes and drove a 1957 lavender Thunderbird.

According to her self-published book, *I Bought and Sold O.J.'s Home in Bel Air,* it was the home owned by O.J. Simpson and his first wife Marguarite. Gloria claimed it needed a lot of repair. She told me, "I bought the house in 1978. The kitchen cabinets looked like they had been punched in with a fist and so did some of the walls." She said in her book; "Never in my life had I seen or would ever see again, a home so rampaged, smashed and trashed. We fixed it up, lived in it for a year or so, and sold it."

Gloria also had her own self-publishing house called *Showgirl Press*. She published over a dozen small books highlighting various times in her career. In 1995, USC's School of Cinema-Television Library, and UCLA's Research Library, purchased three of Gloria's books. USC Library Assistant Ned Comstock said, "They chronicle an aspect of show business that you don't hear much about." Gloria was honored to be part of the collections and in with all the greats of the 1950s.

I met Gloria when I was on the *Montel Williams* television show. She was a paid plant in the audience. Montel let her ask us girl's questions about stripping. Gloria asked us, "What do you do when everything starts to sag?" I responded, "Pray a lot!" Then Dixie Evans said, "I know who that is, it's Gloria, and we go way back. Tell 'em who you are Gloria." So Gloria told the audience she was *Voluptua*. After the show, Gloria came backstage to visit with Dixie. I let Gloria know I was fortunate to have seen her show a couple of times while it was still on the air. We connected and exchanged phone numbers.

Gloria came out to Exotic World for several Pageants. She got on-stage a few times and danced around with her clothes on, just for fun. She did interviews, and sold her pictures and books in the Museum's theater.

Gloria in Exotic World Theatre selling her memorabilia and being interviewed.
Photo courtesy of Authors Collection.

Gloria in Exotic World patio. Photo courtesy of Authors Collection.

She had a lot of fun being a celebrity. She loved the attention and was very approachable.

In 1993, Gloria, Dixie Evans, and I taped England's *Jonathan Ross Show* at Exotic World. Jonathan interviewed Gloria about her career. Dixie talked about her life and did a little strip onstage. I schlepped for Dixie in my little maid's outfit; which means I caught her costume piece by piece in midair, as she tossed them aside.

I gave one of Jonathan's assistants my boa and she got onstage and did a cute mock strip. It was fun to see Jonathan's crew let their hair down. There was something about Exotic World that had that same effect on everyone. Everyone wanted to get into the act.

Gloria and I kept in touch over the years with many exchanged phone calls. She turned me on to Comic Mousie Garner, who was living in Las Vegas. He was kind enough to give me a taped interview. Gloria loved to help out like that. She often sent me pictures of her and me as a surprise. She was a phenomenal person and friend.

Gloria sold a lot of her pictures and books at Exotic World's Pageants. She always took the time to write special inscriptions to anyone who bought her books. She was delighted to be remembered by fans and sought-after by the media. She was in her element and it showed. I have several of Gloria's books and I treasure them.

Gloria at home in front of her Wall of Fame (2000). Photo courtesy of Gloria Pall.

Author and Gloria posing for the *Jonathan Ross Show*. Photo courtesy of Gloria Pall.

Even as Gloria became older, she had beautiful skin. It was the type Marilyn Monroe had; the type the camera loves.

Gloria passed away peacefully December 30, 2012, in Burbank, California; she was eighty-five years young. Gloria was mourned by so many of her fans. Hollywood's younger set saw her as a cult figure and to many; she was also a friend. Gloria died on my birthday, so now I place a lavender candle on my birthday cupcake in her memory.

PETTI VARGA

I met Petti in 1965 when I was working at the Club Pussy-Cat-A-Go-Go in Harbor City, California. She and Burlesque Stripper Jennie Lee were celebrity guests for the grand opening of the Club. The Pussy Cat was one of the first club's who served drinks topless. There were literally block-long lines of people waiting to get in and be served by a topless waitress! Petti and Jennie were a hit with the mainly male clientele, who worked-up quite a thirst just checking out these two sexy ex-stripper's tools-of-the-trade. Petti and Jennie even made an impression on the one other celebrity guest, prominent Attorney Melvin Belli. Belli came all the way from San Francisco. He discussed the legality of serving topless, on a live broadcast from the Club. He was also representing some of the new topless clubs in San Francisco.

Melvin Belli already had some Burlesque connections in his past. He defended Jack Ruby, who owned the Carousel Burlesque Club in Dallas, Texas, and who fatally shot Lee Harvey Oswald, the man that had assassinated President Kennedy. He even defended Burlesque Comic Lenny Bruce for lewd language and drug charges; and Stripper Candy Barr, who was friends with Jack Ruby, and was busted on possession of marijuana charges in Texas.

Well-known New York Disk Jockey Peter Tripp, whose radio show was called *Tripping with Tripp*, owned the Pussy-Cat-A-Go-Go Club. Peter was famous for setting a record by going eight days without sleep while broadcasting live. Peter and his wife Irene knew, and lived by Stripper Jennie Lee in Palos Verdes, California. Irene was a member of Jennie's Exotic Dancer's League of America, was an ex-stripper who was voted Miss Photogenic, and had been a Playboy Model. She was one of the Pussy Cats who served topless.

I remember how sweet Petti Varga was to all the girls who worked at the Pussy Cat. She often commented on how cute our costumes were. We all wore little black bikinis trimmed in fur, with little black cat ears on our heads and little black furry wrist cuffs, and black high heels. Every half-hour the jukebox would play Tom Jones's "What's New Pussy Cat," which had just been released. We were Playboy Bunnies with a twist. Some of the girls went so far as to wear cat-like three-inch false fingernails. *Not me, too hard to pick up tips!*

The Carousel Club shut down the day after Ruby killed Oswald.
Photo courtesy of Authors Collection.

That was the first and last time I saw the vivacious and adorable Petti Varga. She passed away before I had a chance to interview her. My interview came from Petti's daughter Linda Cooke, who lives in Redondo Beach, California, in the same house where Petti had lived.

Linda resembled Petti in many ways. She was like a small firecracker and totally positive about everything. She had her own hair salon where her mother Petti had often acted as receptionist and hostess. I met up with Linda at the hair salon so I could follow her and her partner Michael to their home after they were finished for the day. To be polite, I figured I should at least spend a few bucks on a haircut, and Michael gave me a really great one. *I was grateful Linda wasn't a dentist or I would've had to, at the very least, have a root canal.*

Linda and Michael were very nice to me, and so fun to be with. I took them both out for dinner and wine during the interview. Linda was tired and asked if I could stay over and finish the interview in the morning. She even fixed me a bubble bath and loaned me one of her nightgowns. She showed me all her mother's photo albums and let me choose a few pictures to put in my book. Later on, she had copies made at her own expense and brought them all the way out to Exotic World's Pageant the following year to give them to me. The distance is 100 miles each way. Linda was so much like her mother Petti; she went out of her way to be helpful.

During my interview with Linda, the thing that really struck me the most was not just the love, but also the sense of pride Linda had about her mother's life and career. As we looked through the pictures of Petti dancing, some of Linda's comments were, "Oh, doesn't Mom look cute? She was such a good dancer." "She made this outfit and isn't it gorgeous?" "Here's a tape of Mom showing her seniors class how to Swing Dance."

Petti Varga was born Dolores Maxine Boyd in Joplin, Missouri on February 3, 1930. Her parents called her Maxine or "Tootie".

It was the beginning of The Great Depression and like most people in the south; the Boyd's were financially depleted and homeless. They were fortunate enough to own their own tent, and lived in one of the many so-called Hoover-Ville tent and shack cities; all of which were located on the outskirts of towns across the United States. After nearly a year of roughing it in the tent, relying on soup-lines and handouts from relatives, the family moved to California in hopes of finding employment. They lived in a Hoover-City-shanty town before finding a small living space over a feed store, where they stayed a few years.

By age three, Petti's mother allowed her to roam the streets unattended. Petti was an independent little child. She watched the older kids singing and dancing on street corners for pennies, and imitated them. Sometimes she would wander too far from home and get lost, but she was never frightened; she knew someone would always help her find her way back home.

Petti's mother had two other children and showed the same indifference toward them as she did Petti. As time went on, Petti continued her role as mother to her brother and sister. She was a child raising children. Worse yet, Petti's mother remained silent while her father abused and fondled her from an early age on. Because of this, she was fiercely protective of her sister.

As the Depression lifted, Petti's father found full-time work and was gone from home most of the time. This gave Petti some freedom from the constant fear of her father's abuse.

By her early teens, Petti began a long-running battle with juvenile authorities to keep her siblings from being taken away from home and placed in foster care.

School was a welcome reprieve from her hell at home. She took part in every activity offered. She made friends easily and was admired by her teachers. Petti was Head Cheer Leader during her years at Compton High School. She was athletic, and loved swimming and dancing. She also had a really great voice and sang at special school events.

Eventually, Petti was no longer able to withstand the everyday drama of her home life. At seventeen, she escaped by getting married. By nineteen, she had two daughters and her husband was gone. He'd traded in their family car, an old milk-truck, for a motorcycle, and went on the road.

Petti had already started dancing, and with her adorable face and petite figure she had no problem finding herself an agent. Her new Agent Max Kirkland took one long, look at her perfect legs and derrière, and suggested her stage name be a play on Artists George Petty and Alberta Vargas. Both men were famous for painting those sexy 1940s pin-up girls who appeared in *ESQUIRE* magazine and on calendars.

Petti was living in Long Beach, California, when her agent booked her at the nearby Mandalay Club. Around the same time, he also booked her into the York Club in Los Angeles. Both clubs had very large upstairs dressing rooms situated over the stage. Some of the dancers took their young children to work with them and kept them in the dressing rooms while they worked at night. They took turns watching over each other's kids while their mother's were onstage stripping. There was even a play-pen for the toddlers. The children slept through the night amid beautiful gowns and bouquets of boas, with the sound of horns wailing and drums beating beneath them. Often times, a well-known stripper who was between acts would give the kids a hug or even change a diaper or two.

As an entertainer, Petti was in the public eye but she was very private about her home and family life. Because of her upbringing, Petti was overly protective of her girls. She took them to work with her until they were seven or eight years of age, before finally trusting them to a baby-sitter.

While staying at the clubs, the girls learned how to affix the adhesive onto pasties for their mother and some of the other strippers. They thought it was fun cutting the rolls of Johnson & Johnson's tape and twisting it over and over, sticky side up, until it was shaped like a snake. Afterwards, they slowly placed it inside the pasties, again in the form of a snake, and pressed it firmly so it would stay. Some of the strippers would reward the girls with a bit of spending money for their time.

While working at the Tattle-Tail in Culver City near the M.G.M. Studios, Petti met Tanayo, who later became "The Costa Rican Dream Girl." Tanayo was still going by her real name Maria at that time, and working as a hatcheck and cigarette girl. Petti knew Tanayo worked hard at her job selling cigarettes on commission. She asked Tanayo if she could dance and Tanayo told Petti, "I love to dance! Especially Latin dances!" So, for a few weeks, Petti and three other strippers at the club, Pat Flannery, Heather English, and Stormy Night, tried to talk Tanayo into stripping; but Tanayo was too shy.

Tanayo told me in her interview that Petti Varga was the one who got her into stripping. She explained how one night, Petti's agent Max Kirkland came to the Tattle-Tail to meet with a well-known celebrity who liked to watch strippers, and Petti cornered Tanayo. She convinced her it was her chance to get a job dancing for a lot more money. At that time, Tanayo had never had a taste of liquor in her life. Petti whipped up a costume for Tanayo out of some material from backstage, gave her a couple of drinks, and practically pushed her onstage. The band belted out a Latin beat and Tanayo was on her way.

Tanayo told me that while she was onstage dancing, Petti walked through the audience and sold all of her cigarettes for her. Tanayo also told me, "A week later I showed up for work and the Club had burnt down.

Tanayo. Photo courtesy of Tanayo.

All the girl's costumes went up in flames! Same story with the musician's instruments." The Club had insurance, but everyone else was out of a job and had no money to replace their losses.

Petti's daughter Linda told me, "Mom was a cheer leader in High School and never stopped cheering and rooting for others. Throughout her whole life, she encouraged and helped so many people." Petti's enthusiasm and genuine helpfulness did cheer everyone into bettering their lives. I know this to be a fact, having heard it from so many other strippers from the West Coast. During my interview with my friend, ex-Stripper Cindy Kay, she told me she considered Petti her best friend during her time in Burlesque. Cindy Kay said Petti's help changed her life and got her into a career stripping.

Petti onstage at the Zamboanga Club in Los Angeles, California (early 1950s).
Photo courtesy of Linda Cooke.

Petti was close friends with Jennie Lee, who she met while working at Strip City in Los Angeles. Petti was a Charter Member of Jennie Lee's Exotic Dancers League of America organization. She attended most of the Stripper's Reunions and kept in touch with Jennie until Jennie's death in 1990.

While working at Strip-City, Petti worked with Comedian Lenny Bruce and befriended dancers Jeanne France, Nona Carver, Stormy Night (also known as Fran Laverne), Sheila Rae, Sue Martin, and Stacy Farrell. She became very close friends with Lenny Bruce's wife Honey Harlow while they worked together with Stacy Farrell at the Colony Club in Gardena, California.

Strip City was extremely popular in the early 1950s, partly due to Emcee and Comedian Lenny Bruce, who encouraged hecklers in the audience to interact with him. Some of Lenny's best gags came as a response to remarks the hecklers yelled out. Sometimes the audience came just to be a part of the show. Each heckler tried to out-do the other hecklers and it became a contest of wits, with Lenny one-upping them all. Lenny loved to be baited, and it fed into his wild side. He would tell the band jokes and ignore the audience, or he would throw wild barbs at the dancers while they were onstage. This was his jump-start to both fame and infamy. He found his comfort zone and honed his style at Strip City.

Strip City was a continuous show from open to close, with no cover charge and no minimum of drinks; the only minimum was what the girls left on.

Petti stripping at The Colony Club (early1950s). Photo courtesy of Linda Cooke.

Stacy Farrell stripping at The Colony Club (early 1950). Photo courtesy of Stacy Farrell.

Irving and Murray Ross owned The Colony Club, and it was considered to be the best Burlesque Club in Los Angeles. It had everything going for it, including its location in Gardena. Mainly because Gardena is zoned for legal card gambling and it draws an enormous amount of people to the area. The Colony had dinner shows, classy strippers, and entertaining Burlesque productions. It had the talented Billie Bird, Bub Thomas, Jean Carroll and her Comedian husband Bob Carney, in residence. Billie Bird's Burlesque career began around 1930. In 1932, she was in a revue for the original owner of the Los Angeles Follies Theatre. Even Betty Rowland the redheaded "Ball of Fire," danced at The Colony Club. The combination of fabulous entertainers and great food drew couples nightly, and

Souvenir Mailing Advertisement for The Colony Club (1954).
Photo courtesy of Authors Collection.

earned a reputation as the place to take your date for a night out on the town.]

It was while working at The Colony Club that Petti established a life-long friendship with "Mr. Entertainment" Bub Thomas, and Comedians Billie Bird and Jean Carroll. Petti was not just a stripper at The Colony; she was in many of the productions and worked as a Straight Woman to Bub and Billie's antics, as did her co-workers Honey Harlow and Stacy Farrell.

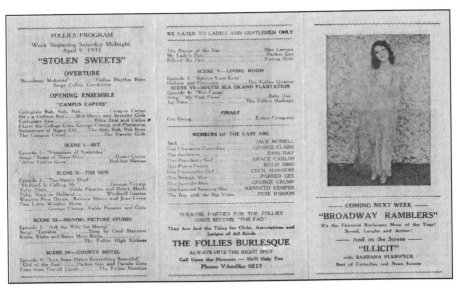

Inside of 1932 Follies Program showing Billie Bird in the cast.
Photo Courtesy of Authors collection.

Betty Rowland. Photo courtesy
Authors Collection.

After many years of entertaining at The Colony Club, Bub Thomas bought his own nightclub named The Roaring 20s, in nearby Torrance, California, where he showcased his Barbershop Quartet called "The Dapper Dans". Not only did he take Billie Bird with him, but also Petti Varga, who sang in his club after she retired from stripping. The Roaring 20s was a really fun place to be; almost like a neighborhood bar, full of regulars on the weekend.

Bub was a renowned Caricature Artist and did thousands of drawings over the years for the patrons of his club.

I grew up near The Colony Club and The Roaring 20s, and spent my twenty-first birthday at Bub's club. After checking my I.D., the doorman told Bub it was my birthday and Bub called me up on the stage and drew a caricature of me as a Gym Instructor. At the time, I was giving exercise classes at the Vic Tanny Health Studios.

Jean Carroll and Billy Zoot Reed. Photo courtesy of Jennie Lee.

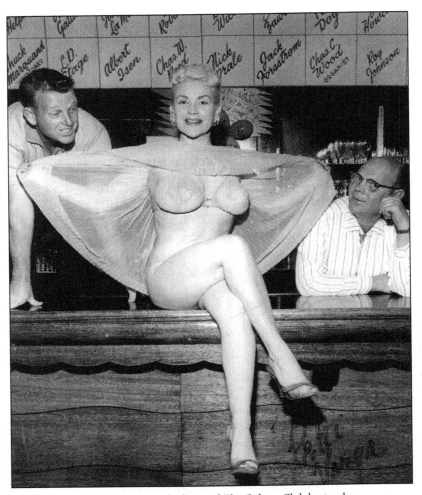

Bub, Petti sitting on the bar, and The Colony Club bartender.
Photo courtesy of Linda Cooke.

Because of her children, Petti mostly worked on the West Coast. She received several offers to dance in Japan with Stripper Jennie Lee, but turned them all down. Among other clubs, she stripped at the Wagon Wheel in Lakewood, The Zomba in Ventura, Top Banana in North Hollywood, The Cobble Stone in Ventura County, Joe Foxe's Lake Club in Bellflower, and The Burbank and The New Follies, both in Los Angeles. She also danced in several strip-shorts filmed at The New Follies Theatre with her friend, Stripper Sue Martin. Sue introduced Petti to her close friend and Costume Designer Gussie Gross. Gussie made several gorgeous, sequined gowns especially for Petti to dance in.

Petti had a nice write-up in the *New Yorker* magazine after retiring from stripping, and for ten years Petti did bit parts in the movies. She was in *Moulin Rouge,* in *Bus Stop* with Marilyn Monroe, and in the movie *Hair.*

In 1956, Petti had an admirer who came almost nightly to one of the clubs where she danced. He sent her flowers backstage, and other small gifts. As time went on, they began to go out for dinner and she found out

Petti working the stripper's panel onstage at The Colony Club. Photo courtesy of Linda Cooke.

he was a policeman. July 8, 1956, Petti and William Pete Ketterer married in Las Vegas, Nevada.

Things were moving smoothly for Petti in her new life. She decided to adopt two small children who were in need of a loving family. Everything started changing shortly afterwards, when a February 5, 1959 article in the *Pasadena Independent* newspaper stated; "Delores Ketterer, a stripper known professionally as Petti Varga, wins custody of seven- and eight-year-old adopted children from law officer spouse." *Imagine the mouths hanging open in that courtroom!*

On March 14, 1993, at the young age of sixty-three, Petti passed away. She raised her own two biological daughters as well as her two adopted daughters, and she did it her way. Those last five words should have been on Petti's epitaph. She was a one-of-a-kind gal and the Burlesque world benefited by her part in it.

Chapter 5

Odds N' Ends

CARRIE FINNELL

At the top of my list is Carrie Finnell, who was known as "The Most Unusual Act in Show Business." Her muscle-bound mammaries made her a fortune! In her act, Carrie would pull forward the elastic top on her low-cut gown, and make her bosoms bounce up and out, and then back into her gown. Carrie's boobs never missed a drumbeat. *Boom-titty-boom-titty-boom!*

For several decades Carrie was quite a popular attraction, and since her act was done with comedic flare, it was never in the least bit distasteful. She would peek inside of her dress, give funny looks and make funny remarks to her boobies and about her boobies. She made comments like "Come on out and say hello to these nice people."

Carrie had a very pleasant speaking and singing voice, and often sang funny, risqué songs as part of her routine. Her theme song was, "It Ain't What You Got, It's the Way That You Use It." She packed the clubs nightly with couples that usually came back several times and brought their friends along with them. Carrie called her act "The Chestcapades." Audiences loved it. In the 1946 World's Fair, Carrie had a bar named "La Do Bust Inn". It was considered the funniest bar at the Fair.

Taking a quote from Gypsy Rose Lee, "Ya' gotta' have a gimmick." Well, this gal had two! She was a large woman who weighed close to three hundred pounds, and had total control of her pectoral muscles. *While other dancers soaked their tired feet; I can't help but wonder what Carrie did.*

Carrie was born Carrie Lee Finnell November 14, 1900, in Covington, Kentucky. Her parents were Thomas Addison Finnell and Martha Finwall.

As a young girl, Carrie was a Teacher's Aid to a Physical Education Instructor in Kentucky. She helped give classes in physical fitness and learned how to develop her muscles.

Carrie went from Teacher's Aid to acting in small plays and later danced in several chorus lines. By 1916, Carrie is listed in the Covington, Kentucky City Directory as an Actress. She was a bit player for Culver Studios.

While performing in a Cincinnati theater, part of the roof caved in and Carrie continued dancing as if nothing had happened. Local newspapers reported that her actions may have saved the lives of those who would otherwise have stampeded out of the theater.

In the 1920s, she worked at Minsky's Winter Garden in New York. In 1923, an Ohio theater manager had Carrie's legs insured for $100,000 as a publicity stunt. She became known as "The Girl with the Hundred Thousand Dollar Legs." *Personally, I think they insured the wrong part of her anatomy.*

In February 1924, Carrie married her first husband, a Pollock named Charles H. Grow, who managed The Congress Theatre in Chicago. They were married for ten years and owned a nightclub in Kentucky named the Villa Venice. In January of 1930, a shooting incident at their club left one man dead and brought police attention to their illegal slot machines. The slot machines were confiscated and Carrie was fined $250, which was a lot of money at that time.

In Kentucky on June 5, 1925, Carrie gave birth to her only child Thomas Finnell Grow, whom she named after her father. Carrie's mother helped raise the boy while Carrie performed, not only in the states, but also in England and Paris.

Carrie loved children and was always buying presents for her coworker's kids, but she kept her son out of the limelight, and even most of her theatrical buddies knew nothing of his existence.

By 1935, Charles Grow was listed in the State Census as a divorced Musician living in the New Kirby Hotel in Ohio. Carrie's marriage was over, and by 1940, she was married to Thomas Morris. In the 1940 Federal Census for Munsey, Indiana, Carrie's son Thomas Finnell Grow was living with Morris's parents and Carrie's sister-in-law, Sadie Morris. Sadie was a seamstress and made some of Carrie's gowns.

At age fifteen, Carrie's son Thomas ran away from home, lied about his age and joined the service. It was during the Second World War; Thomas was big for his age so no one questioned him. He spent most of

Carrie onstage communicating with her moneymakers.
Photo courtesy of Authors Collection.

his life on-and-off in the service, traveling around the world. Carrie seldom heard from him. Thomas Finnell Grow died September 8, 1980, and is buried in Syracuse, New York.

The Encyclopedia of Vaudeville gives credit to Carrie Finnell for introducing the Burlesque routine of twirling two tassels in two different directions at the same time.

Carrie continued entertaining until October 1963. She was a Headliner in Mike Todd's *Star and Garter Revue*, where she worked along-side Gypsy Rose Lee. Gypsy and Carrie quickly became bosom buddies. Her last appearance was at Newport's Galaxie Club in her home State of Kentucky.

Carrie autographing a big-breasted mural at the Gay New Orleans Nightclub (1940).
Photo courtesy of Authors Collection.

Portrait of Carrie Finnell. Photo
courtesy Authors Collection.

At some point in Carrie's career she made as much as $2,000 per week. She was much admired for her down-to-earth attitude, and was generous with the chorus girls and everyone else who was in the Burlesque biz. She lavished money on her friends and she anonymously helped a lot of people in need. When asked concerning her breasts, Carrie would respond, "I made them work for me." *Carrie was truly the "Gland Old Lady of Burlesque."*

October 31, 1963, Carrie's husband Thomas Morris died of a heart attack, and two weeks later Carrie's life came full circle. She died of a heart attack on her birthday November 14, 1963, near the place where she was born sixty-three years earlier.

SPECIALTY ACTS IN BURLESQUE SHOWS

In the 1920s, 1930s and early1940s, along with the comics and straight men that doubled as singing emcees, there were Variety Acts. Some were leftover Vaudeville acts including acrobats, and even young girls twirling batons.

Apache Dancing began in France in 1908. The dance itself is a highly disciplined and choreographed fight between a man and a woman, which depicts the Parisian street culture of that time period. Its dance moves consist of mock violence; with the man dragging the woman across the stage by her hair, throwing her on the ground and over his shoulder, while the woman struggles or pretends to be unconscious. At times, the woman fights back and the two of them throw mock punches and slaps. By the end of the dance she finally surrenders to him; she holds tightly onto his leg as he drags her across the floor trying to leave her, and they exit the stage in this position. The dance is often said to re-enact a violent argument between a prostitute and her pimp.

The Apache Dance is a very rough, but exciting dance, which takes precision timing to perform. It was extremely popular during the 1920s, 1930s and early 1940s. The dance is also a dangerous act and has left many performers with permanent injuries; even one death. It requires a small, slender woman and a strong man, and is a theatrical routine that is not meant for Ballroom Dancers.

A take-off on the Apache Dance was some of the Jitterbug steps. The male, and often a strong female, toss their partners over their shoulders, between their legs and sometimes spin them around like a top, as they lie on the dance floor. It was quite the rage in the 1940s.

Yatava and her partner onstage at the beginning of their famous version of the French Apache Dance (late 1930s). Photo courtesy of Authors Collection.

During 1932 in Chicago, Dancers Francis Woods and Billy Bray began their careers as French Apache and Adagio performers. Adagio is more acrobatic in the way it uses body tossing and catching, and is often done with two men and one woman. What made their act even more special was the fact that Francis was born a deaf mute. She had a good sense of rhythm and picked up the vibrations of the music from the stage floor through her feet. Billy would toss Frances in the air and catch her with one hand.

Billy and Frances married and performed their Apache Dance for ten years longer, then went on to perform Latin dances together until

The famous and fabulous Zorita doing her Wedding Routine.
Photo courtesy of Authors Collection.

they were in their fifties. Afterwards, they had a small studio in their home and taught Latin-style dancing to senior citizens for the next twenty years.

Burlesque performers did a more stylized and sexier version of the Apache Dance, with the female attempting to seduce the male. In the end, the male rips the female's clothes off, a piece at a time.

My favorite act is the Half-and-Half; where the dancer dresses one side as a woman and the other side as a man. There are many versions and variables of this routine, and it takes an extreme amount of agility and practice in front of a mirror to perfect it. The dancer must twist and position her body so it appears to be two people dancing, with the male counterpart caressing and enticing the woman.

Some acts, such as the Gorilla and the Virgin, actually have two people involved, with a man wearing the gorilla suit.

Betta Dodd was a Specialty Dancer who started stripping in the early 1930s. She was known as "Madame Satan" and "The Girl in Cellophane." Betta worked at the New York World's Fair between 1934 and 1940. She performed in Burlesque shows in the 1930s and throughout the1940s. Her routines were especially appreciated at the Gayety in Montreal, Canada, where she had a long run supported by twenty-three chorus girls who were known as the Kuddling Kutties.

Internationally known Dramatic Dancer Diane De Lys, doing her Devil and the Virgin dance. Photo courtesy of Diane De Lys.

At the Café Howard in Bridgeport, Connecticut, Betta combined her see-thru Cellophane Act with her Electric Light Routine. Stage lights were lowered. Flashes of light emanated from special, tiny, battery-charged light bulbs that she held in her fast moving hands, allowing the light to reflect off of various parts of her body, as they accentuated her nudity while she danced. She received rave reviews!

Betta Dodd as "Madame Satan" (1935).
Photo courtesy of Authors Collection.

Pictured ad for Betta Dodd as "The Girl in Cellophane" at the Café Howard in Bridgeport,
Connecticut (1942). Photo courtesy of Authors Collection.

In the 1930s, both the movie industry and theater performers used Cellophane in their scenery and their costumes. At that time, Cellophane was a thin sheet of regenerated Cellulose. It picked up stage lights and reflected them back with a glow that shimmered and sparkled. The effect was spectacular!

Specialty Dancer Maxine Holman worked at the Gypsy Room for many years and packed the place nightly. She was a trained dancer who began her career in Ballet. Later on, she integrated her Ballet training with

Caption: Maxine in her "Wolf Girl" act. Photo courtesy of Jeanine France.

Maxine doing her "Indian Chief and Captive Girl" Act.
Photo courtesy of Authors Collection.

Fan Dancing for many of her routines. Maxine never had to worry about having a roof over her head; she traveled in a full-sized house trailer, with a built-in art studio.

Natoma was a French and Seminole Indian who supposedly was born in the Florida Everglades. Turn-of-the-century French Actress and Interpretive Dancer Gaby Deslys influenced her. Natoma was famous in Paris for her "Dance of the Thunder Bird," which is based on a Pagan

Unknown Half-man/Half-woman Act. Photo courtesy of Authors Collection.

Polynesian girl dancing onstage with a man in an ape costume (Cuba, 1950s). Photo courtesy of Authors Collection.

Sebina Sevan, Turkish Dancer doing Half-woman/ Half-gorilla Act. Photo courtesy of Jennie Lee.

"Lady and the Ape" (1940s). Photo courtesy of Authors Collection.

Burly Ventriloquist Act starring Maude and Woody. The Dummy talks her out of her clothes (1945). Photo courtesy of Authors Collection.

Night Club ad showing Carole Jayne "The Spider Girl" (1958). Photo courtesy of Authors Collection.

Carole Jayne in her spider costume (1949). Photo courtesy of Jennie Lee.

Unknown Specialty Stripper doing her Voodoo Act. Photo courtesy of Authors Collection.

Unknown Specialty Dancer in fabulous costume. Photo courtesy of Authors Collection.

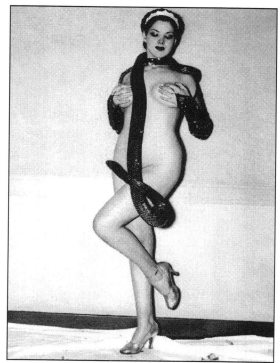

Zorita performing a Snake Dance early in her career (1930). Photo courtesy of Authors Collection.

A very young Zorita walking her snake. Photo courtesy of Authors Collection.

Ritual. Her "Dracula and Vampire" Act is said to have been on the edge of eeriness and mesmerized audiences everywhere she performed it. By the age of nineteen, Natoma was already a Headliner and toured Europe for several years. She had an odd idea about fur coats, and thought buying a fur coat for each of her new acts would make her act successful. It is said she owned seven fur coats.

Genni was a Burlesque stripper from the 1930s to the early 1960s, and she worked as a bit-part Actress and advertising Model in the Hollywood, California area. She danced in the Burlesque movies *Baghdad After Midnight, Strip Around the World,* and *Not Tonight, Henry,* which also starred Burlesque Comic Hank Henry. Genni did a Novelty routine

Genni doing her "Snake-Puppet Dance" (late 1930s). Photo courtesy of Authors Collection.

Rosita Royce at the New York World's Fair (1934). Photo courtesy of Authors Collection.

Rosita Royce and her Doves (1937). Photo courtesy of Authors Collection.

Ad for Rosita Royce and her "Daring Dove Dance" (1936). Photo courtesy of Authors Collection.

wearing a sequined snake on her hand that went all the way up her arm and wrapped around her body. It was cute and it was clever.

Rosita Royce was born August 9, 1913, as Lotus Marjorie Corrington in Lincoln, Nebraska. Her father Dr. Clyde Martin Carrington was a Dentist. Rosita's mother Bertha Belle Brillhart was overly protective of her daughter, due in part to the loss of Rosita's older sister Melba who died before age one.

At a very young age, Rosita was formally trained in the "Denishawn" Dance method, which is an avant-garde, free-form dance style that resembles famed Isadora Duncan's dance style. Rosita began her career at age ten, doing a "Bubble Dance" with the Denishawn Dancers.

Rosita found time to attend Nebraska Wesleyan University, but by age nineteen she was performing in the Crystal Palace Pavilion at the New York World's Fair. The Crystal Palace featured her from 1934 to 1940, and it was there she perfected her "Dance of the Doves."

In 1944, Rosita's mother became a widow, and it was then that she assumed the role of Rosita's chaperone and traveling companion for the duration of her career. She was also an integral part of Rosita's act.

Rosita's dance routine involved doves, which she trained herself. It took several years to train seven doves to come to her and stay on her during her spins and high kicks. Rosita's mother would release the doves from behind the stage; they would fly and land gently on Rosita's outstretched arms, her shoulders, and even on her head. She would playfully interact with the doves, but unlike Yvette Dare, whose birds assisted with her strip; these doves simply added to the ambience of the dance. Before going onstage, Rosita placed some birdseed in her mouth, and now and then the birds would nibble at the seeds. From the audience, it appeared as though the birds were kissing her. Rosita also worked with a large white Cockatoo named Silly Billy and a Macaw named Red. In this case, both the Cockatoo and the Macaw would pull the strings of her cape allowing it to drop to the floor, leaving Rosita in skimpy attire. *I've seen a video of this routine and you can actually see Rosita's training trick. Instead of rewarding the birds with seed, she is seen bobbing her head in the same manner as birds do when interacting with each other. As she goes into her spins and back-bends, she moves her arms in such a way that it causes the birds to open and close their wings while clinging onto to her. The beauty of the birds is part of the act.*

How she kept from being bombarded with biodegradable was a well-kept secret that didn't involve potty training.

Candid of Rosita Royce with her Macaw "Red" and her Cockatoo "Silly Billy" (Worlds Fair 1939). Photo courtesy of Authors Collection.

Dove kissing Rosita Royce (1939). Photo courtesy of Authors Collection.

For a while, Rosita did a Bubble Dance similar to Sally Rand's. Later on, after a long dispute between the two dancers concerning who started the Act first, Rosita finally gave up doing the routine altogether.

During the late 1930s and early 1940s, Rosita was also known for her "Black Butterfly Dance" and her "Parisian Dance in Cellophane." She was an excellent Specialty Dancer and tried to introduce many other forms of dance into her repertoire, but the audience always wanted to see her dance with her doves. Rosita also appeared with her doves in the Chicago, Illinois, San Diego, California, and Dallas, Texas State Fairs.

In the summer of 1952, Producer Mike Todd showcased Rosita and her Doves for eleven weeks in his *A Night in Venice* Revue, which was shown in New York.

On September 24, 1954, Rosita, with her over-protective and ever-loyal mother by her side, surrendered her life to cancer in Dade, Florida. Her mother Bertha lived to be ninety-eight years old and is buried beside Rosita.

One other dancer who worked with a bird was the gorgeous Yvette Dare. She too, danced in New York's 1934 to 1940 World's Fair. Yvette, who was a Hedy Lamarr look-a-like, wore a sarong that the Macaw removed to the sound of tom-toms. When the bird she called Einstein heard the tom-toms start, it would begin removing her sarong.

I still think those birds must have worn some sort of tiny, birdie diapers.

Yvette Dare and her Macaw named Einstein (1941). Photo courtesy of Jennie Lee.

Rare photo of Siska before her bird routines. Photo courtesy of Authors Collection.

Last but not least in the bird business is Siska and her very large Macaw named Pete.

Siska was a tall gal from San Antonio, Texas, with striking good looks. Her real name is Anita Marie Siska. She started dancing with her sisters in Vaudeville at a young age and went from dancing in a chorus-line to stripping in Burlesque. In 1947, she was known as the "Stop, Look and Whistle Girl."

While Siska was working in the Cetlin-Wilson Carnival, it featured a tropical bird exhibit. It was there she developed her love for birds.

Siska found Pete, her beautiful Macaw, in Florida and purchased him for $1,000. It took her nine months to train Pete to pull the ribbons off her gown. In the process, Siska was bit once in the side and once on her cheek; both injuries required stitches.

Beautiful Siska and her Macaw Pete (1950). Photo courtesy of Jennie Lee.

Breathtaking Lili St. Cyr doing her mock Macaw Dance. Photo courtesy of Authors Collection.

She loved Macaws and owned two others that she named Ticky-Tacky and Ticky-Lacky. Sometimes, if Pete was in a foul mood she would have to dance with Ticky-Tacky and Ticky-Lacky, who always worked as a team. Otherwise, Pete would fly around the stage screaming, "Help me!" and, although Siska would try her birdie-best, she couldn't control him.

Sally Rand and her Swan Dance. Photo courtesy of Authors Collection.

Siska used to tell her friends, "If you want Pete to like you, let him remove some of your clothes or untie your shoe laces."

LOIS DE' FEE * 6' 4" * QUEEN OF THE AMAZONS

Lois de' Fee was born August 1, 1918, in Texas. She was the only child of James de' Fee and Ola Mathis. Her mother died when Lois was two and her father died when she was seven. Her father's married sister Mattie Maude Farley took Lois in, but Lois couldn't stand her life with the battling Farley's and at age thirteen, she ran away.

She was completely on her own, yet even though she was young, because of her mature looks and height, people thought she was much older and didn't bother her. Lois had always wanted to be a showgirl and

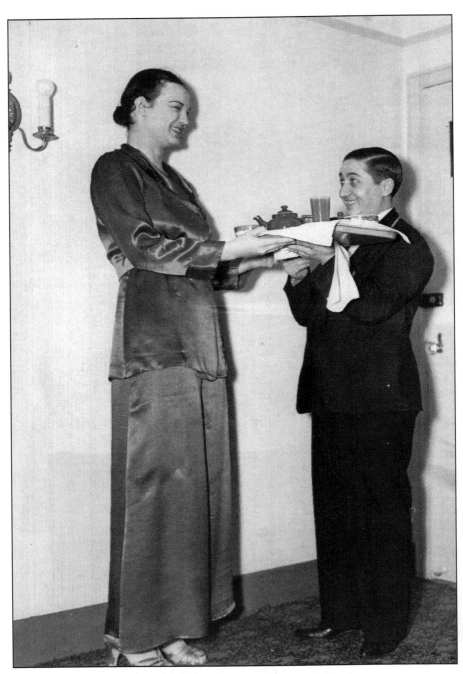

Lois, during the time she worked at Dizzy's (1936).
Photo courtesy of Authors Collection.

she eventually found a job in Miami, Florida, with a traveling Burlesque group that was headed for Havana, Cuba.

By 1933, she was back in the United States and took a job at Dizzy's Club in New York. Because of her size and as a gimmick, they offered her a job as a female bouncer. *You do the math; she was only about sixteen years old.* It was there that she received real recognition. She took her job seriously and was written up in Walter Winchell's celebrity gossip column more than a few times. She then went on to become a bouncer for a lengthy period of time at the world famous Leon and Eddie's.

The beautiful and immensely popular Sherry Britton worked at Leon and Eddie's for several years. Lois formed a lifelong friendship with Sherry Britton, and with Zorita the Snake Dancer who also spent her retirement years in Florida. Lois told me, "Most of the girls were afraid of Zorita's snakes. Not me; I like exotic animals. I had a Woolly-faced Monkey for five years and took it with me when I traveled."

Lois was the 6' 4" "Queen of the Amazon" in the 1938 New York World's Fair Amazon Exhibit, and the leading Showgirl in Billy Rose's *Jumbo.*

One of the Minsky brothers, I believe it was Harold, saw Lois at the Fair and offered her $400 a week to strip in one of his Burlesque shows. She took him up on his offer. Lois told me in my interview with her that it was Sherry Britton who helped her get started with a few strip moves, but that for the most part, she watched some Burlesque shows and picked

Sherry Britton at Leon and Eddie's.
Photo courtesy of Jennie Lee.

Lois de' Fee. Photo courtesy of Lois de' Fee.

Lois, age twenty, rehearsing for the Amazon Exhibit (1939).
Photo courtesy of Authors Collection.

up much of it on her own. She established her own dance style early on in her career, which was an elegant walk around the stage that showed off her stature and femininely demure gowns.

In 1990, Mitzi set me up with a phone interview with Lois de' Fee who owned an antique shop in Florida. Mitzi had worked with Lois and told me, "Just be your funny self with Lois and she'll like you." She added, "Lois really was an Amazon, but she was in perfect proportion for her size. She has a really pretty face and smile, and is fun to be around; and she likes to laugh a lot."

Lois gave me her interview from her shop. She was very open about some elements of her life and rather vague about others. At that time, Lois still thought she might write her memoirs and wanted to save some of the highlights of her career for her own book.

Lois was very much aware of the fact that her 6' 4" stature opened many theater doors for her. She was also aware that she was one of the last living Legends of Burlesque.

Backstage with the lighting man (1940s). Photo courtesy of Lois de' Fee.

The first thing Lois told me was, "Don't ask me how many times I've been married or if I married a midget." She went on to say, "I would rather talk about the old Burlesque days, before it got dirty. You know, it used to be a real show and the girls had what nature gave them. They were all pretty and wore glamorous gowns and costumes. Not like today, where there is no tease, no strip, no comics, no musicians or chorus girls. It's just a cheap bar with a naked broad showing everything God gave her, and some He didn't."

Lois and I talked for several hours about the Golden Days of Burlesque and the many, many people she worked with, in front and behind the scenes. I got the feeling she enjoyed her life but didn't miss being in the spotlight. She told me, "The audience loved me and so did the theater and club owners. I always behaved like a lady onstage. I worked off-and-on for twelve years at the Nocturne Club; they kept bringing me back. I worked at the Gaiety in Montréal, Canada, for several runs; they loved me in Canada. I became a Star right away and I was still a Star when I retired. I didn't retire from Burlesque; it retired from me."

One thing about Lois, she was a matter-of-fact lady with a down-to-earth sense of humor about her life. She knew what worked for her in the Burlesque business and knew how to effectively generate publicity for herself.

In the late 1930s, Lois went a couple of rounds with famed boxer Primo Carnera, claiming to be his sparring partner. On May 25, 1937, a newspaper article stating Fanny Brice's brother Lou, a booking agent, beat-up Lois de' Fee, former Showgirl and Nightclub Bouncer. A photo showing Lois with two black eyes and a broken nose accompanied the article. In 1938, Lois married midget Billy Curtis from the movie *The Wizard of Oz,* as a publicity stunt. She had that marriage annulled.

How many times Lois was married is not clear; some claim five or six, others seven. I do know, besides the munchkin Billy Curtis, one of Lois's husbands was 5' tall Louis Machado, a well-known Jockey. Her last husband was a Mr. Erlanger.

In 1941, Lois adopted a beautiful baby-girl she named Star. The child was the love of her life and she became the center of Lois's world.

Lois was the reining "Queen of the Amazons" until Ricci Covette came onto the Burlesque scene in 1950. Ricci was 6' 8" and Lois had to relinquish her title as the tallest woman in Burlesque. Lois retired from Burlesque in 1959.

About a week after my tapped interview with Lois, I received a large envelope from her. It contained about thirty pages of lists of Burlesque

Lois backstage at a Buffalo, New York, Burlesque theater with newly adopted baby Star and her nanny (January 19, 1941). Photo courtesy of Authors Collection.

Ricci Covette. Photo courtesy of Authors Collection.

dancers, comics, theaters, and a schedule for a Burlesque Road Show. She also enclosed a personal note and three photos; one was an autographed picture inscribed "To Dusty, Good luck and keep that wonderful sense of humor, Lois de' Fee." *It was a total surprise! Was I thrilled? You better believe it!*

Right after we hung up from our interview Lois put on her thinking cap, or maybe it was an old Burlesque bonnet, but she came up with many names of people in Burlesque who were associated with, worked in, and often times worked with her.

Autographed photo of Lois to Author. Photo courtesy of Lois de' Fee.

What a kind, considerate gesture it was, to take the time to hand-write all her lists for someone she only knew a few hours.

It was my good fortune and a great honor to have met Lois. She was unique and truly the Grand Dame of Burlesque.

On February 13, 2012, in Miami, Florida, Lois de' Fee went to that big Burlesque Show in the sky. She was ninety-four years old.

In Lois's first list, she writes exactly what a Traveling Burlesque Road Show consists of. Her second list read, "When I got into Burlesque, the top names were..." Here is her second list: Margie Hart, Ann Corio, Georgia Sothern, Zorita, Rose LaRose, myself, Gypsy Rose Lee, Peaches Strange, Julie Bryan, Amy Fong, Hinda Wassau, Vicky Wells, Jessica Rogers, Valerie Parks, Yvette Dare, Delores Dawn, Louise Rogers, Gladys Fox, Dimples De Light, Trudine, Pat Joyce, Joan Mavis, Naomi, Dorothy Wahl, Countess Naja, Marie Cord, Helen Lovett, Jean Carroll, Irma Vogalee, June March, Myrna Dean, Trudy Wayne, Carol Lord, Carrie Finnell, Sheila Ryan, Roxanne, Lyn O'Neil, Bubbles Darlene, Maxine De Shon, Charmaine, Mitzi, Winnie Garrett, Sherry Britton, Boo La Vonn, Eileen Herbert, Hillary Dawn, Mae Brown, Francine, Ginger Britton, Conchita, Sally O'Day, Sally Rand (who was not Burlesque, but did clubs and fairs), Faith Bacon (Sally Rand's nemesis), Ada Leonard, Marion Wakefield, Sally Keith, Dottie Dee, Nona Ford, Barbara Bond, Tanya, Diane Raye, Connie Fanslo, Marshan, Gloria Dahl, Jean Mode, Marnee Phillips, Nina Louise, Electra, Sally Lane and her monkey Fifi, Ilka De Cava, Lilli St.

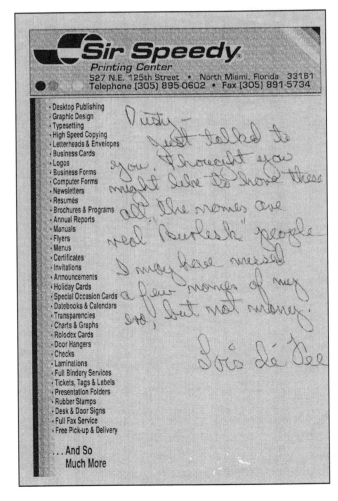

Note from Lois de' Fee. Photo courtesy of Authors Collection.

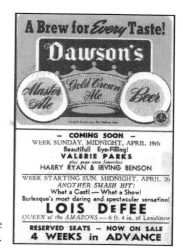

Ad from Globe Traveling Burlesque for Lois de' Fee (1942). Photo courtesy of Authors Collection.

Cyr, Shirley Stanley, Gypsy Rolita, Irene, Inez Clair, Renee Andre', Flame La Marche, Mickey Jones, Scarlett Kelly, Fifi D'Aubry, Evelyn Taylor, Lynn York, Betty Howard, Mary Mack, Ann Powell, Monica Mayo, Dolly Dawson, Lea Wynn, Beverly Ware (who also worked as a Straight Woman for comics), Carmen La Forte, Talia (Specialty Dancer), Margie Kelly, Sigred Fox, Crystal Ames, Ruth Swank, Mona Corey, Barbara Curtis, Princess Lahoma, Lotus Du Bois, Jai-Leta, Margo, Suzanne Daye, Lilli Dawn, Sherry Shannon, Pepper Powell, Jeanne France (who did Strobe tassels), Joan Arline and her Russian Wolfhounds, and Betty Rowland.

Lois's third list is Straight Men and Comics: Lester Mack, Jack Buckley, Joe Freed, Jack Sherman, Bobo Hawkins, Billy Foster, Bobby Burns, Willie Solon, James X. Frances, Harvey Fields, Joe Tempo, Pinky Lee, Billy Frye, Tommy Trinder, Bob Ferguson, Ray Kolb, Tommy "Scurvey" Miller, Max Coleman, Hap Hyatt, Steve Mills, Straight Man Connie Ryan, Peanuts Bohn, Al Golden, Straight Man Lee Trent, Sliding Billy Watson, Bozo Snyder, Billy "Zoot" Reed, George Beetle-Puss Lewis, Little Jack Little, Manny King, George Murray, Bobbie Morris, Singer/Straight Man Paul West, Straight Man Bud Abbot, Comic Lou Costello, Binder and Rosen, Bobby Clark, Zachary Charles, Hal Loman, Bob Ross, Bert Lahr, Walter Dare, Johnny Trauma, Billy Ainsley, Jimmy Pinto, Lee Stuart, Leon De-Voe (who was married to choreographer Lillian Hunt), Monkey Kirkland, Tommie "Moe" Raft, Al Anger, Mike Sachs and Alice Kennedy, Rags Ragland, Phil Silvers, Slats Taylor, Red Buttons, Harry Rose, Bob Carney, Hank Henry and Robert Alda, Lou Arcal, Pigmeat Markham, Dusty Fletcher, Joe De Rita, Maxie Furman, Gus Shilling, Charlie Robinson,

Mac Dennison, Parker Gee, Lenny Gale, Harry Pollard, Looney Lewis, Charlie Harris, Benny "Wop" Moore, Eddie Innes, Irving Selig, Tiny Fuller, Happy Ray, Walter Brown, Bobby Vail, Jack Diamond, Jack La Mont, Lew Black, Marvin Harmon, Bert Grant, Jack Shaw, Al Paar, Shuffles La Van, Bimbo Davies, Joey Cowan, Snuffy Cochran, Billy "Bumps" Mack (who was married to Stripper/talking woman Inez Claire), Lew Fine, Rex Doyle, Harry Savoy, Irving Benson, Eddie Lloyd, Collins and Peterson, Henry Clexx, Harry Levine, Harry Reed, Claude "Say No More Joe" Mathis, Jack Albertson, Sparky Raye, Morty Forman, Jack Roser, Herbie Barris, Bert Carr, Freddie Frampton, Billy "Cheese and Crackers" Hagan, Stinky Fields, Artie Lloyd, Joey Faye, Johnnie Cook, Charlie Kemper, Lew Devine, Murray Leonard, Red Marshall, Billy "Scratch" Wallace, Singer/ Straight Man Charlie Craft, Herbie Faye, Dexter Maitland, Danny Del Rio, Sid Nadel, Charlie Country and Kenny Brenna, Sammie Smith, Curly Burns, Jess Mack (who later became a prominent Talent Agent), Bradford Hatton, Wally Swartz, Moe Gary, Chick Hunter, Don Santo, Dick Richards, Art Baker, Jimmy Mathews, Hi Wilberforce Conley, Joe "Rubber Face" Gallagher, Earl Van, Hermie Rose, Billy House, and Joe Yule (Mickey Rooney's father).

I called Lois to thank her for all her kindness and she told me she had fun remembering the old days. She even looked through her old scrapbooks to see if she had forgotten anyone. She told me that one of her life regrets was that someone had stolen one of her suit-cases and it had over three hundred photos of her with other Burlesque performers, and a large scrapbook of newspaper articles about her.

I asked Lois if she personally knew all these dancers and comics. She said, "I either worked with them or knew them in person." Later on she told me, "In the old days, if you were in Burlesque, you were part of a big family."

Chapter 6

Gilda's Golden Locks and the Three Bares

GILDA

When Gilda was less than two years old her mother, Ruth Evelyn Rickert, entered her in a beautiful baby contest, which she won. This lucky break set off a chain reaction that would eventually end up on a Burlesque stage. Inspired by the baby contest win, Gilda's mother bundled her up and headed for Hollywood where cute little girls and boys became tiny mini-stars; while their hopeful stage mothers managed their careers and spent their earnings.

Gilda's real name is Shirley Jean Rickert, born March 25, 1926, in Seattle, Washington. Shirley had two star-studded careers. Beginning at age three, she was a child Actress in the movies. Her second career was as the gorgeous Stripper "Gilda", lighting up a Burlesque stage.

Shirley acquired her Germanic good looks and natural golden blonde hair from her father's side. She was just the most adorable child. Even silent screen star Mary Pickford posed with Shirley in 1930.

At age five, Shirley played the nameless little blonde girl in several of the *Our Gang* comedies. She was made up to look like a baby Flapper with spit curls and short hair, and was the playmate and love interest of Alfalfa, Weezer, and little Jackie Cooper. In 1933, she played Tomboy Taylor in the *Mickey McGuire* series along side little Mickey Rooney and little Billy Barty. It was the only series to rival the enormously popular *Our Gang* comedy series. Shirley went on to do bit parts in close to one hundred movies, mostly musicals. She was an unaccredited dancer in *Singing in the Rain* starring Gene Kelly, and *Royal Wedding* starring Fred Astaire.

In 1952, at age twenty-five, Shirley started dancing in the chorus line at The New Follies Theatre in Los Angeles. After seven months of weekly

119

Headshot of Gilda showing her crowned signature. Photo courtesy of Jennie Lee.

rehearsals and hoofing it in four to five shows a day, she became the stripper known as "Gilda and Her Crowning Glory;" a title that stresses her tresses. Gilda had the most gorgeous waist-long, natural golden hair, and the sweetest baby-face. Her signature on her autographed photos to her fans was personalized by drawing a tiny sparkling crown over the G in her name. She also liked to sign "Love n' Stuff" before her name.

Although she already knew how to dance, she attended Director and Choreographer Lillian Hunt's Strip College in Los Angeles to learn how to strip. In her bump and grind graduating class were Strippers Blaze Glory, Thunder, Happy Day, Venus The Body, Patti Waggin, Sugar Kane, and a young hopeful named Desire.

The tuition fee ranged from $100 to $150 for a week-long course. Mrs. Hunt taught them how to walk, wiggle, and wear the appropriate costume to showcase each body type. She showed them how to apply the proper make-up for their skin tone and suggested hairstyles that gave each girl sex appeal. Her only free advice was, "Smile ladies, smile!"

Gilda starred in the 1952 stripfilm *The A.B.C.s of Love*, directed by Lillian Hunt. The film included Strippers Blaze Glory, Bebe Hughes, Mae Brondell and Helen Lewis, along with Comics Leon DeVoe and Eddie Ware, and was filmed at The New Follies Theatre in Los Angeles. Gilda was a popular Peeler throughout the 1950s, and worked in Burlesque theaters and nightclubs across the U.S. and in Canada. She was a regular at Minsky's and by 1957; Gilda had fourteen different dance routines.

Glamour shot of Gilda. Photo courtesy of Jennie Lee.

Gilda was married and divorced twice. Her daughter Melody, who was born in 1951, is by her second husband Harold Measures. Until her death in 1957, Gilda's mother Ruth took care of her granddaughter Melody, while Gilda traveled and worked on the Burlesque Circuit. After Gilda's mother died, Gilda quit the Burlesque scene in 1959, taking on an array of various jobs including bartender, secretary, and saleslady; and she even drove a truck. She finally settled into a job on the road, selling nuts and bolts for an industrial company to various small businesses. Sometimes the potential client would grumble, "Oh no, not another nuts and bolts salesman." And clever Gilda would respond by opening up her attaché case showing a shot of herself as a child star saying, "You know me; you grew up with me! I used to be in the *Our Gang* movies." It would always ignite a lengthy conversation and usually cinch the deal.

Years later, Gilda helped managed her own website, making new friends and fans via the Internet. She had lost most of her pictures and memorabilia when the apartment she was living in caught fire. The many fans who visited her website found and sent her copies of her lost photos, ads, and newspaper clippings. She began selling copies of requested photos on her website. She encouraged her fans to write her and she answered all their e-mails. Gilda eventually moved to New York to live with her daughter and help out at her local crafts shop. Gilda even made some of the crafts herself and learned how to knit a mean afghan blanket.

After a lengthy illness, Gilda passed away February 6, 2009, in a nursing home at Saratoga Springs, New York. She was eighty-two years young. She donated her body for medical research to help in finding cures for various diseases.

NONA CARVER

Nona Carver is a statuesque, 5' 11" woman who was known as "The Blonde Venus." She started working in Burlesque at The New Follies Theatre in Los Angeles, California, in the late 1940s. Nona was so popular at The New Follies that she was always booked for twenty weeks at a time. In 1949, Nona worked with Stripper and Talking Woman Inez Clair, and Comic Red Marshall in Bob Bigg's Revue at The New Follies. Talking Woman and Comic Aurora, who later teamed up with Mimi Reed, was part of the Revue and taught Nona the fine art of being a "Talking Woman."

A Talking Woman is a person, often a stripper, who interacts with one or more male comics and has speaking lines. She receives extra pay

Nona Carver (1948). Photo courtesy of Jennie Lee.

for her part in the skit. By November 1953, Nona was still working on-and-off at The New Follies Theatre, but Patti Waggin was the Headliner, along with the glorious Gilda and Her Crowning Glory.

In 1952, while working at the Hollywood Theatre in San Diego, California, Nona became friends with Choreographer/Director/Manager Helen Hunt and her husband, Comic Leon DeVoe. They offered her a role dancing in a stripfilm they were making called *B-Girl Rhapsody*, which featured Frenchy LaVon, Ginger DuVal, Chili Pepper, and Lili St. Cyr. The film was produced by Roadshow Productions and was just one in a series of strip-shorts that featured well-known strippers. The films were shown between acts or during intermission in Burlesque theaters during the late

1940s and throughout the 1950s. It was a way to cheaply show more strippers at a time and draw a bigger audience.

Rose La Rose was not only a popular draw in her own Town Hall Burlesque Theatre in Toledo, Ohio; she was a shrewd businesswoman. She was the first to show strip-shorts in a Burlesque theater. It was something of a gimmick, and instead of taking away from the live strippers, it added new interest. Some of the films had complete Burlesque shows, including comics and Specialty dancers.

It was to be the first of many movie roles Nona would play. The 1952 Strip-Short *Girlesk Show* featured Nona as "Queen of the Glamazons." The film also included Beverly Reynard, who was known as Champagne Sparkle; Paula D'Arcy the Flamingo Girl; and Tandalaye doing her exotic Slave Dance.

In the early 1950s, Nona met and became close pals with Stripper Jennie Lee, who was a member of The American Screen Actors Guild. Jennie talked Nona into joining The Guild and to try out for bit parts in nearby Hollywood studios.

Jennie Lee formed her Exotic Dancers League of America in 1955; Nona became a member shortly after. She was on the E.D.L. stripper's softball and bowling teams, both aptly named "The Barecats," and came to many of Jennie's stripper Reunions.

By 1958, Nona was still stripping and dating Actor Kenne Duncan, who was featured in many of Writer/Director Ed Wood's bizarre films. In 1959, Nona played an Indian girl named Yellow Gold in Ed Wood's movie *Revenge of the Virgins*. In 1963, she played a waitress named Nona in Ed Wood's movie *Terrified*. During the late 1960s, Nona was doing non-speaking bit parts for various television series, including several episodes of *Dragnet*. Then, in 1970, Nona played sleazy Maisie Rumpledinck in her last Ed Wood film, *Take It Out In Trade*. The movie has been lost and only rare clips remain, but it made Nona a cult figure.

Nona remained close friends with Jennie Lee and spent the last few months of Jennie's life in Lee's home at Exotic World, taking care of Jennie in her last stages of cancer. During the final weeks, Dixie Evans came to Exotic World and helped Nona care for Jennie.

In March 1990, during Jennie's last month, I went to see Jennie and she introduced me to Nona. Because of the circumstance, Nona was cordial but aloof; she was preoccupied with attending Jennie's every need. I could see the special bond and the respect these two women had for each other. It was an extremely touching scene that spoke volumes to me about

Nona Carver and two unknown strippers in *Las Vegas Revue* (1953).
Photo courtesy of Authors Collection.

the sisterly love, understanding, and loyalty that is prevalent among so many strippers I've known.

Once, I asked Charlie Arroyo, Jennie Lee's last husband, what Nona was like. He told me she was hard to figure out and wasn't real friendly with him. Then he said, "She had an odd habit of always keeping exactly $700 hidden on her person. It was her lucky number and she thought it brought her good luck."

It turns out that while working in a small nightclub in San Francisco, the owner refused to pay her and she was stranded. After that incident, Nona always carried what she called "my get-away cash."

KARLA FLAME

In 1960, Karla Flame, whose real name is Beverly, was a pretty and petite stripper who worked at Chuck Landis's famous Largo Club on the Sunset Strip in Hollywood; and she also worked at the popular Moulin Rouge in San Francisco. At The Largo, she worked with well-known Strippers Miss Beverly Hills and Candy Barr. The Largo is where Candy Barr

Karla, while dancing at San Francisco's The Moulin Rouge (1960).
Photo courtesy of Jennie Lee.

met mobster Mickey Cohn, who she had a long-term relationship with. Later on, Miss Beverly Hills also had a lengthy relationship with Mickey Cohn.

Karla became a member of Jennie's Exotic Dancer's League of America and rallied around Jennie in some of her publicity stunts. In the spring of 1961, Karla Flame and Stripper Baby Lulu Wilnot the "Pocket Pin-Up Girl," helped Jennie Lee picket a topless bathing suit show in Hollywood. They carried signs saying, "Topless Bathing Suits Unfair to Strippers."

Around 1967, Karla danced part-time at Jennie's Sassy Lassy Club along with Stacy Farrell, Jeannie Anderson, and Jeanine France. While working at The Sassy Lassy, Karla befriended one of the dockworkers in the San Pedro area. It was a relationship that would have an affect on the rest of her life.

Jennie's husband Charlie Arroyo was the Clubs bartender and he kept an eye on the girls' safety. He told me in my interview with him, "I warned Karla about going anywhere with that guy; he was drinking too much and acting wild. I threw him out of the Club, but later on she met him somewhere." No one knows exactly what happened that night; Karla was roughed-up, gang-rapped by six or seven men, and thrown out of the car in front of The Sassy Lassy. Jennie always came to work at her Sassy Lassy Club around 9 p.m. It was around then that a regular customer entering the Club found Karla lying, half-dressed near the front door. He got Jennie and some of the other girls to help Karla inside.

Karla was never the same person after that terrible incident. She became an empty shell with a vacant look in her eyes; she was distrustful of everyone, and men in particular. She had a small daughter that someone took in and raised. The state paid for Karla's care and the medication to keep her calm. Jennie took on the responsibility of caring for Karla, and Karla was still living with Jennie at Exotic World when Jennie died in 1990.

After Jennie died, Dixie Evans took over as Curator for the Exotic World's Museum and she replaced Jennie Lee as Karla's caretaker. This was no easy task because Karla missed Jennie, who was the one person she trusted. Jennie had always been the only person who could handle Karla and get her to take her medication. Without her meds, Karla could become combative and often did. Neither Charlie Arroyo nor Dixie could convince Karla to take her medication everyday, and if she thought it was hidden in her food, she refused to eat.

When I met Karla at Exotic World in 1988, she was like a zombie wandering all over the forty-acre grounds. Ziggy, who had worked part-time for Jennie at her Sassy Lassy Club, was Jennie's long-time friend and now caretaker for her horses, dogs, and cats. He had been working at the Club the night Karla was raped. Because of it, he was protective of Karla and kept his eye on her. Ziggy was old enough to be Karla's grandfather and was the only man Karla trusted. She followed him around like a puppy.

When Dixie had the yearly Miss Exotic World Pageants, Karla would be on the prowl but she was unapproachable. Sometimes, a journalist visiting the Pageant would ask one of the dancers who Karla was, and they would simply say, "She used to be a stripper," and walk away. Karla was Exotic World's best-kept secret; yet she was always in plain sight.

Sometime in 1999, Karla took a turn for the worst. It may have been all the extra activity at Exotic World combined with the Pageants, or maybe she was no longer taking her meds. Jennie was gone, Ziggy was gone, there was a constant flow of visitors to The Museum, and there was tension between Dixie and Charlie concerning financial issues. Dixie wanted Karla's family to take over the responsibility of her, but Charlie insisted they needed the money the state paid them for Karla's care. Dixie had to watch Karla more closely now, and she even took her to some of the documentary tapings. She would dress Karla up and try to pass her off as an old stripper saying, "Karla doesn't do interviews." It was sad.

Karla had started pulling Dixie's hair, even shoving and slapping her on occasion. Then, Karla got real scary and bad things started happening. Karla would boldly approach a visitor and ask for a cigarette and a match, or even a cigarette lighter. She didn't smoke, but she would hide the matches and light small fires on the property. We were all worried she would burn down the Museum and its thousands of pictures, gowns, personal belongings, and memorabilia.

Dixie finally reached the point where she could no longer take the stress of monitoring Karla around the clock, and then what we feared most happened. Karla set the neighbors ranch on fire. Luckily, someone saw her do it and they put it out right away, but the Firemen had to report

Barb Burrows and Karla (with boa) in the main house of E.W.
Photo courtesy of Authors Collection.

the fire to the police and they took Karla away. It was actually a blessing in disguise. The court declared Karla a danger unto herself and to the public.

I don't know what became of Karla, a once attractive, talented, and sweet girl whose life was ruined by trusting the wrong man. I do feel she became a lost soul, living in the midst of that Museum full of past reminders of what her life had once been. Sadly, there was not one photo of Karla hanging on those Museum walls. I asked Dixie why that was. She told me Karla would always find them and rip them off the wall.

Patti Waggin

Patti Waggin, whose real name is Patricia Artae Hardwick or, according to some records, Heartwig, was born January 17, 1926, in Los Angeles, California. Her parents Alfred James Hardwick and Artae Patricia Hillyer were rumored to have been Adagio Dancers in the latter part of Vaudeville. After Patti was born, her father took on a steadier job; and in the 1932 Los Angeles City Directory he is listed as working as a Chauffer for a wealthy family. In the 1940 census, Patti's parents are divorced and her mother is remarried to a man named Alfred Anderson who was a steel worker, and they are now living in San Francisco.

Growing up, Patti was something of a tomboy. She and her younger brother Al were born a year apart and Patti liked to hang out with him and his friends. They were interested in baseball, racecars, and motorcycles, and so was Patti. She was one of those girls who thought, *why let the boys have all the fun?* In her teens, Patti played second base for the Welsh's Golden Crust Bread Baseball Team in Chico, California.

By the time Patti was fourteen, she was a skilled rider and already winning trophies for competing in local motorcycle races. By 1949, Patti had married the popular Bill Brownell, motorcycle racer and owner of a local motorcycle dealership. Brownell had an interesting background. Supposedly he had been a member of The Booze Fighter's Motorcycle Club; the club who partied hardy on a Fourth of July weekend in 1947 at Hollister, California. The incident was in *LIFE* magazine and later became the inspiration for the 1953 movie, *The Wild One* starring Marlon Brando.

Patti was very popular in the field of motorcycle racing and in 1950, she presented many well-known racers with their trophies. During her marriage to Brownell, Patti continued her education at Chico State College in Chico, California, where she majored in acting and dancing. She is listed as Patricia Brownell in the 1949 Chico State Yearbook. She had an

Patti sitting on her red wagon. Photo is autographed to a fan of
Patti's (1956). Photo courtesy of Jennie Lee.

acting part in the play *Our Hearts Were Young and Gay,* in the 1949 Chico
State Dramatic Festival.

While going to Chico State during the day, Patti had taken a job stripping at night to help pay for her education. At that time she was known as
"The Girl with the Educated Torso" and "The Stripping Coed." With her
dark, shoulder-length hair and pageboy bangs, Patti resembled Bettie Page.

Articles concerning her riding abilities and marriage to Brownell
were covered in several men's magazines in the 1950s. They served to
boost both her popularity and her stripping career. Readers of the magazine articles who came to see her strip out of curiosity, often returned in
admiration. Patti was pert, energetic, and wholesome looking. Her mil-
lion-dollar smile was dazzling on the stage and off. It was real, and she
was one of the friendliest girls in Burlesque.

Patti and Brownell divorced after only a few years, and Patti continued stripping. While working at The New Follies Burlesque Theatre in Los Angeles, Patti was managed and choreographed by Lillian Hunt, who suggested Patti use the name Patti Cake or Patti Waggin. Patti Waggin was her choice and it became her best career move. Except for Strippers Candy Barr and Tempest Storm, Patti Waggin's name is one of the most remembered names in Burlesque in the 1950s and 1960s.

Patti worked off-and-on at The New Follies Theatre during the 1950s. She had a great relationship with Bob Biggs, the Owner and Manager, as did her new Agent Milton Schuster. Biggs was a Manager who was quick to spot "Star" material and always had the best strippers and comics at his theater. Tempest Storm worked for him often, and Lillian Hunt was her choreographer.

Patti and hubby Don Rudolph by his team's dugout. Photo courtesy of Jennie Lee.

Patti was one of the few Burlesque stars who took the time to personally answer all her fan mail. She even befriended a few fans, sending them much-appreciated personally autographed photos of herself. Patti retired from stripping around 1961, but she kept boxes of all her fan letters. In 2009, Bob Brill, who is Patti's number one fan, published a book based on Patti's fan mail. The book, *Fan Letters to A Stripper, The Patty Waggin Tale*, has received rave reviews and is said to be the consummate source of Patti Waggin information.

In 1955, Patti married left-handed baseball pitcher Don Rudolph, who played for the Cleveland Indians and the Chicago White Sox. The marriage was a home run and lasted until September 1968, when, at age thirty-seven, an accident caused Don's truck to rollover on him, crushing him to death. Patti was devastated and never married again. The perfect couple had one child, a daughter.

Patti passed away February 24, 1992, in Granada Hills, California. She left behind a daughter, grandchildren and many, many adoring fans. She was only sixty-six years young when she died.

Chapter 7

Strippers Who Help Rescue Animals

Zabrina, the Swan Girl

Because everyone in my circle of friends is aware of my Animal Rescue and Lifetime Sanctuary, I often receive phone calls or notes with information regarding other animal welfare organizations, or newspaper articles on out-of-the-ordinary situations where pets are being saved. This is how I found out about Zabrina in the summer of 1995.

I had spent a couple of days interviewing well-known Burlesque Stripper Patti Starr at her beautiful home in Arizona. A few weeks later, Patti's daughter Raven, who was also a stripper, sent me a sweet letter telling me about Zabrina, whose real name is Triva Slote. Triva had been a stripper from 1950 to 1955, and she founded the Arizona Humane Society in 1956.

I immediately dashed off a note concerning the book I had started about Burlesque, and I included a tape of myself working with animal rescue. A few weeks later, I received a letter and gorgeous photo of Triva when she stripped under the name Zabrina the Swan Girl.

Triva had a lovely figure and the face of an angel, but don't let her femininity fool you; she had the heart of a lion and for almost fifty years Triva was ferociously dedicated to the welfare of animals.

Triva was raised in the Midwest and started her stripping career in Kansas City, Missouri, in 1950. By 1954, Triva was working in San Francisco and Los Angeles. She came to Arizona in 1955, while she was still working the nightclub circuit. She told me, "I danced to Clair De Lune covered in feathers; and as I stripped, I molted!"

While dancing at The Gilded Cage, the most prestigious nightclub in Phoenix, Arizona, Triva met Ed Slote, a doctor in the area who became fascinated by the lovely Triva and began courting her. They hit it off, got

Patti Starr during our interview in her Scottsdale, Arizona home (1995).
Photo courtesy of Authors Collection.

Zabrina (1953). Photo courtesy of Triva Slote.

August 25, 1995

Dear Dusty,

I was surprised and delighted to receive your video and note. I would have answered sooner but I had to track down my "8x10 glossies" as well as supervising the day to day operation of the Arizona S.P.C.A. I'm enclosing a copy of our latest "Up-date" to give you an idea of our programs.

I "stripped" from 1950 to 1955 when I married a doctor here in Phoenix. Yes, I met him at the "Guilded Cage", a really lovely little club here in Phoenix. I was lucky enough to be working at the top of the club and theatre action with live bands and some of the best "bananas" in the business. Lenny Bruce, Billy Reed, "Lord" Dick Buckley (he was beaten to death by the San Francisco cops), etc., etc. I bought wardrobe and broke it in (heaven help you if the zipper jams) in L.A. but traveled from coast to coast being careful to jump over Texas. (I still remember when they busted and jailed Beverly Hills).

I have been working in the humane field since '55 as a doctor's wife not only couldn't take off her clothes in public, she couldn't even be employed .. it was a sign of a failing practice if your wife worked. As I am a "workaholic", I jumped in with both feet. I founded the Arizona Humane Society in '56 and the Arizona S.P.C.A. in '60.

I would love to talk with you. Give a call .. any-time (602) 943-8802.

Sincerely,

Treva Slote (Zabrina, the Swan Girl)

Triva's letter to me. Copy courtesy of Authors Collection.

married, he clipped her wings and Triva retired. At the same time, Triva had a cat named Demon who was part of one of her acts. He too, retired and became part of the Slote family.

While stripping in San Francisco, Triva worked with two really far-out comedians who later became icons in the world of stand-up comedy; Lenny Bruce who talked dirty and influenced everyone, and the eccentric 6' 4" Lord Buckley. Both Comics had L.P. record albums on the market, which are now highly collectable; and throughout their careers, both men were continually harassed by the police.

Lord Buckley was the hippest cat of all and is credited as being an influence on George Carlin, Robin Williams, Jerry Garcia, Frank Zappa, and many other stand-up comics.

I had many phone conversations with Triva over the years; most were interrupted by urgent calls for emergency rescues or advice needed for a sick animal, etc. Her phone rang constantly around the clock, plus she kept busy with her own menagerie of eight cats, two dogs, two ducks, guinea pigs, five rabbits, rats, and a pot-bellied pig named Patrick.

Triva won many humanitarian awards over the years, including the coveted National Humanitarian Award presented by the American Veterinary Medical Association. (A previous recipient was actress Betty White.) In 1960, Triva founded the Arizona S.P.C.A., which is The Society for the Prevention of Cruelty to Animals.

In 1997, five days before Christmas and sometime after midnight, Phoenix Police called Triva to help officers rescue a badly injured dog from the side of the road. While she and the officers lifted the dog into the back of her car, a drunk driver crashed into her, pinning her against her vehicle.

As the ambulance attendants were putting Triva into the ambulance, she told them, "Never mind me, get help for the dog."

Her leg was crushed and she needed thirty-one pints of blood to survive. She spent three weeks in the hospital recuperating from her amputated leg, but in just a few months Triva, with only one leg, was rescuing animals again.

Her work with pet rescue continued for ten more years, and in March of 2007, at age seventy-five and surrounded by her husband and her family of furry friends, Triva lost her battle with cancer. In her lifetime, Triva rescued close to 2,000 animals. *She is my hero.*

JOAN TORINO AND FRIENDS

Starting in the late 1950s, striptease stars Joan Torino (who was known as "Torrid Torino") and her close friend and showgirl Ellye Farrelly, donated their time and energy to the Animal Protective League of Hudson County in New Jersey. Joan was Vice-President of the League and Ellye was a member. Both girls were involved in many campaigns, benefits, and other fund-raising projects to support the needs of rescued animals awaiting new owners.

Joan's real name is Joan Trusso; she was born October 6, 1933 in Jersey City, New Jersey. Both her mother and father were professional Exhibition Ballroom Dancers. Her mother won over a hundred dance contests and for a while, she was a showgirl at The Hudson Theatre in New Jersey. When Joan was thirteen, she wandered into The Hudson Theatre and saw her mother onstage dancing. Joan was so impressed; she would hide in her family's attic, dress-up in filmy curtains, and dance around in front of an old mirror.

At age fourteen, Joan lied about her age and auditioned for a job in The Hudson chorus line. To her surprise, she was hired. Even as a Chorus Girl, Joan did Specialty numbers; she danced the Can-Can and a jungle dance called the Banana Wiggle, a take-off on Josephine Baker's Banana dance.

At fifteen, Joan performed her first striptease and claims it was more teasing than stripping. She recalled, "We wore pasties covered by a net bra and little net under-pants covered with fringe."

Joan Torino and Maria Bradley, "Toni Twins". Photo courtesy of Joan Torino.

About the same time, Maria Bradley, her classmate from school, also took a job dancing at The Hudson Theatre. According to the November 25, 1950 issue of *Billboard Magazine*, the two girls were chosen by Dance Director Paul Morokoff to perform a special double strip routine wearing identical costumes, and were to be known as the Toni Twins. Their act was something of a gimmick, but it was such a huge hit that the girls received many offers to take their act on the road. Joan turned down these offers, not wanting to be away from her family. The girls performed their Toni act at The Hudson for quite a long run.

For you youngsters' information, Joan and Maria's stage names were a play on the 1950s Toni Home Permanents that were all the rage. Their advertisements read, "Which Twin has the Toni?" along side a picture of twins. The ads were in almost every woman's magazine and on T.V. The Toni Home Permanents put a large dent in the beauty shop business.

Around 1954, Joan became known as the "Queen of the Bubbles." The bubble-making machine was a new addition to theatrical numbers and Joan, along with The Hudson's house Choreographer Paul Morokoff, worked out an innovative dance number involving bubbles. There was a big bathtub in the middle of the stage with bubbles coming out of it and floating everywhere. The lighting man would pan the stage with a pink light and focus on Joan with her gorgeous red hair, sitting inside the tub amid hundreds of bubbles, wearing red pasties, a net bra, and little red-fringed pants. Her strip routine was nothing short of spectacular!

Paul Morokoff was considered a genus in his field. He turned strippers into dancers. When he choreographed a dancer's routine, it was almost always a guaranteed hit. Paul also choreographed for The Empire Theatre in Newark, New Jersey, which was torn down in 1957. Paul was the original Stage Manager and Choreographer for Burlesque Queen Ann Corio's long-running, off-Broadway smash hit, *This Was Burlesque.*

Paul was born in 1904, and became a dancer in his teens. He later developed a close friendship with Master Costume Designer Rex Huntington. Paul passed away in Weehawken, New Jersey, in 1978. He was living in an apartment he rented from Rex Huntington.

Joan remembers how she idolized Paul, and so did the rest of the strippers and chorus girls. Joan told me in her interview that Paul would go to see Broadway shows, come back to The Hudson and adapt the dancer's routine to resemble the shows he reviewed. She said, "He taught us girls six routines a week and we performed two to three shows a day. Since we were always learning new routines for the following week, it meant

HUDSON THEATRE
Week Beginning Sunday Matinee, February 21st, 1954
OVERTURE...GEORGE PONZONI ORCHESTRA
Staged and Directed by **PAUL MOROKOFF**

LOIS DeFEE

ACT ONE

1—OPENING — THERE'S NOTHING LIKE A DAME
  a) THE TIME, THE PLACE, AND OUR GIRLS
  b) A SAILOR WHO KNOWS WHAT HE LIKES .... JIMMY ADAMO
2—Scene — Ice Cream .... Bert Carr, Charlie Harris, Jimmy Adano, Dottie Deane, Ann Powell, Jeannie Allen
3—Specialty..Ann Powell
4—Scene — First Drink ....Benny Moore, Charlie Harris, Dottie Deane
5—Divertissement — In A Persian Market .... Morokoff's Pals Offer Oriental Swing
6—Before the Drapes .... Miss Dottie Deane
7—Scene — The Lost Flyers................. Bert Carr, Charlie Harris, Jimmy Adano, Ann Powell
8—Vodvil At Its Best .... King Johnson —Just Rolling Along
9—Scene — Trying To Get Arrested .... Benny Moore, Charlie Harris, Jimmy Adano, Dottie Deane, Ann Powell
10—BALLET EXTRAVAGANZA — "A CHAMPAGNE BUBBLE SHOWER"
  a)Lost In Paradise.. Girls in White
  b)My Voice In Song .... Jimmy Adano
  c)QUEEN OF THE BUBBLES ....LOVELY JOAN TORINO
11—Scene — Muchacha .... Bert Carr, Charlie Harris and Joan Powell
12—FEATURE — THE QUEEN OF THE AMAZONS...................... LOIS DeFEE
13—Finale — Stars In Review .... The Cast

ACT TWO

1—Opening — Those Wild Flappers of The Roaring Twenties
  a) Five Foot Two, Eyes of Blue...............................Our Girls, with Ora Mae
  b) Ricochet Romance .... Jummy Adano with Delores Fisher
    Reprise — There's Only One .... Ora Mae
2—Scene — A Policeman Objects ....Benny Moore, Charlie Harris, Jim Adano, Dottie Deane
3—Specialty...Ann Powell
4—Ballet — Swinging To The Blues .... The Morokoff Girls
5—Scene — The Drugstore........................... Bert Carr, Harris, Powell, Deane, Adano
6—FEATURE — OUR STAR RETURNS..................... GLAMAZON LOIS DeFEE
7—Finale .... MISS DeFEE and Girls

Program for The Hudson Theatre, listing Joan as the "Queen of the Bubbles" (1954).
Photo courtesy of Joan Torino.

JOAN TORINO

Publicity shot for a young Joan Torino.
Photo courtesy of Joan Torino.

we always had to remember twelve different routines." She added, "Paul got along with everyone. We all loved him and when he died, it was like losing family. Everyone pitched in and helped buy his headstone." Paul Morokoff's headstone read, "We all love you."

Joan told me, "For $1 you could see a complete Burlesque show with thirty chorus girls, accompanied by an orchestra, baggy-pants comics, and the featured resident stripper. Every weekend there was the added attraction of a touring Burlesque road show. The Hudson was the best Burlesque theater in New Jersey."

Joan became one of the featured resident strippers up until 1957, when The Hudson Theatre put on its final Burlesque show and closed its doors forever. It was torn down in 1965 and turned into a parking lot.

After The Hudson Theatre closed, Joan went on the road for a while, but she was lonesome and missed The Hudson, which had been like a second home to her. She also missed working and socializing with her close friends, Showgirl Ellye Farrelly, Stripper Helen Morrison who was known as "Athena The Grecian Siren of Sex," Maria Bradley, and Stripper Hope Diamond the "Gem of Exotics." Most of all, she missed her baby son and her grandmother.

Joan retired from Burlesque in 1958. She worked as a waitress, a car-hop, went to Cosmetology school, and was a Real Estate Agent for twelve years. She was both ambitious and resourceful.

In 1983, Joan mortgaged her home and opened her own nightclub in Hoboken, New Jersey; she named it Red Heads.

Joan enlisted her four best friends and strip-sisters from The Hudson Theatre days to help out part-time, and join in the fun. On the Red Heads walls were enlarged pictures of Joan and her friends in their hey-day at The Hudson. On Sundays, Joan had a free Champagne and Jellybeans brunch.

The Red Heads was an immediate success, thanks in part to publicity by local newspaper reporters who had a field day interviewing Joan about her past. She conducted the interviews in her club while sipping Cham-

Joan, standing behind the bar at the Red Heads (1983).
Photo courtesy of Joan Torino.

pagne and popping Jellybeans into her bright red mouth. In March 1994, Joan sold the Redheads and retired.

In 1985, Joan performed the role of a stripper in a nostalgic production of *Gypsy,* staged at The Hoboken Civic Theatre. She wore one of her 1950s Rex Huntington creations, a rhinestone-studded costume complete with beaded opera-length gauntlet-gloves, feathered boa, and feathered headdress. Aside from going from a size nine to a size eleven, Joan hadn't lost her va-voom or her hubba-hubba appeal. She did a marvelous mock-strip with the skill and flair of the consummate Burlesque entertainer, and received standing ovations every night.

Starting in February 1995, I conducted several phone interviews with Joan. She was such fun to talk with; her enthusiasm and eagerness to discuss her part in Burlesque's past was infectious. I could have listened to her all day.

Joan arranged for my interviews with her two strip-buddies, Ellye Farrelly and Athena. Talking to them was like talking to old friends. They even tried to get me to come to New Jersey and hang out with them, but I couldn't get away. *It is one of my biggest regrets!*

Joan continued her close friendships with her stripper gal-friends and with noted Costume Designer Rex Huntington, who made many of her beautiful costumes.

Rex Huntington's costume designs have often been compared to the designs of Bob Mackie, the "Sultan of Sequins." The only difference being, Rex was self-taught.

Rex was born Rexford Jay Huntington on March 25, 1907, in Richmond, Indiana. His parents were Vaudevillians who toured with different circuits. Rex traveled with them, and as soon as he was able to walk he became part of their act. In his teens, Rex performed at the well-known 606 Club in Chicago, but as Vaudeville waned, Rex found less work in Vaudeville shows.

He moved to Michigan to work as a drill-press operator, but was quickly hired by Mr. Clamage, who ran Minsky's Avenue Theatre in Detroit. Still in his early teens, Rex took this job working as a dancer in the chorus line and soon became fascinated with everything involving costume making. He watched and took note of the wardrobe makers' designs and use of fabric; the seamstress's measurements and careful handling of sequins, bangles, and Bugle beads, and the way the costumes moved with the dancer's body. He had never studied sewing; it was a natural talent he learned thru observing and doing.

In the beginning, Rex danced at night and sewed costumes by day. He had a female dance partner and they sprayed their bodies' silver. Gradually, and after a few years, Rex developed his own style of design and eventually became the best-known Costume Designer on the East Coast. When Minsky purchased The Newark Theatre in New Jersey, they hired Rex and his assistant Bob Greenwood as Costume Makers.

Rex was the Costume Designer and Wardrobe Master for Ann Corio's long running *This Was Burlesque*. Some of his famous customers were Burlesque Queens Georgia Sothern, Zorita, Tempest Storm, Ann Corio, Lili St. Cyr, and Margie Hart. Among many other famous women, Rex made costumes and gowns for dancer Denise Darcel and Actress Patrice Wymore, who was married to Actor Errol Flynn.

Burlesque Star Yvette Paris, Rex Huntington and Joan Torino in Rex's Weehawken home (late 1980s). Photo courtesy of Yvette Paris.

Denise Darcel was in a 1969 Burlesque Revue that also starred body-builder Mickey Hargitay, who had been Jayne Mansfield's husband. *I wonder if he wore a G-string?*

Rex passed away September 13, 1992, in Weehawken, New Jersey. He had owned his three-story home since 1950. It still contained his wardrobe shop over-looking the Manhattan Skyscrapers, along with his five sewing machines, his special sequin sewing machine, sketches, business records, and photos of performers wearing his fantastic costumes. It was virtually a catalog of his life-long achievements. He left his whole costume archive to his beloved and devoted friend, Joan Torino.

Rex's costumes are showcased in Liz Goldwyn's fabulous book on Burlesque, *Pretty Things, The Last Generation of American Burlesque Queens.*

Publicity shot of Joan with her favorite Champagne. Photo courtesy of Yvette Paris.

Joan passed away on August 29, 2009. Her obituary reads in part; "Joan will be remembered for her love of animals and lifetime commitment to Animal Rights Groups."

Champagne and Jellybean toast to Joan Torino, a beautiful Burlesque baby and a remarkable lady!

ELLYE FARRELLY

Ellye Farrelly's real name is Elinor Margaret Farrelly. She was born January 9, 1934, in Hudson County, New Jersey, and was the youngest child in a family of six girls and three boys. Her mother died when she was six years old and at nine, she was sent to live at Sacred Heart Academy where Nuns raised her. Her father died when she was fifteen leaving her an orphan. At age eighteen the Nuns sent her out on her own.

The Nuns helped her find work as a telephone operator; a job she didn't like. Ellye soon quit that position and found one as a waitress in a White Castle hamburger shop.

One afternoon, Ellye and a friend stopped for a drink in the Red Robin bar across the street from The Hudson Theatre. The bartender over-heard Ellye complaining about not liking her job and how little it paid. He took one look at Ellye and said, "With your looks, you should go over to The Hudson and try out for a job." Being raised by Nuns, Ellye was shocked at the idea!

After a week more of bussing burgers, Burlesque didn't sound so bad. In fact, it was starting to sound a little exciting to Ellye. She decided to go to The Hudson and see what happened. For a young girl who lived nine years among Nuns who never exposed more than fingers or face, this took guts!

Ellye was scared, but she got up enough nerve to go into The Hudson Theatre and ask for the Manager. She told him she wanted a job and he asked to see her legs. It just happens that Ellye is 5' 7" and most of that IS her legs! As it turned out, it wasn't the Manager after all, but the House Choreographer Paul Morokoff who hired her. He asked Ellye,"When can you start?" She answered, "I can't dance," and he replied "I'll teach you. Come back tomorrow at noon."

Within a few days, Ellye learned enough basic dance steps to get her started in the chorus line. She was soon rehearsing right along with the rest of the girls and being fitted for costumes. She danced background in the chorus line-up for six months, before becoming a chorus line feature.

Ellye also made extra money as a Catcher for the Headliners. Her job as a Catcher entailed waiting behind the stage curtain during the star's act, and catching their costumes as they removed them, piece by piece and tossed them behind the curtain. The Headliner paid the Catcher out of her own money. It was worth the extra $5 or $10 to keep their expensive costumes from lying on the floor of the dusty stage.

Ellye told me: "For some reason, Paul liked to show-case me on high platforms as part of the chorus girl's numbers. Once, he put me ten feet in the air on a scaffold with stairs in the back. I was wearing a low-cut peasant blouse and a 10' long and 5' wide blue, crepe paper skirt that was tied around my waist. When I pulled the strings, it opened down the middle and the girls would come strutting out in their little blue outfits and dance to "Sweet Little Alice Blue-Gown," but, when they came out, the scaffold would start shaking and I'd be terrified. The girls would dance in and out of my skirt and I'd be shaking. I had to stay up there and smile until the number was over and the curtain closed."

Ellye also told me: "Another time, Paul had me sit in the middle of a big silver star hanging eight feet off the ground. The star would swing back and forth while the girls danced to "Swinging On A Star." It was all I could do to hold on and smile."

She went on to say, "The scariest time was when Paul put me on a 6' high platform with stairs going up the front. I wore a sparkly gypsy costume and held a crystal ball as part of the backdrop for a carnival scene. A couple of other chorus girls were the "hoochie-coochie" dancers on pedestals beside me. In front of us was Zorita with two of her boa constrictor snakes. She was doing her act and didn't notice that one of her snakes was slowly crawling up the steps toward me. I froze! Tears were rolling down my face and I thought it was going to squeeze me to death, or at least bite me. Than someone near the stage got Zorita's attention and she caught the snake and went on with her act."

I've heard rumors from other strippers that Zorita enjoyed it when her snakes frightened the dancers.

Ellye eventually became a stripper and she recalled the first time she stripped. She told me the girls called stripping "exotic dancing" back then. Rex made her a rather sweet outfit for her debut; he put tiny roses on her gown and orchestra leader George Ponsonie chose her music. It was "Stay as Sweet as You Are" followed by "Sugar Blues", and the finale was "Flash Bam Ala-Ka-Zam". It was on her twenty-first birthday and the cast gave her a party after the show. An admirer sent her a bouquet of twenty-one

Zorita and her snake. Autograph shows Zorita's snake signature.
Photo courtesy of Jennie Lee.

Zorita and her snake in the movie *I Married a Savage*.
Photo courtesy of Authors Collection.

Seductive Zorita and jeweled Scorpion. Photo courtesy of Jennie Lee.

Zorita with her daughter Tawny. Photo courtesy of Jennie Lee.

red roses with a five-dollar bill wrapped around each rose. *That was big money in the 1950s.*

She never forgot it, and although it was strictly platonic, Ellye and her admirer were still friends at the time of my interview with her. She told me he called her every holiday and sent her roses with five-dollar bills wrapped around them. She added, "He would always write; Ellye, you will always be a Star."

Ellye became good friends with dancer Choreographer/Straight Woman Ilene Murray and her husband, Comedian George Murray. They would always use Ellye in their skits when they played The Hudson, and Ellye earned extra money for her part. Ellye said she considered Ilene the best Talking Woman in Burlesque. She said Ilene had perfect timing, and a voice like Ethel Merman that could be heard in the back row.

Ellye said she knew both Jennie Lee and Dixie Evans from The Hudson, but her all-time favorite stripper was her close friend and mentor Georgia Sothern, who called Ellye ". . . my adopted daughter." Georgia tried to get Ellye to join her traveling Burlesque show, *Sothern's Red-Headed Revue,* and go with her on the road. Ellye declined not wanting to travel, but she considered Georgia to be the greatest stripper that ever lived and went on to say, "Georgia had energy coming out her kazoo."

In 1956, Ellye left The Hudson for Buffalo, New York, to work at The Palace Theatre where she both danced in the chorus and stripped.

The Palace Theatre opened in 1898 and had seven hundred seats; it was a real moneymaker. When Ellye worked there, the owner drove a chartreuse Cadillac convertible, promoted prizefighters, and auditioned the strippers personally. He made enough money in Burlesque to send his kids to Harvard. The Palace Theatre closed its doors in 1977.

While Ellye worked at The Palace, her favorite comics were Bert Carr and Charlie Robinson. Ellye said Charlie Robinson used her in his skits. She would just stand there looking pretty and he would try to crack her up. When he did, her boobs would bounce up and down and the audience would roar! She also worked with Billy Ainsley, who took his teeth out while working onstage; and Billy Hagan, who used the term "cheese and crackers" instead of cuss words. She said that when she worked with Comic Al Baker, he called her "Scoop-It" because she could never do a proper bump. He used to stand in the wings while Ellye was dancing and yell, "Scoop it, Ellye, scoop it!" She also worked in one of the nightclubs with Comedian Shelly Berman, who called her "Long Sam" after one of the Little Abner characters.

Al Baker was one of Burlesque's best. He worked with Abbott and Costello and toured with Joe De Rita, who was Curly in the Three Stooges. In 1956, Al won $140,000 in the Irish Sweepstakes and semi-retired. He married Singer Marcel Jones in 1932, and they remained married until her death.

Ellye worked at The Palace off-and-on for the next five years, until she fell in love with a bass player and he didn't want other men looking at her. She received an offer for a screen test, but Mr. Bass Player scared her with casting couch talk so she declined the offer. Ellye stayed with Mr. Bass Player for a couple of years, working as a secretary for some firm.

She then dated well-known Actor Mickey Shawnessy for a while. At age thirty-seven she finally married, because people kept bugging her about it. The marriage to a man she referred to as "Nameless," was short-lived.

In 1971, she enjoyed working as a waitress in a high-class sports bar wearing a Joe Namath Jersey and shorts that her friend Rex Huntington made for her. By the time I interviewed Ellye, she was working as a secretary for her friend and ex-Stripper, Hope Diamond's Real Estate Brokerage.

Ellye told me her years in Burlesque were the most wonderful time of her life, and she has no regrets. She said she wasn't the least bit ashamed of working in Burlesque and thought it was pretty innocent back than. The comics made fun of sex and so did the girls. Sadly, she lost most of her photos and couldn't locate the few she had left. As luck would have it, Joan Torino supplied me with a fabulous picture of Ellye.

Ellye continued to assist Joan Torino in her quest to raise money and civic awareness of animal abuse until Joan's death in 2009. On October 19, 2010, at age seventy-six, Ellye joined Joan.

Miss Athena

Athena was born October 18, 1930. Her real name is Helen Morrison. Her mother had been a beautiful Latin Dancer who danced with castanets and died giving birth to Athena. Her father was a trumpet player in Benny Goodman's Band and because of his work, he was always on the road; so Athena and her two brothers were put in an orphanage. As a child, her father visited her when he was playing in the area. But he too, died when Athena was nine years old. No one adopted her, so she had to stay in the orphanage until she was eighteen.

Ellye Farrelly in one of her chorus-line costumes (1950). Photo courtesy of Joan Torino.

At that time, she was given a job at the telephone company just like her friend Ellye Farrelly. While working at the phone company, Athena developed a painful cyst on her gluteus maximus from sitting too much. While on disability, Athena was walking near The Hudson and heard the sound of horns coming from the theater. It reminded her of her father. She was more curious than brave, so she walked in and took a back-row seat. As fate would have it, the chorus line was in full swing. She remembered thinking to herself, *I can kick higher than that.*

After the matinee Athena, who was the only girl in the audience, decided to wait until all the men filed out of the theater before she left. Once again, Paul Morokoff, with his eye for new talent had been watching. He approached her, asking if she was looking for a job. Athena surprised herself by saying yes. Paul told her, "Get up on the stage and show me what you can do." Athena told me she almost knocked herself out auditioning, and was very excited when Paul asked her, "When can you start?"

Athena had been living with her aunt and uncle in Union City, near The Hudson. She went home and told her aunt about her new job as a dancer and her aunt was furious! First off, because of Athena's employment her aunt had been getting her phone bill half-price, and secondly, she didn't want her husband living around a Burlesque dancer. So she threw Athena out on the street, calling her ungrateful garbage.

Athena, Joan Torino, and Ellye Farrelly quickly bonded on and off the stage. Ellye and Athena stayed in the chorus the longest; Joan was the first one to become a Specialty Dancer and a Feature.

Athena told me a funny story about her and Ellye's Friday night escapades at The Hudson. "For a long time, Ellye and I would take turns bringing a bottle of vodka and hiding it in the dressing room," she said. "No one could smell the vodka on our breath, so now and then we'd sneak a few nips. Paul Morokoff had taught the chorus a new routine and Rex had made our costumes. We all wore gowns that were black on one side and white on the other, and we all had to turn in unison showing first the black side and then the white side. Paul was pretty pleased with this idea and was on the sidelines watching. I had a few more nips than usual and I got mixed up and couldn't remember which side to show; so I kept showing the wrong side. I heard Paul say, 'Get her off the stage; she's drunk.' Down went the curtain and they pulled me off the stage. Well, very few people knew that Paul wore a toupee, so I screamed at the top of my lungs, telling him to take his toupee and shove it where the sun

Miss Athena sitting on the piano (1978). Photo courtesy of Athena.

didn't shine!" Athena continued, "Of course, he fired me and I cried for two weeks; until he forgave me and let me come back to work."

Athena stayed at The Hudson for several years. She was a Catcher for Lili St. Cyr, became close friends with Georgia Sothern, and Rex Huntington made all her costumes. She said she had a ton of fun at The Hudson.

Athena had an abusive marriage at age twenty-three, and left both the marriage and The Hudson to become a Headliner in a Pittsburgh nightclub. The nightclub owner asked her to flash and she told him to shove it; but after a few weeks of starving, she decided she had to take it off after all.

Athena met her second husband at one of the nightclubs. He came in to watch the comics and Athena caught his eye. He sent an Orchid pinned to a black lace hanky, to her dressing room. Everywhere she played he would have the florist send the same little gift to her dressing room. Finally, out of curiosity, Athena agreed to have dinner with him between shows. They hit it off, and eventually they married and had two children. The marriage lasted until her husband's death. Athena told me she still had all the black hankies and orchids pressed in a book.

Athena spent eight years in Burlesque theaters and quit stripping in 1973 because she didn't want to go nude. After her marriage, Athena became a Belly Dancer at The 500 Club and the La Bistro Club in Atlantic City, where she worked weekends for fifteen years. She worked with Frank Sinatra and his Rat Pack, and Comic Jackie Mason.

Athena found time to work as a swimmer and high diver for different Water-Shows and Aquacades. She would dive into a large see-thru tank and perform acrobatics while inside it. She even gave swimming lessons to pre-teens.

Athena had an amazing career and remained friends with Joan Torino, Ellye Farrelly, and Hope Diamond. She said the girls all got together at least once a month for hamburgers and a movie, followed by a few drinks and chitchat about their old Hudson days. Athena told me the girls all agreed that Burlesque was the most misunderstood form of entertainment.

Athena was very accommodating in her interview, especially considering she was having chemotherapy at the time, but she didn't tell me until our two sessions were finished. She was both feisty and sweet, with a great sense of humor.

Athena passed away September 5, 2001, in North Bergen, New Jersey. She was seventy years young.

HOPE DIAMOND

Hope Diamond's real name is Leona Bonaccolta. She had a hard childhood; her family was poor and her mother was an alcoholic. She left home at the age of seventeen to escape her abusive stepfather.

Auburn-haired Leona had a lovely face and a dazzling smile; she easily found work in the chorus line at The Hudson Theatre. It wasn't long before she became a stripper, a job that paid $50 extra per week. She took on the stage name Hope Diamond, Precious Gem of Burlesque.

Hope's strip routine banished the myth that Burlesque is naughty, not nice and bristling with vice. Her act was flirty and feminine. Hope was on the tall side and her measurements were: 37" bust, 25" waist and 37" hips. She had one of those hourglass figures that men love. Hope often played the Burlesque theaters in Montreal, Canada, but mostly she worked here in the states on the East Coast. She got into stripping during the last vestiges of Burlesque in the 1950s and 1960s, just before the popularity of Topless Dancers replaced the Peelers.

Hope married Jazz Musician/Singer Al Beldini. They later divorced and she married Singer Bobby Colt with whom she had a son. Hope had a messy break-up with Colt, naming well-known Turkish Belly Dancer Nejla Ates as correspondent in her divorce. Afterwards, Hope went on with her life, but a short time later the Belly Dancer had a big fight with Colt and she attempted suicide by an overdose of tranquilizers.

Rare photo of a young Ann Corio. Photo courtesy of Authors Collection.

In 1962, Hope went on tour in Ann Corio's *This Was Burlesque*. She did a cute satire of Lili St. Cyr's famous Bathtub Strip and received wonderful reviews for her part in the show. Hope remained good friends with Corio, until Corio's death in 1999.

After retiring from Burlesque, Hope went into the Real Estate business, which proved to be highly lucrative for her. She also got into politics and became the Jersey City Deputy Mayor. Years later, Hope was arrested as part of a massive bid probe/sting operation that dealt with municipal officials and candidates for office. In March of 2012, at age seventy-six, she was convicted of taking a bribe. Hope was fined $30,000 and sentenced to three years in a Federal Prison in Texas. *Was it the curse of the Hope Diamond? Or just bad luck.*

Sunny Dare * Val Valentine * Joni Taylor

After retiring from Burlesque, these three gals reconnected with each other in Toledo, Ohio. Sunny Dare was known as the "Girl with the Blue Hair" and was the most well-known of the three. Sunny's real name is Roberta Bauman, Val is Carole Licata, and Joni is Joanne Di Rando. All three worked during the 1950s, 1960s, and 1970s.

Both Sunny and Val traveled across the states working in nightclubs. Val also worked in carnivals where she was called "Cupids Cutie." Sunny's parents spent most of their life working on the Carnival Circuit; her father was a Carnival Barker and her mother worked in various acts including routines with snakes. Joni was a dancer, but she was never a big-featured stripper like Sunny and Val. She was a popular Talking Woman who worked with some famous old-time comics. While still in the strip scene, Sunny went through four husbands. Val had three and Joni had two. Strippers and marriage is a hard mix.

By 2002, Sunny was working at a local hospital; Val was taking care of an elderly aunt and working as a waitress; and Joni, who is a cancer survivor, counsel's women who are undergoing cancer treatments. All three of these terrific ladies were involved in animal rescue. They met once a month to discuss better ways to improve their rescue operation, like raising the funds needed to house and feed the dogs and cats in their care; and find each and every animal lifetime homes.

All three are members of Jane Briggeman's Golden Days of Burlesque Historical Society. Sunny Dare passed away in 2008.

Sunny Dare. Photo
courtesy of Authors
Collection.

Val Valentine. Photo
courtesy of Mitzi.

YVETTE PARIS

Yvette Paris was born Barbara Ann Baker in Patterson, New Jersey. She married at age nineteen and endured an abusive marriage to a man who broke her nose twice. She divorced at age twenty-seven, and met and married her soul mate David March. They have two great kids, Jack and Juliet. Juliet is drop-dead gorgeous and plays in her own band named "Steel March". Yvette is now a grandmother and lives in Cheyenne, Wyoming.

Leola Harlow and Ann Corio (1988). Photo courtesy of Leola Harlow

Yvette is a freelance writer speaking out against animal abuse. She is also a prolific author, having written *Queen of Burlesque,* the Revised Edition of *Queen of Burlesque,* and *Dying To Be Marilyn,* which is a book about Marilyn Monroe impersonators. She also authored *Suffer Not a Witch, Lost in the Sixties, Everyday Angels,* and *March's Ark,* which is about their rescued animals.

Yvette and her husband are both animal activists and have spent their lives together rescuing and mending abused animals, letting them live out their remaining lives in the peace and love of the home they refer to as March's Ark. At one time, Yvette and her family had one hundred twenty-two cats, thirteen dogs; ferrets, rabbits, birds, rats, hamsters, guinea pigs and Yvette's beloved wolf.

When Yvette was fourteen, she was a skinny, buck-toothed kid. Her classmates voted her the ugliest girl in school. Well, the jokes on them. Yvette went on to pose for over one hundred men's magazines, eight magazine covers, and matching centerfolds. *How's that for a skinny, buck toothed kid?*

Yvette started out as a Go-Go Dancer and went on to be one of the most popular strippers in New Jersey and New York City. She has been on numerous television talk shows, including three times on *Sally Jessy Raphael, Morton Downy Jr., Joe Franklin,* and her favorite *To Tell the Truth,* where she was the featured star. In 1988, Yvette was on Sally's show with Jennie Lee, Dixie Evans, Leola Harlow the world's oldest stripper, Bambi Vaughn, Annie Sprinkles, and Burlesque Legend Ann Corio. It was around that time Yvette received the Fanny Award from Jennie Lee. Yvette was also on a show with Strippers Bambi Sr. and her daughter Bambi Jr., who later married television host Montel Williams; and Kelly Everett, who strips for God.

Yvette is featured on a 1989 calendar where she portrays Marilyn Monroe, Jayne Mansfield and Jean Harlow.

Yvette knows more celebrities than I have space to mention. One I will name is Tiny Tim, who was close friends with both Yvette and her family. I recommend Yvette's revised edition of *Queen of Burlesque* for a great read that's loaded with personal pictures and interesting antidotes.

Leola doing a Spanish Bullfight Dance in 1942. Photo courtesy of Leola Harlow.

Yvette as Jean Harlow (1989). Photo courtesy of Yvette Paris.

Yvette holding her lucky Boa, standing in front of her gowns and photos on display in the Exotic World Museum (2005). Photo courtesy of Yvette Paris.

DEBB BRENTON

I can't forget to mention Debb Brenton who started rescuing animals in 1969. She has spent most of her life saving exotic and domestic animals; has rehabilitated snakes, hawks/falcons, and wild burros, and founded a desert tortoise preserve. She worked as a veterinary assistant, and for a while she turned her home into a lion's den so she could baby-sit a cougar cub. In 1968 and 1970, Debb supplemented her income as a Go-Go Dancer at the Copper Penny in Ohio. She was also photographer's model in Riverside, California.

Although she was never a Stripper, she deserves honorable mention for being forced to watch strip films until she screamed, cast a cautious eye on all the curvy cuties in the gallery of gorgeous gams, listen to my ramblings on Burlesque, and proofread every word of Burlesque babble in this book to render it readable.

Debb modeling with her Burmese Python.
Photo courtesy of Debb Brenton.

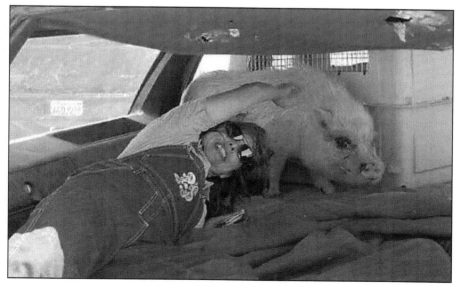

Debb "bringing home the bacon" in her pup-mobile. (Wilbur, an abandoned pig)
Sorry *Debb, I couldn't resist!* Photo courtesy of Authors Collection.

Chapter 8

Tidbits N' Teasers

BECAUSE OF AN OLD SUPERSTITION, every Burlesque theater housed one or two cats. They lived out their lives lapping up milk amid the glitter and glitz, while being petted and protected by a bevy of Burlesque beauties. *Personally, I think it had more to do with mice than superstition.*

In 1964, Tempest Storm withdrew her bank account because the bank balked at printing her semi-nude picture on her checks.

Stripper Rose La Rose and a few of the chorus girls who danced in her theater, holding the next generation of theater kittens. Photo courtesy of Authors Collection.

The timeless Tempest Storm. Photo courtesy of Tempest Storm.

In 1945, Gypsy Rose Lee earned $5,000 per week in addition to 25% of the box office gross. She traveled with her own house trailer so she didn't have to rent a hotel room; and she cooked most of her meals in her home on wheels.

Gypsy had a real knack for drumming up publicity. On October 29, 1936, for instance, while Gypsy was both Burlesque Queen and Star of the Ziegfeld Follies, she was chosen Queen of the annual formal Senior Ball at Columbia University in New York City. In 1937, she married her first husband, manufacturer Arnold Robert Mizzy. For publicity, they wed in a water taxi on the now-defunct Venice Canal in Santa Monica, California. In her wedding to

Tempest with Maynard Slote, Owner of Strip City in Los Angeles (early 1950s).
Photo courtesy of Authors Collection.

another husband, Gypsy used a chimpanzee as her ring-bearer. At the wedding reception, Gypsy informed reporters, "I don't tease; I tantalize."

One horticulturist named a red rose after Gypsy. It is called the "G-String Rose," and it still blooms every year in Brampton, Ontario, Canada.

Gypsy was an animal lover, too. She had cats, small turtles, guinea pigs, goldfish, and Chinese-crested dogs that she often took with her on the road. Her main companion was her Chihuahua named "Stud."

There is an etching of a rose and Gypsy's stage name Gypsy Rose Lee, on her headstone in Inglewood Memorial Park Cemetery, in Inglewood, California. Anyone can visit it and pay their respects to Gypsy. *You might want to leave a red rose.*

In 1929, the movie industry took advantage of the public's interest in regards to Burlesque. Paramount Studio decided to capitalize on the general public's morbid curiosity concerning naughty, bawdy Burlesque

Gypsy wearing the costume she made. Photo courtesy of Authors Collection.

babes. Paramount put together a film based on a past-her-prime Burlesque Queen who fears that her daughter (who was raised in a convent) will end up like her. The movie titled *Applause* depicts the Burlesque world as a decadent and sleazy life, both on and off the stage. The crowded runway scenes show shoddily costumed Burlesque dancers leaning over the stage and interacting with the all-male audience, who are eager to grab anything they can reach.

The film stars well-known Torch Singer Helen Morgan, and was a sell-out in 1929 and 1930. After seeing the movie, one gets the feel-

Gypsy and her Chihuahua. Photo courtesy of Authors collection.

Gypsy Rose Lee's headstone. Photo courtesy of Authors Collection.

ing that not only is Burlesque bad for public morals, but the men who frequent it are all a bunch of sex-crazed degenerates. The bible beaters had a field day using this movie as an example of what sinfulness was about. In later years, because of its historical and cultural significance, the National Preservation of the Library of Congress selected *Applause* for preservation.

In the 1941 movie *Ball of Fire*, Barbara Stanwyck starred as nightclub dancer and Singer Sugar-Puss O'Shea. The movie had some comparisons to real-life Burlesque Queen Betty Rowland, who was known as the "Ball of Fire." One of the costumes Stanwyck wears in the movie is almost an

Betty Rowland showing Lt. Edward Tetrick where a lighted cigarette was pushed into her thigh (1943). Photo courtesy of Authors Collection.

exact replica of one of Betty Rowland's. In fact, Rowland unsuccessfully sued the studio

On November 18, 1943, a woman forced her husband to show him where he had been spending his time and money. The man took his irate wife to The Follies Theater in Los Angeles to see dancer Betty Rowland do her striptease. The wife got so worked up, she leaned across the stage and jabbed a lit cigarette into Rowland's thigh. The following day, Betty appeared at the city attorney's office and waged a complaint of assault and battery charges against the little wife of her number one fan.

Pinky Lee and chorus girl. Photo courtesy of Authors Collection.

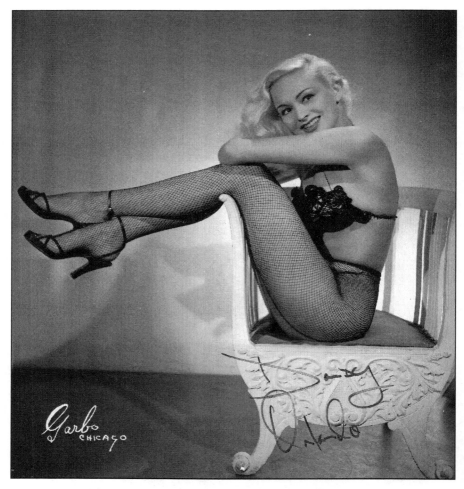

The exquisite Dardy Orlando. Photo courtesy of Jennie Lee.

Oddly enough, Barbara Stanwyck, whose real name is Ruby Catherine Stevens, began her career in a 1927 Broadway musical play called *Burlesque*, where she starred with Actor/Comic/Dancer Hal Skelly and a young character actress named Marjorie Main.

The 1943 movie *Lady of Burlesque* was based on Gypsy Rose Lee's book *The G-string Murders*. It takes place in a Burlesque theater where one of the strippers has been murdered by strangulation with her G-string. The movie is unique in its use of three ex-chorus girls and an actual Burlesque comic. Stanwyck, Iris Adrian, and Marian Martin were all ex-Ziegfeld dancers before going into the movies. Pinky Lee was a Burlesque Comic before having his popular children's television program, *The Pinky Lee Show*.

Harold Minsky at his Rialto Theatre in Chicago, presenting Dardy Orlando with The Anatomy Award. (1950). Photo courtesy of Authors Collection.

Dardy Orlando, whose real name is Rosemary Dardy Blackadder, was both Lili St. Cyr's half-sister and Harold Minsky's wife. She won the coveted Anatomy Award for the best body of the year. The winner is chosen by the press and the award is a gold statuette of Venus.

The 1944 movie *Casanova in Burlesque* is about a Professor of Shakespeare who moonlights every summer as a Burlesque Clown. One of the strippers threatens to reveal his secret, unless he gives her a starring role in his upcoming school play *Romeo and Juliet*. He agrees, but she is so bad the whole cast walks out. In the end, the Professor solves the problem by staging a Swing version of *The Taming of the Shrew,* using numbers from Burlesque routines and skits. It stars rubber-faced, bigmouth Comic Joe E. Brown and Gypsy Rose Lee's sister June Havoc, along with cowgirl Dale Evans. *This is a fun film and it was made during Burlesque's hey-day. Wow, Dale Evans in Burlesque!*

In the 1945 movie *Doll Face,* a popular stripper played by Vivian Blaine goes to great lengths to prove to the press that strippers can have a high IQ, but she does it with a ridiculous Brooklyn accent. Carman Miranda plays the Specialty Dancer who steals the show, and a very young Perry Como is part of the Burlesque scene. Although the story line is somewhat silly, it's worth seeing for the wonderful Carman Miranda dance scenes.

Candid shot of Natalie Wood and Gypsy Rose Lee on the set of *Gypsy.*
Photo courtesy of Authors Collection.

Blaze Starr. Photo courtesy of Blaze Starr.

The year 1962 brought us the fabulous movie *Gypsy,* based on the life of Gypsy Rose Lee. Natalie Wood and Rosalind Russell are a perfect match-up as Gypsy and her mother Rose. This is a movie to see over and over. It's not only a glimpse into real life behind the scenes of a Burlesque stage, but its wonderful entertainment.

The 1963 movie *The Stripper* is based on an aging actress-turned-stripper, and a young admirer played by Richard Bymer. It stars Joanne Woodward, whose strip-costume consists of a bunch of balloons. The film has Gypsy Rose Lee cast as Madame Olga. In real life, Gypsy gave Joanne some tips and instructions for her strip scenes. The original casting was

Marilyn Monroe and Pat Boone, but for moral reasons Pat opted out. *Pat Boone infatuated with a Stripper? Wow, this can't be April Love!*

For her efforts on this film, Stripper Jennie Lee presented Woodward with the Woman of the Year Award on behalf of the Exotic Dancers League of America. The 1968 movie *The Night They Raided Minsky's*, is part musical and mostly farcical. It is based on the book of the same title, written by Rowland Barber in 1960. The story line is set in 1925, and is a supposed account of the real Minsky Brother's who owned Burlesque theaters in that time period; Billy Minsky in particular. It is a theatrical production of how the striptease came about. *If you believe a young runaway Amish girl was the first Burlesque dancer to bare her breasts on the stage, you'll love this film.*

The 1989 movie *Blaze* is about her life as a stripper and her affair with Governor Huey Long, starring Paul Newman as Huey Long. Paul, who is married to Joanne Woodward in real life, is a hoot; especially when he wears his boots to bed-down with Blaze, claiming they gave him traction. Blaze Starr herself has a cameo in the movie and was a technical advisor for the filming. All of the movies background photos of strippers were on loan from Jennie Lee's Exotic World Museum.

Blaze was known for her wildly uninhibited dance style. Audiences loved it when she came onstage wearing a sexy jungle outfit and began beating on her bongos. Her face was every bit as sexy as her body. She had a great gimmick that has never been duplicated. Blaze would start out by sitting on top of her satin couch. Before long, she'd begin to writhe and squirm around as she teasingly peeled off her clothes; and just as she reached the point where she was only clad in her pasties, G-string, nylons, and garter-belt, she would start bouncing on the couch. This would trigger a mechanism that sent smoke billowing out from beneath it. Blaze called her act "Spontaneous Combustion," and it drove the audience wild!

Blaze Starr's real name is Fannie Belle Fleming. She was born in 1932, in Wilsendale, West Virginia, and was one of eleven children. One of her sisters was a stripper whose stage name was "Sheba Queen." She never reached the popularity of Blaze. In 1969, Blaze spent a few days at Walter Reed Hospital passing out her pictures, signing autographs, and cheering-up wounded soldiers. It was the hospitals highlight of the year and made mention in the *Stars and Stripes* bulletin. Sadly, Blaze passed away June 15, 2015.

Dixie Evans, Stripper and Curator of the Exotic World Museum, tried for years to acquire Blaze's smoking couch to add to the Museum's collection, but for several reasons it never came to pass. One issue was the condition

Blaze beating on her bongos (1950s). Photo courtesy of Author's Collection.

of it. Everyone involved in the efforts thought it might be too fragile to ship. Jennie Lee purchased Jane Mansfield's heart-shaped love seat for the Museum; it was a popular seat to pose for pictures.

Speaking of Jennie Lee, she had small roles and an even smaller wardrobe in the B- films *3 Nuts in Search of a Bolt* and *the Secret File of Detective X.*

Jennie Lee's sister-in-law was a stripper. Her stage name was Nadia and she was Jennie's first husband Danny Wanick's, sister. Nadia's real name is Evelyn Wanick. She and Jennie Lee went to high school together in 1947 in Wyandotte, Kansas City, Missouri.

"News Flash: Stripteasers Husband Fined." Shortly after Jennie and Daniel Lewis Wanick were married, Jennie Lee, along with two other strippers, found themselves in Judge McQueen's courtroom. The police testified that the girls danced in the nude. The girls argued they were wearing flesh-colored nylon and their dances were artistic and exotic. The Judge fined them each $250. Twenty-three-year-old Danny Wanick, who was with the girls, was fined $100 for driving his wife to the show. Asked by the Judge, "Do you think it's alright for your wife to strip before three hundred men?" Wanick replied, "As long as she's not violating the law." The Judge responded, "These women are to be pitied. I know what a striptease dance is. It is nothing artistic or exotic. I just can't understand a man taking his wife out there. I'll raise his fine to $300 and discharge these women.".

In 1962, Jennie Lee hired a bodyguard when she played the New Follies in Los Angeles. After appearing on a local television show, a threatening call came into the studio complaining she revealed too much about the strippers in the East Coast, and about their mafia boyfriends.

In 1948, redheaded stripping dynamo Georgia Sothern, known as the "Wow Girl," had some bumps with the law. She sued the New York Police to force them into returning her entertainment permit. The police thought her wiggles and bumps were too ferocious and revoked her permit. Georgia quipped, "They accused me of doing bumps and grinds. I couldn't do a grind for a million dollars. I do a few bumps; they called them ferocious bumps, but what I do is a burlesque of Burlesque." *Georgia was built for speed.*

Glorious Georgia Sothern. Photo courtesy of Authors Collection.

Flier advertising Georgia Sothern playing at The Howard Athenaeum in Boston, Massachusetts. Note Winnie Garrett and Mimi Reed on the same bill (1938). Photo courtesy of Authors Collection.

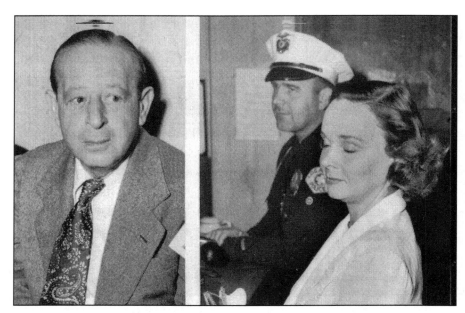

Press photo of Maurice Rosen, police officer, and Betty Rowland in court (May 8, 1952). Photo courtesy of Authors Collection.

Talking about run-ins with the law, Stripper Betty Rowland and Maurice Rosen, Manager of the Los Angeles Follies Theatre, were sentenced on September 18, 1963, to one hundred and twenty days in jail. It seems a certain prudish Judge Byron J. Walters deemed her act a lewd picture come-to-life. Judge Walters said, "The striptease is more dangerous than lewd or filthy pictures, because of the movements of the feminine form." *Oh, pooh!*

Betty Rowland stripped at The Follies Theatre in Los Angeles more times than any other stripper. One reason could be that, for several years, she was married to wealthy Owen Dalton who, along with his brother Roy, were the original Owners of the Follies Theatre in 1920. Before 1920, The Follies Theatre was named The Republic Theatre. The Dalton brother's and their family were prominent lumber magnates during several of Real Estates big building booms. Even after Betty divorced Dalton, she continued to be the House Stripper. For well over a decade, Betty was the most popular stripper in Los Angeles.

After retiring from Burlesque in the 1960s, Betty Rowland and longtime musician friend Mel Thompson worked together for close to twenty years at The Lightning Room in Santa Monica, California. Mel played the piano while Betty did some be-bopping around, or sometimes she would get someone to Jitterbug with her. Once in awhile, Mel and Betty would sing, nothing professional, just having fun. It was all very casual. Betty and Mel both helped tend bar and mingled with the customers. They brought in the clientele and kept The Lightning Room doors open. Most everyone who frequented the club knew that Betty had been a Burlesque Queen in the past, but Betty wasn't one to flaunt it, nor was she ready to pull up a rocking chair and retire. Although she genuinely liked the nightlife and seeing people have fun, she kept a sign on the front door that read, SHOES, SHIRTS and YOUR BEST BEHAVIOR. A sign on the wall near the pool table read, NO FOUL LANGUAGE! NO EXCEPTIONS!

When the original club owners died, they left The Lightning Room to both Rowland and Thompson. Betty and Mel changed the club's name to Mr. B's. For many more years Betty and Mel kept the club going. Then, after Mel died, Betty took on a couple of new partners and they changed the name again. It became Lounge 247.

Author Richard Lamparski wrote about Betty Roland and Mr. B's in his series, "*Whatever Became of. . . .*"

The club was still named Mr. B's in 1991 when I first met Betty Rowland. After being on the *Montel Williams* television show Dixie Evans, Sa-

Betty Rowland and Author at Betty's club in Santa Monica (1991).
Photo courtesy of Authors Collection.

die Burnett, and I stopped in to see Betty at her bar. She was just the most gracious host. It was hard to believe we were in the company of Burlesque royalty. She took us all to the Mexican restaurant next-door and insisted on paying for our meals. Betty lived in an apartment in Burbank. She gave me her home phone number so we could keep in touch. *I thought I was dreaming, and about a week later I called her to see if it really was her number.*

December 21, 1951, four days before Christmas, a robber tried to hold up a casher in a Detroit, Michigan, Burlesque house. The Cashier screamed out that she was being robbed and Comic Walter Menke, who was in the middle of his act, heard the screams, jumped off the stage, and chased the robber for two blocks before catching him with a flying tackle. The crook, weighing two hundred pounds, was a bloody mess, while the one hundred twenty-five pound Walter was unscathed. When the police arrived on the scene, Walter was still wearing his doctor's gown and the big silly necktie he used in his act. He later told the cops, "I didn't want the chorus girls and comics to be broke for the holiday because some of them have children to buy presents for." Walter later married cashier and Stripper Dawn Marie in-between shows at the Empress Theatre.

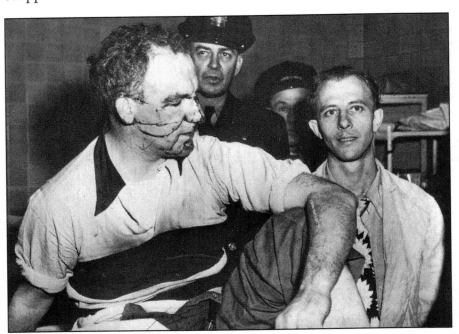

Press photo December 21, 1951, showing the bloodied robber, the cop, and Comic Walter Menke (whose stage name was Buddy DeVault). Photo courtesy of Authors Collection.

Gene Gemay with her Genie (1954). Photo courtesy of Authors Collection.

Stripper and Specialty Dancer Gene Gemay had an unusual act. It revolved around romantic intentions with a 6' 2" rubber man who was dressed like a Genie. Her routine was right out of the Arabian Nights, magic lamp and all. She would rub the lamp and smoke would surround her. As the smoke dissipated, the life-size Dummy would appear behind her. Gene would then go into her alluring dance routine to entice the Genie to grant her wish for some sort of rubber romance.

Stripper Gilda wasn't the only Hollywood child-star to perform on a Burlesque stage. Actress Charlotte Henry, who portrayed Alice in the movie *Alice in Wonderland*, was a chorus girl in the late 1940's at The Hollywood Theatre in San Diego.

Many of the strippers posed for magazine covers, earning extra money, publicity or both. Magazines such as *True Detective* often showed

Author on the cover of *Easyriders* Motorcycle Magazine (June 1976)].
Photo courtesy of Authors Collection.

anonymous half-dressed strippers on their covers, being tied up or choked as incentive for buying the book. There were scores of men's magazines filled with pin-up girls and Burlesque dancers. Some strippers even posed for motorcycle and racecar magazines.

Stripper Kitty Kelly the "Irish Venus," whose real name is Stella Marie Flaherty, worked mostly on the West Coast. She was in demand in Los Angeles, San Francisco, and Spokane, Washington. She had been stripping for close to eight years when she met Bandleader and Jazz Musician Billy Tipton. His group was playing at a club called Tin Pan Alley in Spokane, where Kitty was stripping. Billy was smitten by Kitty and pursued her for weeks. Finally, Kitty told him to forget any ideas of romance; she wasn't into sex. She had just had a hysterectomy to rid her of cancer of the cervix and it left her with some physical problems. To Kitty's surprise, Billy assured her his relations with women were strictly platonic because of an accident that left him unable to have sex. He further added, "I was so disfigured that I won't even allow anyone to see me naked."

To make a long story short, Kitty and Billy got together and were married for eighteen years. They adopted three children and it was only after they divorced that Kitty discovered Billy's secret. One of Kitty and Billy's adopted children found Billy lying on the ground dying of a bleeding ulcer, and called for an ambulance. When the paramedics opened Billy's shirt, they discovered Billy was a woman!

Yvette Paris on the cover of a Magazine. Photo courtesy of Yvette Paris.

Kitty Kelly, photo taken in San Francisco by Electra's husband Al Grey.
Photo courtesy of Al Grey.

Billy Tipton's real name was Dorothy Lucille Tipton. She lived all of her adult life as a man and married three women, including Stripper Kitty Kelly. His/Her entire story is in Diane Wood Middlebrook's book entitled, *Suits Me: The Double Life of Billy Tipton.*

After retirement, many well-known strippers supplemented their income by selling their photos to admiring fans. Three of them are Jennie Lee, Blaze Starr, and Lili St. Cyr. Most of the photos were accompanied with handwritten notes. Lili wrote her notes on her own stationary with the heading, "The Fabulous Female, Lili St. Cyr." Blaze not only sold her pictures, but also made custom jewelry that she marketed to the public.

Blaze liked to rouge her lips and leave her lip-print by her signature, along with a drawing of a shooting star.

While dancing in the chorus line at Nils Granlund's Florentine Gardens, Lili St. Cyr was part of an unusual act involving a man in a gorilla suit. Specialty Dancer Emile put on a nightly skit as a Harem Master who controls a gorilla with a whip. Unbeknownst to the girls, the ape is kidnapping wives for his Master's Harem.

Both Georgia Sothern and Jennie Lee had their own strip school and gave classes to wannna-be strippers. The most popular strip college was at The Follies Theatre in Los Angeles. Director/Choreographer Lillian Hunt taught it.

Talented Lillian Hunt never really retired. She remained personal manager for several strippers, and because she still wanted to be a part of The Follies Theatre, she became the box-office cashier.

Some strippers like to cook in little more than an apron. *I suppose if the food is a flop, no one will notice.*

Harem and Gorilla skit onstage; Emile with whip, Lili second from right. Nils Thor Granlund far right (1943). Photo courtesy of Authors Collection.

Jennie Lee doesn't need
a stove to heat her coffee.
Photo courtesy of Jennie Lee.

Garter Girl Lyn O'Neil burned her leg
while getting her cookies in the oven.
Photo courtesy of Authors Collection.

Lois de' Fee would rather compete in an eating contest than cook. Photo courtesy of Authors Collection.

While half-naked Zorita sets the table for guests, she fiddles with her nutcracker; look out gentlemen. Photo courtesy of Authors Collection.

At least Rita Grable wears an apron to stir her soup.
Photo courtesy of Authors Collection.

In 1952, Evelyn West filed a lawsuit in San Francisco against Tempest Storm, claiming unfair competition and trademark infringement. West claimed, "Tempest does not have a policy covering her bosom." *I think this was just a clever publicity stunt.*

January 18, 1935, a group of Burlesque performers escaped with little to no injuries when a blazing fire broke out backstage at The Shubert Theatre in Philadelphia. The fire gradually encroached into the front of the house. Six people in the audience were injured and one thousand five hundred others filed out in an orderly fashion. The Burlesque troupe was

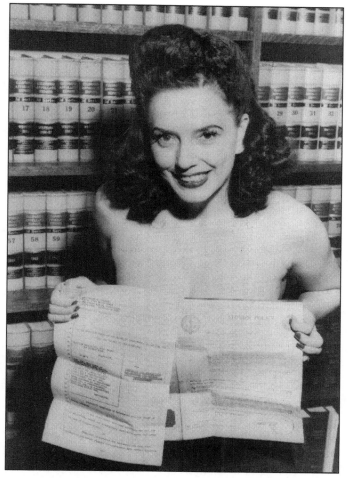

Evelyn West displays a copy of her complaint and a copy of her Lloyds of London policy, which covers her $50,000 Treasure Chest. Photo courtesy of Authors Collection.

only able to save a few pieces of clothing before the flames drove them out of their dressing rooms. They lost all their music and costumes.

In the late 1930s and early 1940s, strippers designed a new style of costuming to compete with the tired trend of Fan Dancing. They replaced the fans with gauntlet gloves that went all the way to the shoulder, and they sewed floor-length boas made of rabbit fur, from the shoulder to the wrist. Sometimes they did the same thing with floor-length tassels; the girls wore nothing else but a G-string. The dancers twirled round and round, opening and closing their arms in such a way that the sleeve costumes covered their almost-nude bodies.

Burlesque dancers wearing their fur coats and holding the few pieces of clothing they were able to save (1935). Photo courtesy of Authors Collection.

It would be a distraction to have a stripper wearing a low-cut dress, register to vote, especially if it's Tempest Storm! *I'll bet she's an Independent.*

Up until the attack on Pearl Harbor on December 7, 1941, Fan Dancer Sally Rand had her beautiful ivory handled Ostrich feathered fans made in Tokyo, Japan, by Master Fan Maker Fusayo Nagai. Afterwards, for patriotic reasons, Sally refused to allow her fans to be made in Japan. Sally Rand had her own club in El Cerritos, California called the Hollywood. After running her club for three years Sally walked away, owing three years in back taxes.

Gwen Marlow wearing a tasseled sleeve costume (1940). Photo courtesy of Authors Collection.

Ming Toi wearing fur sleeve costume (1941). Photo courtesy of Authors Collection.

Tempest registers to vote (1950s). Photo courtesy of Authors Collection.

The Lenz-Gazecki Post 152
of the American Legion — Menasha

PROUDLY PRESENTS

The

Cavalcade of Amusements

"The Nation's Greatest Show"

6 'Til Midnight Each Evening

ALL THIS WEEK

Featuring

Sally Rand in Person

At The

OLD AIRPORT SHOW GROUNDS

On Highway 47 Between Appleton and Menasha

Plenty of Rides and Shows for Young and Old
Free Parking on the Show Grounds.

SPECIAL MATINEE FOR THE CHILDREN
SATURDAY AFTERNOON — 1 to 6

Bus Service and
Special Union Cab Taxi
Service to the Grounds.

● SINGING AND DANCING MINSTREL MEN ● DARE DEVIL MOTORCYCLE
RIDERS ● TRAINED CHIMPANZEES ● FABULOUS MECHANICAL
KIDDIELAND FOR THE LITTLE FOLKS

Ad for Sally, at the Cavalcade of Amusements (1942). Photo courtesy of Authors Collection.

Sally Rand's Headstone. Photo courtesy of Authors Collection.

SO MANY STRIPPERS HAD GIMMICKS, which became part of their trademarks. Gypsy used safety pins to hold the sides of her gowns closed; she than slowly unfastened each one while reciting humorous poems to the audience, and she often threw her garter belt into the orchestra pit at the end of her routine. Not too many strippers talked to their audience during their act, but Gypsy and Evelyn West were the exceptions and it was part of their popularity. It's the personal touch that sets them apart from other strippers. The stripper uses her voice to draw the audience up onto the stage, and for a split second she makes eye contact and locks in with someone in the crowd. Bam! They've created a lifetime fan, who feels like the stripper is dancing only for him.

Many of the 1930s and 1940s strippers wore a flipper as part of their costume. A flipper is a G-string shaped like a flap that is worn over a smaller G-string. As the stripper does her bumps, the flipper goes up and down giving the audience a peek. When the stripper removes the flipper exposing her tinier G-string, the audience realizes it was a trick. No matter how many times they saw the flipper go up and down, they never gave up peeking, just in case the tiny G-string was missing. Five feet nine inch Winnie Garrett the "Flaming Redhead" really knew how to work a flipper!

In 1950, Winnie Garret sued big-time photographer Murray Korman for $50,000, claiming mental anguish and distress because he sold her photos for use in a Penny-a-Peep machine. Murray Korman remarked, "I'm not worried; she signed a release form. She's always suing someone." Winnie Garrett's real name is Winnie Ruth Houghton. She started in Burlesque in 1937 at age seventeen, and she was still going strong into the

Winnie, wearing a flipper and gauntlet sleeves (1940s). Photo courtesy of Authors Collection.

late 1950s. She worked mostly on the East Coast. Throughout the 1950s, she stripped off-and-on at the Club Ha Ha, which is located in Manhattan, New York. Winnie was the only stripper ever invited to the Press Photographers Ball. To relax, she was an avid golfer and a member of several country clubs in Florida where she had her winter home. In 1989, at age seventy, Winnie married architect Robert Vogal.

A dancer with a unique act was Sandra Farrell "The Pony Girl," who earned $100 per performance. Sandra worked in the 1940s at The Folly Theatre in Kansas City, Missouri. She was a popular Specialty Dancer who had been a chorus girl early in her career. Believe it or not, Sandra actually wore sequined horse hooves on her hands and Ostrich feather plumes for a mane and tail. Her act consisted of her prancing around like a pony. *Somehow, I can't picture this, but at least no one had to clean up after her.*

The whispers and rumors surrounding Burlesque kept a lot of reporters, photojournalists, and printers of pulp working around the clock. Newspaper columnists devoted their resources and space to juicy or not-so-juicy tidbits about Burlesque; it's shady ladies and corny comics. Some gossip columnists like Walter Winchell and Earl Wilson, could practically make or break a Burlesque babe's career. Both were fond of nightlife, and showgirls in particular.

Earl Wilson's column, *It Happened Last Night*, was widely read by people in the Biz. His book *Show Business Laid Bare* is loaded with gossip and pictures of showgirls and strippers. Earl often mentioned strippers that he was chummy with in his column.

Walter Winchell helped the careers of many, many strippers with mentions in his syndicated column, *Broadway Through A Keyhole*. In recognition of his efforts, Winchell was the first recipient of the Jennie Lee

Fanny Award. The Fanny is made of plaster of Paris and cast in the shape of Jennie's fanny.

Billboard Magazine carried Charlie Uno's Burlesque Column *Uno*; it was literally the Burlesque bible when it came to finding out who was who, how they were, and where they were playing. Charlie, whose real name is Charles M. Feldhiem, wrote his column for more than three decades. He was considered the Dean of Burlesque Journalism and revered by everyone in the Biz. His career began around the time Al Jolson and Eddie Canter were in vogue.

Then there was Jennie Lee's column in *Continental Flash Magazine* called *Who's Who In Burl-Le-Que*, which Jennie wrote for several years. After Jennie quit, Stripper Blaze Starr wrote the column for a while, and Stripper Rita Atlanta succeeded her.

Rita Atlanta typing her column. Photo courtesy of Rita Atlanta.

Some odd little pamphlets loaded with innuendos came onto the Burlesque scene as early as the 1930s. One thirty-five-page booklet written in 1937 was *Chorus Queens or Private Lives of the Hotcha Chorus Girls.* The book expounded on the life-styles and drawbacks of being a social outcast. The author writes about his booklet; "I have been connected with the stage for more than twenty years and have tried to give an unbiased picture."

Some strippers had really clever stage names. My close friend Stacy Farrell was called "Eartha Quake." Just to list a few: there were strippers named Sunny Day, Sunny Smiles, Virginia "Ding Dong" Bell, Stormy Knight, Mysty Knight, Bee Sweet, Candy Barr, Honey Bee, Tornado Tonya, Gee Whiz, Tedi Bare, Kinda Bare, Penni Cillen, Penny Bright, Crêpe Suzette, Cupcake Cassidy, Powder Puff, Tinker Bell, Giggles, Bubbles, Criss Cross, Cherry Bomb, Melba (the Toast of the Town), and a stripper named Murine, the girl who was "Easy on the Eyes." *Sorry, I made up the last one.*

Melba's real name is Dottie Faye. She was a smash hit in the 1940s and early 1950s. Throughout her career, she showed real class in all her performances. Her bubble bath routine was way before Lili St. Cyr created her famous Bath Act in the 1950s. Melba bathed in a mirrored art deco bathtub surrounded by bubbles from a bubble-making machine. *I don't think the tub had any water, just bubbles coming out of it.*

Steve Allen, television host of the first *Tonight Show*, held an honorary membership in the Exotic Dancers League of America. The Fanny Award was given to Steve for having more strippers on his show than any other television personality. Jennie Lee presented it, along with her Strip Kit, which consisted of a G-string, pasties, naval jewel, and instructions.

Jennie Lee's Fanny Award was given to Actor Tony Curtis for his portrayal of the chorus girl/musician in the movie *Some Like It Hot.* The same Award was given to Mickey Rooney for his comedic role in the long-running Broadway musical, *Sugar Babies.* Jennie also presented Mickey with a cake in the shape of her fanny. Mickey sent Jennie an autographed copy of a picture showing the presentation. The autograph reads, "Best piece I ever ate."

Faith Dane received the Fanny for her role as Mazeppa the trumpet-playing stripper in the 1959 Broadway show *Gypsy,* and the 1962 movie *Gypsy.* Patsy Darling, stripper and friend of Jennie Lee, received the Fanny in the 1970s for her lengthy Burlesque career working in Japan, and for her many humanitarian contributions. Other recipients were Tullah Hanley, Tommy Noonan, Ann Corio, Jeanine France, Lita Paul, and for a

Autographed photo of Mickey and Jennie with the Fanny cake.
Photo courtesy of Jennie Lee.

joke, Bull Winkle. Stripper Yvette Paris was the last recipient of the Fanny Award before Jennie passed away. Yvette's Award was for Humanitarian Work via her incredible compassion and dedication toward the cause of animal rescue.

Faith Dane was a member of The Exotic Dancers League of America. Years later, and on nine different occasions, Faith ran for Mayor of Washington D.C. Her campaign posters had a younger photo of herself playing a bugle. Marlon Brando endorsed her in 2002. The last time she ran, she was ninety years old.

Maxine Martin was another very tall stripper. She was 6' 4" and known as the "Skyscraper of Burlesque." She stripped in the early 1950s.

Maxine Martin. Photo courtesy of Authors Collection.

SPECIALTY DANCERS

Burlesque enthusiasts not only remember the pretty Peelers, but many have fond memories of the Variety and Specialty Acts.

There were two well-known strippers that worked with little Capuchins, also known as the organ grinder's monkey. The monks not only removed the stripper's costume one piece at a time, but they were delightfully fun to watch. After each piece was removed, the monks would turn their tiny heads towards the audience and wait for applause. When the audience clapped, the little monkeys would mimic the audience by gleefully clapping

Specialty Stripper Sue Christy, danced with three Parrots (1947).
Photo courtesy of Authors Collection.

their hands in approval. The girls would try to coax the monkeys to remove parts of their costume in the proper sequence, but instead they would chatter in objection, which was all part of the routine. These particular types of acts were a favorite with both men and women, and kept couples coming to see their shows. *For obvious reasons, the girls always used female monkeys.*

Diane Ross and her monkey Squeeky started out as strictly a Specialty Act in the late 1940s. She later worked out a strip routine using Squeeky as her gimmick. Diane also worked with her monkey in carnivals in the middle 1950s.

Sally Lane, also known as "Sally Majestic," worked in the early 1950s. She actually had two different monkeys during her stint in Burlesque; both were named Fifi. Additionally, Sally was a model for fetish Photographer Irving Klaw, who was famous for his Bettie Page series.

Another well-known Novelty Act was Dagmar's Half-and-Half "Devil Seduction" routine. Dagmar was born in Boston, Massachusetts; her real name was Virginia Dagmar Blair. She worked the Hirst Circuit in the early 1940s. Dagmar fell in love with San Francisco and adopted it as her home. She and Specialty Stripper Electra worked together in San

Lovely Bonnie White doing her "Demon and His Mistress Act" (1948).
Photo courtesy of Authors Collection.

Diane with Squeeky in their Specialty Act. Publicity photo taken at The Palace Theatre, Buffalo, New York (1946). Photo courtesy of Authors Collection.

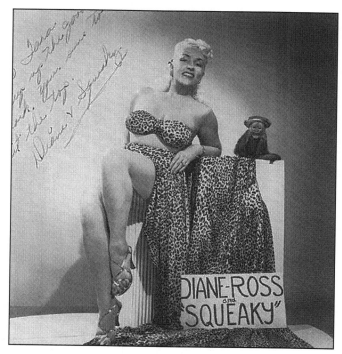

Diane and Squeeky in Promotional Photo (1950s). Photo courtesy of Authors Collection.

Sally and Fifi in matching costumes (1951). Photo courtesy of Authors Collection.

Dagmar's Devil offering her a box of pearls (1942).
Photo courtesy of Authors Collection.

Francisco and became close friends, sharing innovative dance ideas. Both were trained dancers. Dagmar died in 2004.

Some Half-and-Half acts were more creative than others, adding special signatures to their routines. One such act included a cigarette placed in the Dummy's mouth that actually blew smoke. There was a rubber bulb filled with smoke behind the Dummy's head; and when squeezed, it emitted the smoke through a hole in the Dummy's mouth.

In the early 1950s, a lovely stripper named Francis Dubay came onstage wearing a long blonde extension, even longer gown, and riding a beautiful Palomino mare named Melody Lady. Her act, aptly named "Lady Godiva," was an immediate hit. Research tells me the horse nibbled and tugged at her gown until it dropped to the floor. *Wonder where she hid the carrots? Before show time, the horse was trained to relieve itself in a bucket in the alley behind the nightclub. I knew you'd wonder.*

Unknown dancer and Dummy with cigarette (early 1940s).
Photo courtesy of Authors Collection.

Zorita wasn't the only stripper who used snakes in her Burlesque acts. Many other gals worked snake charming into their routines as well. Lonnie Young and her python named Lindo worked mostly in New York and New Orleans nightclubs throughout the 1950s. She always danced to the slinky sounds of a blues band.

Lonnie started out in the late 1940s as a pin-up model. She was often referred to as the "Vixen of Venomous Vipers." She bred and raised her own snakes on her farm in upstate New York. Lonnie was an animal lover owning many exotic animals, and often kept her monkey or puma with her in her hotel room when she was on the road. Lonnie starred in the 1954 film *Side Show Burlesque*.

Francis on Melody Lady (1950). Photo courtesy of Authors Collection.

Headshot of Lady Godiva and her horse (1951). Photo courtesy of Authors Collection.

Girls who worked with snakes had to be both agile and strong. They were either taught the trade from other dancers or learned it from Carnival people. This was the case with Zorita. The dancer must learn to move with the snake and not against it, gracefully stretching her arms for flair and to support the snakes' natural movements. The snake must be allowed the freedom to undulate and slither, yet wrap itself around the dancer in a safe manner in order to prevent it from coiling itself too tightly around the neck of the performer.

In the 1920s, 1930s, and early 1940s, twins were a big Specialty hit in both Vaudeville and Burlesque shows. The Lamar Twins were so very

Lonnie removing her snake from its trunk before a performance (1953).
Photo courtesy of Authors Collection.

Cuban Dancer working with two different species of snakes, one is very heavy (1950s). Photo courtesy of Authors Collection.

small; they were sometimes billed as midgets. Their only competition was the acrobatic dance team of Leona and Naomi Krummel, known as the Keen Twins; and twin sisters Maude and Ethyl Ross, who were Fan Dancers in the late 1920s.

The most famous twins of all were Daisy and Violet Hilton. They were Siamese twins who were joined at the hip and the buttock. The girls were born in Sussex, England, on February 5, 1908. Their unwed mother was a barmaid who gave the girls to the woman who owned the pub where she worked. Starting at a very young age, the girls were exploited.

Sadly, they spent most of their life working in sideshows and other forms of entertainment.

Another set of beauties, the Dolly Sisters. Photo courtesy of Authors Collection.

The Lamar Twins (1933). Photo courtesy of Authors Collection.

The Hilton Twins and actor Robert Montgomery (1936).
Photo courtesy of Authors Collection.

Daisy and Violet Hilton. Photo courtesy of Authors Collection.

Daisy and Violet Hilton's headstone in Forest Lawn West, Charlotte, North Carolina. Photo courtesy of Authors Collection.

In reality, the Hilton Twins were talented singers, dancers, and musicians. One sister played the saxophone and piano, while the other sister played the clarinet. They both tap-danced in unison. Their managers and so-called family profited by selling souvenirs of the girls. Years later when they were older, the girls did Specialty numbers in Burlesque theaters. Of course, they never removed their gowns, but they still found it an unpleasant experience.

The girls had boyfriends and Violet even had a couple of short-lived marriages. Daisy was always the Maid of Honor at the weddings. Violet's first attempt at marriage to a man named Maurice was foiled in 1936 when their request for a license was denied in twenty-one states.

The girls died of influenza in January 1969, at age sixty-one. When they were found, it was noted that one sister had died at least four days before the other sister succumbed. Almost all the money they had earned in their lifetime went to the people who raised them and the managers who stole their earnings. The girls had worked the last four or five years as checkers in a local market. One sister rang up the bill on the cash register while the other sister bagged the groceries. They were so broke; there was nothing left for a burial. A friend donated a plot.

BURLY TROUBLES

Starting in 1934, New York's 5' Mayor Fiorello La Guardia, began his war on what he called corrupt Burlesque houses. Local police in every city with a Burlesque theater were commissioned to keep a close eye on the so-called sordid activities associated with strip-teasers. Theater managers were constantly harassed and in fear of a raid that would culminate in the arrest of the dancers. In the year 1937, the police activity accelerated, and on May 3, 1937, the Mayor banned all Burlesque House Licenses, which resulted in the shutting down of New York's Burlesque Business.

On April 29, 1937, three Burlesque dancers working the evening performance at Minsky's Emporium on Forty-Second Street in New York were arrested for indecent exposure. They were forced to leave, clad only in their skimpy stage attire, and were booked at Poplar Street Police Station. When the newspaper cameramen arrived to take pictures of the barely concealed strippers, they found that the artists had already donned the street clothes the Theatre Manager had brought in, and were at the casher's booth paying their bail. The girls refused to reveal their faces to the cameramen.

Two of the three anonymous Burlesque dancers bailing out of the police station (1937).
Photo courtesy of Authors Collection.

The three anonymous strippers in Court (1937). Photo courtesy of Authors Collection.

More Tidbits

Souvenir from a Burlesque club called The Oasis Cabaret in Baltimore, Maryland (1936).
Photo courtesy of Authors Collection.

ED SULLIVAN

LEADING COLUMNIST OF THE

N. Y. DAILY NEWS

IN HIS COLUMN

•BROADWAY•

Wednesday, May 6th, 1936, says:

Most unusual night club I've ever seen, and your reporter has seen a lot of 'em, is the Oasis here . . . It is located in a cellar, and for the past nine years, it has proven a gold mine for the inventive owner . . . The feature is a line of chorus girls, whose ages range from 23 to 47 . . . They sit around at tables, in evening gowns, but when the Master of Ceremonies starts the show, they stand up at the tables, peel off their evening gowns and are revealed in their chorus costumes . . . When they finish a number, they wriggle back into their evening gowns and sit at the tables again . . . John Barrymore, on one of his Baltimore visits, spent hours at the Oasis, and wound up on the floor reciting Hamlet's soliloquy . . . The patrons were pretty mad at him for introducing a melancholy note, and Barrymore had to square himself with the irate customers by buying drinks for the house.

SEE FOR YOURSELF

THE OASIS

BALTIMORE AND FREDERICK STREETS
BALTIMORE, MD.

NO MINIMUM OR COVER CHARGE

You may take this card with you.

Ed Sullivan's critique of The Oasis Club in his 1936 newspaper column.
Photo courtesy of Authors Collection.

Chorus line at Minsky's National Winter Garden (1916).
Photo courtesy of Authors collection.

Chapter 9

Burlesque's Top Bananas

MANY OF THE BURLESQUE COMICS got their start in Vaudeville, but as Vaudeville died out, Burlesque became the most likely platform to ply their trade. The 1900s and 1930s were the early days of Burlesque and for a while it was still more of a variety show. Usually, the Emcee was also a singer who interacted with the Chorus Girls and sang during some of their numbers. The Headliner also danced in several of the show's revues, which were sandwiched in-between the Comic's skits. She only performed solo towards the end of the show, just before the finale and when the whole cast took their bows.

Joe Yule, father of Mickey Rooney, typing up a comedy skit while working at The Follies Theatre in Los Angeles, California (1938). Photo courtesy of Authors Collection.

Burlesque comics were a unique breed of people. They had a different way of viewing things, and found humor in every facet of life. Burly comedians tended to have a special camaraderie among themselves. They were seasoned performers whose friendships were steeped in Burlesques' rich history, resulting in an enormous admiration and respect for each other's talents. Of course, that didn't stop them from stealing a joke or two, twisting it around and making it theirs. Comics were notorious for petty pilfering and recycling each other's lines, ditto with complete routines.

With or without the big flapper shoes, putty-noses or baggy pants, comedians were the real source of early Burlesque entertainment; the pretty girls were simply eye-candy. The comic's material was somewhat corny and yellowed with age from Vaudeville stages, but it was not yet blue or risqué, as necessity would dictate by the 1930s. As the social climate changed, so did the publics views on sex; it was no longer a taboo subject. In fact, it was not only permissible to discuss, but people discovered it had a funny side, too. So the comics injected risqué situations where they rolled their eyes and stared at the straight girl's breasts. The audiences not only loved it, they were eager for more. Burly-Q's clientele was more than happy to embrace the naughty gleam in the comic's eye and the silly sexual innuendos woven into their old skits. It brought renewed interest in Burlesque shows. The old Vaudeville jokes were reworked to fit into the Burlesque comic's personality and style. The skits were never dirty; it was simply a matter of removing the improper notions about sex and having a good belly laugh at its absurd side.

The word Burlesque itself signifies an attempt to take a serious subject or incident, and turn it into something silly through comical exaggeration, parody, or satire. Burlesque was really the casting couch that produced not only the crazy antics of the Burly comics, but later found a whole new audience via television's comedy shows. Stars like Milton Berle, Red Skelton, and Sid Caesar all used some form of Burlesque-based humor. Jackie Gleason's show *The Honeymooners* was based on a Burlesque sketch called *The Friendly Neighbors*. Jackie started in Burlesque at The Empire Theatre in New Jersey and developed his split-second timing while working in these shows.

Burly comics knew when to wait long enough between the lines for the laughter to build or subside. Some had comical expressions that made the audience laugh the minute the spotlight hit them, or sometimes, it may have been their body language and even the funny clothes they wore.

They knew how to mug or do a double take, and developed qualities and quirks that distinguished them from other comics. They had a large repertoire of bits, skits, shticks, scenes, and one-liners; most were handed down from comic to comic. Some comics were known for their use of dialects, which added emphasis to the punch lines. Others had a tag line or catch phrase that was their signature. For example: Joe Penner's "Wanna buy a duck?" Lou Costello's "I'm a baaad boy;" Billy Hagen's "Cheese and Crackers;" Claude Mathis's "Say no more, Joe," and Jackie Gleason's "Awaaaay we go." Others had nick-names like Tommy "Moe" Raft whose tag-line was "I never get a break;" and Benny "Wop" Moore, Lou "Stinky" Louis, Jack "Check" Hayes, "Little" Jack Little, Billy "Bumps" Mack, Harry "Boob" Meyers, and Bob "Box Car Benny" Nugent.

There are far too many comics to mention all of them. Some of the comics were already over-the-hill when they went into Burlesque; they retired and were soon forgotten. Other, more memorable ones were in demand throughout their entire careers, which for some, like Steve Mills, Jimmie Matthews, Claude Mathis, and Irving Benson, turned into a lifetime. Many of the younger comics were drafted into the service during WWII. Some were placed in U.S.O. programs where they helped entertain the troops and boost their morale.

Others like old-time Comic Joe Emerson, retired and went into business for themselves. Emerson owned a small haberdashery in Ocean Park, California. Another old Burly, Harry "Zoup" Welsh retired in 1947, and operated his own general merchandise factory in Los Angeles. Harry had played a Burlesque comic in the 1936 film *King of Burlesque*. In 1943, Jack "Tiny" Fuller retired and became a bartender. He later opened a Bar and Grill called Chicken in a Haystack in Flatbush, New York. Comic Joe Burton retired from Burlesque in 1942 to become an elevator operator in The Palace Theatre Building. When Straight Woman/Choreographer and Director Helen Hunt semi-retired, she remained at The Follies Burlesque Theatre working as a ticket-taker in the box-office. While working at The Kansas City Follys, Comic Happy Ray fell out of a hotel window breaking both an arm and a leg. Afterwards, Happy semi-retired to Emcee and manage Stripper Connie Raye.

Burly's oldster Comic Joe Seidler retired in the 1940s, to own and operate a neon-sign shop. The year 1941 saw Comic Ray Read and his wife Dot retire to their restaurant in Bronson, Michigan. Stripper Margie Lee retired in 1947, to work as a cashier at Warner Brother's Bowling Alleys in Hollywood, California. Straight Man Jack "Check" Hayes owned

VERY RARE one-of-a-kind candid shot; front row, left to right, Straight Man Dudley Douglas, Comic/Juggler Jean Badini, Comic Rags Ragland, and Comic Benny "Wop" Moore. Back row, Comic/Juggler Joe Madden, and Comic Harry Bently in The Hudson Theatre's basement dressing room (1940). Photo courtesy of Authors Collection.

an eatery in Oceanside, California, and Bob "Box-car" Nugent retired in the early 1940s to run the Warner Brother's movie houses and concession stands in New Jersey. In 1944, Burly Comics Max Colman and Bob Birch became joint-owners of a small hotel in Los Angeles. Max also owned a small barbeque spot in Hollywood and well-known Comic Jimmy Pinto owned a small nightclub in the east.

Dudley Douglas started out as a Vaudeville Comic and Eccentric Dancer in 1918. He went into Burlesque in the late 1920s, where he worked with and married a dancer/straight woman. Together they did a poor-mans George Burn's and Gracie Allen routine with his wife playing the role of a Dumb-Dora. Dudley was also Straight Man for Harry Bently, Joe Rose, Jack "Tiny" Fuller, and Joe Lyons. He stayed in Burlesque until the early 1950s, working mainly in the New Jersey area where he and his wife had a home.

Jean Badini was originally a product of London's music halls. His Juggling Act was then called Badini and Arthur. After coming to the United States in 1917, Badini, a bottle and plate juggler, performed in Vaudeville. He went into Burlesque around 1921, where he combined his juggling skills with comedy. He partnered with Joe Madden in 1926, in an act known as 'Badini and Madden." Badini at one time owned and produced his own shows on the old Columbia Circuit. His 1921 show starring Clark and McCullough earned $350,000 in a year. Badini was a Stage Director for many of Minsky's Burlesque shows from the 1930s into the 1940s. For a time, Badini tried unsuccessfully to revive Burlesque's original venue of big, costlier productions. While in Vaudeville, Badini worked with some of the brightest luminaries in show biz; namely Fanny Brice, Fred Allen, and Eddie Cantor. Sadly, in later years Badini became a frail and pitiful Straight Man, trading lines that no longer got a laugh with strippers who smiled back from a squatting position. He stayed with Burlesque until the early 1950s; it had been his whole life.

Ole Olson and Chic Johnson in Zoot-Suits (1944).
Photo courtesy of Authors Collection.

Joe Madden was a Juggler who started in Vaudeville in 1924. He went into Burlesque in 1926 and teamed up with Jean Badini. They were a well-known Comedy/Juggler Team for thirty-five years. Madden was famous for his deadpan look that was similar to Buster Keaton's. In 1945, Joe Madden became the official clown in Olson and Johnson's second zany Broadway Revue *Funsapoppin'*, which played in Madison Square Gardens, New York. Among other well-known comics, Madden worked with Burlesque Comedians Benny "Wop" Moore, Hank Henry, Harry Butler, Billy "Scratch" Wallace, clown-faced Harry Bently, and Straight Woman Barbara Bond. He quit the Burley Biz sometime in the 1950s.

Burlesque Comic Billy House and Straight Man Eddie Garr in *Hellsapoppin'*.
Eddie Garr is Actress Terri Garr's father. Photo courtesy of Authors Collection.

Funsapoppin' was a take-off on Olie Olson and Chic Johnson's first hilarious and enormously popular 1938 Broadway Musical hit, *Hellsapoppin'*, which ran for three straight years. Basically, it was something of a crazy Variety Show. The shows plot line was loosely based on a lot of talented people who were trying to break into show biz. The revue was chuck-full of sight gags and risqué jokes, with everything moving at a fast pace. Its 1941 Road Show version had Jackie Gleason in its cast. Although Olson and Johnson never actually hit the Burly Boards, their comedic style was Burlesque in full throttle.

Harry Bently got his start working in Vaudeville using a Dutch dialect with his mouth painted like a clown. By 1919, Harry was doing Burlesque skits at Minsky's National Winter Garden alongside Burly Comedians Jack Shargel and Eddie Fox. In December of 1943, Harry worked The Palace with Benny "Wop" Moore and Freddie Lewis. On the same bill was ill-fated Strip-Star Dian Rowland who died at age twenty-nine, all alone in her hotel room of a congenital heart problem. She was the "Ball of Fire" Betty Rowland's younger sister.

Throughout 1948, Harry Bently toured the Hirst Wheel with his own comic unit consisting of himself, Slats Taylor, George Murray, and Bobby Burns. Bently retired in the 1950s.

Dian's real name is Thelma May. She was one of two other stripping Rowland sisters, Betty Jane, and sister Rozelle Rowland who married into Royalty. The oldest sister Lorraine never became a dancer; she married young and raised four children.

Rags Ragland is a legend in the world of Burlesque Comics. Rags was born John Lee Morgan Beauregard Ragland on August 23, 1905, in Louisville, Kentucky. Somewhere around 1934, Rags arrived like a comet, shooting across the stage of Minsky's National Winter Garden Burlesque Theatre. His looks, demeanor, and way of talking made him an immediate stand-out. Rags' good-natured oaf character fit his persona perfectly. He made people not only laugh at him, but *with* him. Other Burly comedians wanted him to be their best friend and drinking buddy, and the chorus girls and strippers wanted to take him to bed. Rags had a certain saviorfaire with all the ladies; he and Gypsy Rose Lee were quite an item for awhile. In 1924, Rags and Sabina "Muff" Vanover were married in his home state of Kentucky. The union produced a son, John Griffin Ragland, in 1925. The couple divorced in 1926. John Griffin Ragland died in 1990.

Rags rose quickly up the ribald ranks to become Minsky's House Comic, and remained so off-and-on for over ten years. He worked in

Dian Rowland (1930s). Photo courtesy of Authors Collection.

all of the Minsky's theaters, including The Republic. The Minsky brothers, who were Jewish, thought Rags was the funniest comic in Burlesque. Behind their backs, Rags called them "The Bagel Brothers," and he called their shows "Burlesque on a Bagel". Billy Minsky was a stickler when it came to stipulations and proper signatures on his contracts, so Rags used to rib him by saying "I won't write my name in Yiddish." Even offstage, Rags was in comic mode. *Joey Faye told me these funny anecdotes about his friend Rags when I interviewed him in 1995.*

Before Burlesque, Rags was already accustomed to hearing the sound of applause, and had gotten his first taste of show-biz as a comedic dancer and singer in the 1928 and 1929 *Flapper Follies Revue*, working along-side old-time Comic Jack Montague. Rags, whose real first name is John, originally used the stage-name Johnny "Rags" Ragland. He was in the 1929 Metro Movie Revue Short titled *The Hotdog*, along with a Burley Comic named Harry Rose. Harry sang a bizarre rendition of a song about a frankfurter sandwich, while Rags made slightly lewd, but funny gestures.

Rags became a member of the National Vaudeville Artists Union and sang, danced, and clowned around in several off-Broadway revues with beautiful showgirl Maxine De Shon, who he fell in love with. On December 8, 1930, Rags opened in a show called *The New Yorker* at The Broadway Theatre in New York. The show ran for twenty weeks and starred Jimmy Durante, Fred Waring, and well-known Specialty Dancer Ann Pennington, who stood only 4' 10" and wore a size 1-1/2 shoe. Rags sang a Cole Porter song called "I Happen To Like New York" and did a bit of hoofing. Around 1931, Rags played New York's Irving Place for three straight years at a $150 a week, which was a bundle for a comic. In 1938, Rags was in another film short about a hotdog vender where he was teamed up with Comic Joey Faye. In the clip, Joey and Rags get wild with one of Joeys favorite skits, *The Susquehanna Hat Company*, which Joey played with a stutter.

Again in 1938, Rags played the Hudson Theatre in a musical play called *Who's Who*. Ragland did twenty-three performances along with a very young Imogene Coca, who he again worked with in Broadways *New Faces of 1938* Revues. Coca was funnier than hell in *New Faces*! Her role was performing a mock striptease in which she hams it up by mugging sultry looks and making absurd gestures while she tries to remove a very long opera glove that just won't come off. She stretches and struggles for about four minutes before finally figuring out a way to pull off the glove by stepping on it. In the end, it's the only item she manages to take off. The routine was hilarious and the critics singled her out with great reviews. Coca went on to costar with Comedian Sid Caesar from 1950 to 1954, in Television's *Show of Shows*. From 1954 to 1955, Coca had her own variety show. She received a Lifetime Award along with George Burns. Imogene Coca lived to be ninety-one years young. She was married twice to other comedians.

While working at Minsky's, Rags formed a lasting friendship with Comic Phil Silvers. Rags and Phil both grabbed the Hollywood golden

Sid Caesar and Imogene Coca (1950). Photo courtesy of Authors Collection.

ring and made it big in the movies. Phil also made it big in television; his *Sergeant Bilko* series is still in reruns.

Rags broke into the movies in a 1942 film called *Panama Hattie*, where he starred with ex-Burlesque Comic Red Skelton, Funny Man Ben Blue, Ann Southern, and a young singer named Lena Horne. It had been a smash hit musical on Broadway in 1940 starring Ethel Merman, and ran for five hundred performances. The Writers, Buddy De Silva and Herbie Fields were good friends of Ragland's, so when M.G.M. Studios asked Buddy and Herbie to buy the rights and turn it into a film, they thought immediately of Rags.

De Silva and Fields wrote a part for Rags and sold the rights to M.G.M. Studio with a clause that Ragland had to be included in the film. Rags talked the Studio heads into giving his old Burlesque buddy Joe Yule a small, un-credited role as a waiter in the film. Rags said later that he gave De Silva and Fields about two thousand of his Burlesque sketches to rework and use in the movies plot.

This particular film was Rag's second try to make it in the movies. The first time, he had been doing Burlesque routines at The Follies Theatre on Main Street in Los Angeles, when a talent scout offered him a screen test.

Phil Silvers, unknown Emcee, and Rags Ragland on the radio show "Command Performance" (1942). Photo courtesy of Authors Collection.

Rags Ragland, Red Skelton, and Ben Blue in the movie version of *Panama Hattie* (1942). Photo courtesy of Authors Collection.

Rags said, "They threw a script at me and told me to memorize it. I said I couldn't learn off paper. So they said, 'We can't use this bum, he can't even read!' So I went back to Minsky's."

Panama Hattie was a springboard for Rags's movie career. He went on to make twenty more movies for M.G.M. playing beside old Burlesque buddies Abbott and Costello, Zero Mostel, Bert Lahr, and was in three films with Red Skelton. Additionally, he played in films with Martha Raye, Lucille Ball, Judy Garland, and child-star Margaret O'Brian. One of his favorite films was *Anchors Away* with his pal Frank Sinatra.

Rags had just returned from a big drinking binge in Mexico with Actor Orson Wells when he became ill and was taken to Cedars Sinai hospital in Los Angeles. He went into a coma and died a few days later of uremic poisoning (Uremia). Rags passed away August 20, 1946, three days before turning forty-one. His buddies Phil Silvers and Frank Sinatra were at his bedside in the hospital when the final curtain fell for Rags. Ragland had spent twenty of his forty-one years in Burlesque. At the time of his death, M.G.M. Studio slated Rags for a renewed contract of seven movies per year.

Benny "Wop" Moore started out in Burlesque around 1930. He was a Dialect Comedian who worked with a broken Italian accent, but he was really Jewish. Chico Marx, who was also Jewish, used the same type of broken Italian accent throughout his career. It made everything sound even funnier. Benny worked in almost every Burlesque house across the states. He was one of those funny men that could team-up with other Comics or work alone. He was a favorite with Burlesque audiences and remained so up until he retired sometime in the 1950s. Benny lived in Rochester, New York with his wife and son Bernie.

Rags and Margaret O'Brian rehearsing a Jitterbug dance for a scene in *The Canterville Ghost* (1944). Photo courtesy of Authors Collection.

Comic Jimmy Matthews also began his career in Burlesque sometime around 1930. According to *Playbill Magazine*, Matthews married his Straight Woman, a gal named Sue Gaye. Both Gaye and their son Tommy toured with Matthews until the early 1950s. Matthews worked on the same bill with Sophie Tucker, Carrie Finnell, Harry Arnie, Claude Mathis, Billy Foster, Harry J. Conley, Straight Men Berl Saunders and Harry Vine, and Comic Hermie Rose, just to name a few. Matthews was in both of the long running Burlesque Musicals, *This Was Burlesque* and *Sugar Babies*. Jimmy Matthews passed away in October of 2004.

Straight Man Harry Vine and Comic Hermie Rose at The Capital Theatre (1954). Photo courtesy of Authors Collection.

Comic skit about a Candy Butcher. Left to right: 6' 7" Stripper Denise Darnell, Comic Pat Harrington Sr., and Stripper Naomi (1950). Photo courtesy of Authors Collection.

Bobby Clark was born in 1888. At the age of twelve, he teamed with his school-chum Paul McCullough and they worked out a tumbling routine. They hired themselves out to local lodges and grand openings, and in 1906, took their act on tour with the Ringling Brother's Circus. Later, they formed a team in Vaudeville called "Clark and McCullough." The two worked together for thirty-six years, until McCullough committed suicide. Paul had been suffering from depression, and while sitting in a barber chair he suddenly grabbed a straight razor and slit his wrists and throat. He died in a hospital three days later on March 25, 1936. After the loss of McCullough, Clark went into a lengthy period of seclusion.

Bobby Clark worked on stage, films, and television. In 1942, he was in Mike Todd's Musical Revue *Star and Garter,* at Broadway's Music Box Theatre. The Revue ran for six hundred and nine performances, during which time Clark performed every night in eight of the Revues comedy skits. Also in the Revue were Gypsy Rose Lee, Georgia Sothern, Carrie Finnell, Rosita Royce, and Comedians Pat Harrington, Joe Lyons, and Gil Maison. Bobby Clark died of a heart attack in February of 1960, at age seventy-one.

Candid of Straight Man/Comic Berl Saunders, Stripper/Straight Woman and Vocalist Dorothy De Haven, who were a Burly Team, and Comic Billy Foster in Toledo, Ohio (1942). Photo courtesy of Authors Collection.

Harry Conley worked as a comic during the Golden Age of Vaudeville and headlined at The Palace Theatre so many times he considered it his home away from home. During 1918 and 1919, Conley was the Principal Comedian for Fred Irwin's musical comedy *Razz Jazz*, plus numerous other short-lived, off-Broadway shows. In 1928, Harry starred in a popular Vitaphone film-short called *The Book-Worm*, for which he received $1,100 for his weeklong effort.

After the decline of Vaudeville, Harry took his great comedic talent onto a Burlesque stage and soon became a Headliner. Conley and Billy Foster were the House Comedians for The Capital Theatre in Toledo, Ohio, from 1940 until 1942. Conley had his own touring unit consisting of Comics Harry "Shuffles" Le Von, Billy Foster, Lew Brown and Stripper-

Clyde Bates on left, Jack Hunt on right. Both men began their careers in 1918, working as Tramp Comics in Vaudeville. Clyde originally wore a putty nose. He teamed-up with Burly Comic Benny "Wop" Moore for 1936 and 1937. Photo courtesy of Authors Collection.

Rare candid of a very young Harry J. Conley in Toledo, Ohio (1942). Photo courtesy of Authors Collection.

turned-Comic and Straight Woman Peggy Bond. He worked with blind Comic Mike Sachs and his Straight Woman and wife Alice Kennedy, at The Hudson Theatre in 1950.

In May of 1965, while doing one of his comic scenes in Ann Corio's *This Was Burlesque* in Louisville Kentucky, Harry was overcome by a stroke, leaving him with a severe paralysis on one side. He proved himself to be a real Burlesque trooper by returning to Corio's Revue in January of 1966. Conley and his wife Edith owned a nine-room home in Atlantic City, New Jersey, where Conley lived to be ninety-eight years old.

Burly Comic Steve Mills was born in Boston, Massachusetts in 1896. At age fourteen, Mills began entering and winning Amateur Night con-

Ann Corio and Morey Amsterdam using a plunger for his cane (1979).
Photo courtesy of Authors Collection.

Unique female Comic Thelma Lu Havvadash.
Photo courtesy of Authors Collection.

tests alongside future Funny-Men Fred Allen and Benny Rubin. After being an Army Bugler during WWI, Mills and some of his Army buddies
formed a group and went into Vaudeville. In 1924, Mills worked with
stuttering Billy Gilbert in the Burlesque Revue *Whiz Bang Babies*. He also
worked as a Candy Butcher in Burlesque theaters and by 1928, he was a
Top Banana in Billy Minsky's Burlesque shows in New York. After Minsky's closed down in 1937, Mills worked in different comic units in the
Hirst Circuit and had movie roles in the late 1940s. In 1977, Steve joined
the cast of Ann Corio's *This Was Burlesque*. After working with Corio,
Mills had a stroke and was semi-confined to his home in Boston until his
death March 13, 1988, at age ninety-two.

Benny Rubin started out in both Vaudeville and Burlesque; alternat-
ing whichever venue paid the most money. He worked in Vaudeville with
dance-man Jack Healy, who later became the Tin-Man in the *Wizard of*

Mills, starting out

Steve Mills starting out in comedy.
Photo courtesy of Authors Collection.

Oz. Rubin was born in Boston, Massachusetts, where he learned to tap-dance by watching the neighborhood kid's dance for pennies on street corners. He had a little act where he tapped and told jokes with a Jewish dialect. This earned him from a quarter to fifty cents in local amateur contests. In 1923, Benny got a break at a New York Burlesque theater. He played The Palace twenty-four times in the 1920s. While working The Palace, Benny helped George Burns and Gracie Allen get booked on his bill. For a while, Rubin teamed up with Jack Benny. In 1929, Rubin went to Hollywood where for thirty-years he worked in movies, radio, and later he had parts in television shows. Sadly, after he got older, the offers for work stopped and his financial well went dry. He ended up running a dress shop and selling barbeques to his friends. In July of 1986, Benny Rubin died in Los Angeles of a heart attack. He was eighty-six, at the time of his death.

Danny Thomas was also in Ann Corio's *This Was Burlesque,* for one season. He too, got his start in show biz at The Empire Burlesque Theatre in Toledo, Ohio. Danny Thomas's father was a candy maker and by age eleven, Danny and his brother Raymond were selling their father's candy by working as Candy Butchers; a job Danny kept for seven years while helping to support his nine siblings. While working at The Empire Theatre, Danny was influenced by an old Hebrew Burlesque Comic named Abe Reynolds, who was an expert in dialects.

Thomas worked hard to make it up the ladder to fame via movies, as a nightclub singer, on radio and finally, his own television series *Make Room for Daddy*. Here is a bit of Thomas trivia regarding how his show got its name. In 1936, Danny married his wife, Singer Rose Marie, and he was working on the road in clubs. While away, Rose Marie stayed home

Benny Rubin (1935). Photo courtesy of Authors Collection.

in their small apartment and would place their young toddlers in large dresser drawers to sleep. When Danny returned from his nightclub tours Rose would clean out the drawers and say, "Let's make room for Daddy," and that's how he came up with the show's name.

Beginning in 1965, Thomas starred in four different television specials, all called *The Wonderful World of Burlesque,* with Mickey Rooney, Phil Silvers, Carol Channing, Lucille Ball, and many other celebrity guests that included Milton Frome. Milton was born in 1909. He started his career in Vaudeville and Burlesque, working as a Singer and Straight Man at The American Burlesque Theatre in St. Louis, Missouri. Frome later played Straight Man to Milton Berle's antics on Berle's Texaco Television

Show and he toured with Mickey Rooney in *Sugar Babies*. Milton Frome died in 1989 in Woodland Hills, California. He was eighty years old at the time of his death.

Danny Thomas died in 1991. His legacy is the St. Judes Children's Research Hospital in Los Angeles, which he founded in 1962.

Burly Comic Dick Bernie, whose real name is Richard Bernstein, claimed Burlesque was in his blood. He found a job as an accountant's assistant at age sixteen, and finding it boring he took a job working as a stagehand in a local theater. After watching the comics perform, Bernie wanted to try his hand at comedy, and to his own surprise he was asked to fill in for a comic who'd downed a few too many drinks between shows.

Thomas 'Scurvy' Miller. Photo courtesy of Authors Collection.

Bert Lahr and Burley Comic Bobby Barry in *Burlesque* at the Balasco Theatre (1946). Photo courtesy of Authors Collection.

Bernie was hooked on show biz, but since he was still living at home, he didn't tell his family he was working in Burlesque until he moved out six years later. Bernie was both Straight Man and Comic; he danced and did a routine with a fiddle. He worked on Broadway, in television, and in nightclubs. Bernie was associated with Burlesque close to forty years, and was in Ann Corio's *This Was Burlesque* in 1965.

In the original 1927 musical *Burlesque* starring Barbara Stanwyck, Hal Skelly played Skid, the good-for-nothing hoofer. Hal started in the circus at age fifteen and eventually ended up in films. He was known for his eccentric style of dancing. Skelly died in 1934 while out searching for his lost St. Bernard dog; a train crushed the truck he was driving. Hal's real name is Joseph Harold Skelly.

Scene from the musical *Burlesque;* Actress and accomplished Stripper Joan Andre, and Bert Lahr (1947). Photo courtesy of Authors Collection.

Joe Frisco was from Chicago. He began his career in Vaudeville working as an Eccentric Dancer and Comic. Frisco performed both solo and with his longtime girlfriend Loretta McDermott, in New Orleans, where he started gaining notoriety by inventing dance steps he called "Jazz Dancing". In 1915, Joe became a hit in The Ziegfeld's Follies. It was during the Roaring Twenties that Joe's dance style made him a popular item with the Flappers who were crazy about new dance crazes like the Black Bottom, the Lindy, and especially the Charleston with its eccentric movement. Joe had a dance named after him called "The Frisco."

Famous and infamous alike wanted to mingle with Frisco, including bootlegger Al Capone, who had his picture taken with Joe. Mae West

Hal Skelly in the Broadway musical *Burlesque* (1927).
Photo courtesy of Authors Collection.

was fond of Joe and wanted him to be in one of her films; and Writer F. Scott Fitzgerald made reference to Frisco in his 1925 novel *The Great Gatsby*. Joe's personal life was that of a rogue and a rascal who liked to dance on and off the stage and chase the ladies. His love of gambling on the pony's later led him to a long and strong friendship with like-minded Bing Crosby.

Frisco was a stutterer, and when he went into Burlesque he used this unbecoming trait to make his lines sound even funnier. He worked with Straight Man Benny Davis, Comics Tommy "Moe" Raft, and Harry Steppe who was Bud Abbott's first partner and the person who introduced Bud Abbott to Lou Costello. According to Phil Silvers, Steppe coined the

Actor Michael O'Shea in the movie *Lady of Burlesque* (1943). He is dressed as a typical Burly Comic from the 1920s. Photo courtesy of Authors Collection.

phrase "Top Banana" from a funny sketch he used to do. Joe Frisco was also in some Hollywood films during his long career in the entertainment biz.

Burlesque comic Joe DeRita began his career entertaining on a Vaudeville stage at age seven. He worked alongside his mother Florenz Wardell, who was a dancer. Joe's father Frank was a Stage Technician. DeRita's real name was Joseph Wardell, but he later took on his mother's maiden name of DeRita. Joe was only 5' 4" tall. He began in Burlesque in 1921, where he met and married Chorus Girl/Stripper Betty Brooks. He continued working in Burly until 1942, when he left for a U.S.O. tour of Britain and France along-side stars like Bing Crosby, Bob Hope, and Singer Frances Langford. After returning to the states, DeRita guest-starred on some radio programs and in 1946, he was offered a contract with Columbia Studios to star in his own comedy series. He later joined the outrageously silly antics of the Three Stooges in 1959, and it became his legacy. DeRita once told an interviewer, "I don't think the Stooges were funny." DeRita died of pneumonia on July 3, 1993, nine days before his eighty-fourth birthday, and is buried in Woodland Hills, California.

Left to right, candid of Bud Abbott, Donald O'Conner, Eddie Cantor, Jimmy Durante, and Lou Costello (early1940s). Photo courtesy of Authors Collection.

Joe DeRita and unknown. Photo courtesy of Authors Collection.

Joe DeRita's headstone showing Joe as a "Stooge." Photo courtesy of Authors Collection.

Some of the Burlesque comedians used stage backdrops and props for their comedy scenes. These types of sketches involved several strippers and straight men interacting onstage at the same time. This form of comedy sans the strippers had been popular in Vaudeville productions, but later spilled over into Burlesque where the theme was always "Girls, Gags and Giggles."

George "Beetlepuss" Lewis was what is known as a Comic's Comic and a favorite with audiences. He worked with all the best Burlesque comedians and had an unequaled, individual style that made him a standout no matter who he partnered with. Lewis was born January 2, 1901. He went from Vaudeville to Burlesque. In March of 1938, George played The Palace Theatre in the *Revels of Burlesque* Revue with fellow Comic Claude Mathis and a cast of forty. That same year, "Beetlepuss" starred in the film-short *Pardon My Accident* and went on to play in four other Burlesque shorts in the early 1950s. He was featured in the *A.B.C.s of Love* with Stripper Gilda; *Moulin Rouge, Ding Dong/Merry Maids of the Gay Way,* and *International Burlesque* with Betty Rowland and Don Mathis.

Left to right: unknown Straight Woman, unknown Straight Man, Comic George "Beetlepuss" Lewis, Stripper/Straight Woman Doreen Gray, Stripper/Straight Woman Pat Flannery, and Comic "Little" Jack Little (Follies Theatre in Los Angeles, 1952). Photo courtesy of Jennie Lee.

He had a small part in the 1948 movie *When My Baby Smiles at Me* starring Betty Grable and Dan Dailey.

"Beetlepuss" spent most of his Burlesque career working on the West Coast, in particular, The Follies Theatre in Los Angeles. He lived with his wife Leona and their two pooches, Freckles and Ameche, in the San Fernando Valley of Southern California, until his death, August 8, 1955, at age fifty-four.

Red Buttons was born Aaron Chwatt. By age sixteen, Red was working in the Bronx as a Bellboy earning extra tips entertaining while delivering messages and carrying luggage. Because of his red hair and the shiny brass buttons on his uniform, he acquired the nickname Red Buttons.

Comic Hermie Rose, Straight Man Don Mathers, and unknown Straight Woman/Stripper (1950). Photo courtesy of Jennie Lee.

Don Mathers, unknown Stripper/Straight Woman, and Comic Hermie Rose who finally bags a broad with his shoe. Photo courtesy of Jennie Lee.

Billy Hagan, Irving Benson and Murray Briscoe from the film *Scantie Panties*. Photo courtesy of Authors Collection.

Comic Professor Lambertini, Straight Man Charlie Craft, Mimi Reed, and unknown comic sitting. Photo courtesy of Jennie Lee.

Unknown comic, Singer/Comic Charlie Craft and Stripper Petti Varga playing a Straight Woman (1953). Photo courtesy of Jennie Lee.

Red Buttons, Minsky's youngest Burlesque Comic (1959)
Photo courtesy of Authors Collection.

Soon after, Red worked the Borsht Belt with the handsome Straight Man Robert Alda. In 1939, Red worked at Minsky's in a Revue called *Wine, Women and Song*, written by Billy Rose. Sometime later, Red was onstage when the cops had one of their many raids on The Minsky's Republic Theatre.

Red worked off-and-on in Broadway shows until he was drafted in 1943, and was designated to serve his time entertaining in U.S.O. shows in Europe. After his tour was served, Red was offered movie roles and had his own T.V. Show. In 1958, Red won the Academy Award Oscar for his supporting role in the film *Sayonara*. Red Buttons lived to be eighty-seven years old. He was very much loved by his peers.

Burlesque's old-timer Walter "Schultz the Butcher" Brown claims to have played every Burlesque house in the states and some in Canada.

Popular Comic Jimmy Pinto. Photo courtesy of Authors Collection.

Brown started out in Vaudeville in his early teens. He teamed up with Straight Men/Comics Ed "Clothes" Norton, who was known for his snappy outfits and classy demeanor; and George Le Maire, whose real name was Meyer Goldstick. Brown was one of the original Keystone Kops for the Mack Sennett studio, along with Buster Keaton and Roscoe "Fatty" Arbuckle.

Walter started in Burlesque in 1900 at The Old Howard Theatre in Boston, and went on to Minsky's National Winter Garden in New York, where he stayed on the bill for seven years. It was while working for Minsky that Brown acquired his nickname "Schultz the Butcher." The name came from an old Burlesque skit that Brown reworked and made his own. The scene takes place in a butcher shop, and Brown is the butcher waiting on several strippers who come in to purchase meat. *If you can imagine the naughty innuendos and double-entendres involved in this skit, you are already smiling.* One stripper says, "Do you have pig's feet?" Walter stares at his own feet, scratches his head saying, "No." Eventually, one of the girls asks, *here it comes,* "Do you have any weenies?" And pulling out a big salami Brown says, "No, Lady, but have I got a big salami for you!" Walter goes on to ask, "Do you want me to wrap it and put it in a bag?" The stripper says, "Yes, please." Walter says, "Do you want a regular-sized one or a huge one?" Stripper: "I want a huge one. Do you have a huge one?" Walter: "Oh, I've got a huge one, alright!" The whole shtick is done with a German dialect and lots of, *you know what I really mean,* facial expressions.

In 1941, Walter received a telegram-wire in his dressing room at The Eltinge Theatre. It read: Saw your act. It was great. Will see you tomorrow. Signed: Edward G. Robinson.

Walter worked in Burly well into his seventies. He was married five times; each wife was a show-biz gal.

Born on February 26, 1914 in New York City, New York, Robert Alda was one of the best looking men in show biz. He had talent and charisma, which he passed on to his famous son Alan Alda, star of the television series *Mash*. Robert started out singing and dancing in Vaudeville sometime around 1929, where he worked in the Catskill Mountains in New York. He eventually went into Burlesque as a singing Emcee and Straight Man. Alda played Straight Man to Phil Silvers, Rags Ragland, and Hank Henry, and he worked with Bud Abbott and Lou Costello.

In 1932, Robert married ex-show girl and former beauty pageant winner Joan Browne, who was crowned Miss New York. On January 28, 1936, baby Alan Alda was born and soon began touring with a Burlesque Troup along with his show-biz parents. It was an interesting education for the skinny little kid nick-named Allie, who the stripteasers teased while he was in their dressing room. The comics would hang out at Alda's family home trading jokes, while a young Allie was learning through osmosis

Robert Alda and wife Joan, dancing at *Redbook*'s Annual Trophy Awards party held at The Clover Club in Los Angeles (January 17, 1945). Photo courtesy of Authors Collection.

the importance of perfect timing and delivery, which he would later use in his own career. When Alan Alda was in his teens, he and his father used to rehearse Abbott and Costello's skits together. Alan adored his father and they remained close during Robert's lifetime.

Robert did radio and Broadway shows in 1945, and made a splashy film debut in Gershwin's *Rhapsody in Blue*, where his singing helped to make the movie a big hit.

After several more films and a sad divorce, Alda moved to Italy, re-married, and had one more son named Antony. He made a few other films in Italy that were never distributed in the states. After his return, he was in several television series, including guest starring twice on *Mash* with his son Alan. Robert was a Mystery Guest on *What's My Line* when Alan was working on the panel. Robert Alda passed away May 3, 1986 in California, at the young age of seventy-two.

Burlesque Comic Jack Diamond began working in Vaudeville about 1920; he was twelve years of age and stayed with it for ten years. He worked in Burlesque from 1931 to 1955, when he developed a heart affliction. After taking time off to get stronger Jack tried to make a comeback, but after just two performances at The Empire Theatre in Newark, New Jersey, Diamond was forced to retire from Burlesque, which had been his life.

Jack married strip Headliner Ethel De Voe in 1933, and she eventually became his Straight Woman. The two remained married and made their home in Seaford, New Jersey. Jack was always a top-billed comedian who often partnered with Mandy Kaye, Charlie Harris, and Boo Le Von. Jack claimed his jokes were so old they were moldy, but were still getting a laugh.

Mary Murray and Bob Ferguson started making audiences laugh in the 1920s, and stayed at it for over forty years. During this time, they were a featured part of many Burlesque units with other well-known comics. Ferguson was an expert camera-man who had worked for Kinagram's si-lent film newsreels, and for over thirty-five years he had filmed 16mm candid footage of Burlesque behind the scenes. His films showed not only the dancers, chorus girls, comics, and variety acts, but also the stage man-agers, electricians, ticket-takers, and everyone in between. It was virtually a visual history of the people who were part of Burlesque in 1920s, 1930s, and 1940s. In the 1950s, the Fergusons retired to their home in Detroit, Michigan. Sadly, no one knows what became of his film collection.

Ed Wynn, whose real name is Isaiah Edwin Leopold, was born in Philadelphia, Pennsylvania, November 9, 1886. Like many other poor boys of his generation, Ed ran away from home at age fifteen. He held a

Ed Wynn in his dressing room applying his make-up in the early 1930s.
Photo courtesy of Authors Collection.

series of minor jobs before going into Vaudeville in 1903, where he found his niche in comic roles. Wynn was a natural born comedian with his tittering voice, silly expressions, and visual sense of humor. He wrote all his own material. He was featured in the 1914 and 1915 Ziegfeld Follies and had a long career in Radio. He also did Burlesque. Later, Wynn guest starred on many television series, including a memorable role on the *Twilight Zone*. He is the father of actor Keenan Wynn. Ed passed away June 19, 1966, at age seventy-nine.

Jack Albertson was born Harold Albertson June 16, 1907, in Massachusetts. He started out in Vaudeville as part of a Variety Act tap-dancing, singing, and doing little funny bits. Eventually, as Vaudeville went into

Phil Silvers as the *Top Banana*. Photo courtesy of Authors Collection.

Comic/Hoofers Phil Silvers, Jack Albertson, and Joey Faye shuffle off to Buffalo in the musical *Top Banana* (1953). Photo courtesy of Joey Faye.

decline, Albertson went into Burlesque where, for two years he worked as Straight Man to Phil Silvers' rapid-fire comebacks. While at Minsky's, Jack and Phil became close friends, and both would go on to make movies and be in television series.

Albertson worked on-and-off Broadway and was in forty motion pictures. He is remembered for his role in *Willy Wonka and the Chocolate Factory,* but won an Oscar in 1965 for his supporting role in *The Subject Is Roses.*

Jack and Phil teamed up again for the 1951 Broadway musical hit *Top Banana,* which was made into a movie in 1954 using the same cast.

Jack Albertson co-starred in the television series *Chico and the Man* with a very young and talented Freddie Prinze, and the two became very close. Sometime later, Prinze, who suffered from bouts of depression, put a gun to his head and shot himself. He died a few days later at the young age of twenty-two. Albertson was devastated.

In 1972, Jack starred in Neil Simon's Broadway play *The Sunshine Boys,* which was later made into a movie. The movie, about two old crotchety ex-Vaudevillians, was right up Albertson's alley and it touched a soft spot he held for his early days in Vaudeville. The story line was said to have been inspired by either the partnership of Vaudevillians Weber and Fields, or the team of Smith and Dale.

Jack Albertson died of cancer in his Hollywood Hills home on November 25, 1981. He was seventy-four years young.

For many years, Lew Fine was an outstanding Comedian and Master of Ceremonies. He was famous for his fast-talking dialog, impressions, and pantomime. Fine was well known for his riotous performance of a skit he wrote in 1944 called, *This Ain't the Army*. Lew Fine not only worked on many of the Burlesque Circuits, but also traveled with J.C. Michaels Carnival and Circus Revues in the late 1940s and early 1950s. Lew

Actor, dancer, and Burlesque Comic Jimmy Savo (1935).
Photo courtesy of Authors Collection.

Charlie Robinson and Joel Yale. Photo courtesy of Authors Collection.

played several different musical instruments and he worked in a Novelty Act with a life-sized Ventriloquist Doll named Suzy. He was classy and versatile. Once, Columnist Walter Winchell referred to his act as a "Mirthquake of fun and laughter."

Frail looking little Charlie Robinson with his big expressive eyes started in Burlesque around the late 1930s, and was still going strong in the 1960s, when he clowned it up in Ann Corio's *This Was Burlesque*. Robinson was a very popular comic and a likable person. He was quite agile and his type of humor and skits were particularly funny in a slapstick style.

In the 1940s, Charlie worked mainly in the Midwest, playing long runs at The Capital Theatre in Toledo, Ohio. Later, when Stripper Rose LaRose bought The Capital and changed its name to The Town Hall, Billy Foster along with Charlie were two of Rose's favorite Comics. She called Charlie her "little pantaloony."

Al Anger started working as a Burlesque Comic in the late 1930s. While playing at Minsky's, Al worked with Phil Silvers and Pinky Lee. Anger toured the Hirst Circuit holding his own among many of Burly's great comedians. He married the lovely Margie Davis who started danc-

Al Anger in his Burlesque prime.
Photo courtesy of Authors Collection.

ing as a chorus girl alongside her sister Babs in The Globe Theatre. Margie stripped under the name Justin Vain. Eventually they divorced, and in 1952, Al married the pretty Stripper/Talking Woman Barbara Curtis. They were wed at The Follys Theatre in Kansas City, Missouri. Although they kept their clothes on, Al and Barbara both starred in the 1964 nudie film *Lullaby of Bareland.*

Comic Hank Henry, whose real name is Henry Rosenthal, was born in New York City July 9, 1906. Hank was a partner with Straight Man Robert Alda in the 1930s. In his younger years, Hank Henry was a Rodney Dangerfield look-a-like. During the 1930s, Hank had a tall crush on 6' 4" Stripper Los de' Fee, whom he dated in between her marriages. He used to send funny love notes to her dressing room. *I've seen several pictures of Lois and Hank together, out on the town.*

Hank was drafted into the service sometime in the early 1940s, and toured in the U.S.A. with U.S.O. shows. In 1943, Hank was cast in the big Irving Berlin film *This is the Army,* along with fellow Burly Comics Dick Bernie and Pinkie Mitchell.

Hank worked in the Burly Biz for most of his life, and after Burlesque stopped using comics in the 1950s; he thought he was washed-up. In 1957, he was on the Colgate Comedy Hour. In 1959, he was on *The Thin Man* television series playing Peanuts Noonan in "The Case of the Baggy Pants." In 1960, Hank made a Burly movie titled *Not Tonight, Henry* that was quite popular. Around the same time, he took a chance and moved with his wife Jo Ann to Las Vegas where, to his surprise, he was a big hit in nightclubs and hotel shows. Then, in 1963, Henry was on *The Red Skelton Hour*. He made two movies with Frank Sinatra; one was *Pal Joey*, and also did *Robin and Seven Hoods* with Peter Falk, Dean Martin, Bing Crosby, and Sammy Davis, Jr. Hank was in six more films. He continued to work in Las Vegas through the 1970s, where he died in 1981 at age seventy-four. Hank Henry used to say he loved Vegas and Vegas loved him.

Leon Errol was born July 3, 1880, in Sidney, Australia. Errol toured with his dance partner Stella Chanteloene, who he married around 1904.

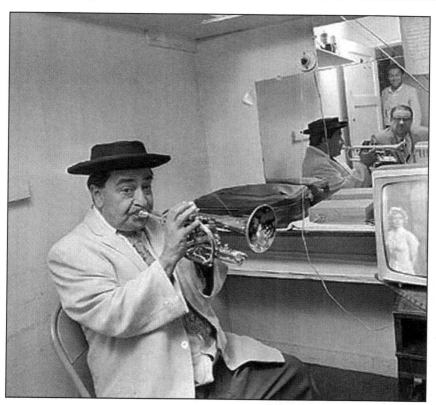

5' 4" Tommy "Moe" Raft in a 1970 Minsky's Burlesque Show.
Photo courtesy of Authors Collection.

Comic Leon Errol (1936). Photo courtesy of Authors Collection.

The two came to the U.S. and in 1909, Leon became a singing/dancing waiter in San Francisco. He soon got into Vaudeville and Burlesque. Around 1910, Errol was Production Manager and Circuit Owner for traveling Burlesque revues. He wrote and starred in Burly houses for a couple of years. While playing in Portland, Oregon's Orpheum Theatre, Errol worked with an eighteen-year-old Fatty Arbuckle.

Errol's shtick was playing a rubber-legged drunk. Due to his early dance training, it was a routine he excelled in and one he did for most of his career. Errol was in several of Ziegfeld's Follies along with Fanny Brice and the talented black entertainer Bert Williams. He worked with

WC. Fields and Burly Comics James Barton, Jack "Clothes" Norton, Burly tramp Tommy "Bozo" Snyder, and Dusty "Open the Door, Richard" Fletcher. Errol was very close friends with Lew Fields, who was one-half of the famous Vaudeville Team Weber and Fields. Errol went on to acquire 160 film credits. Leon Errol died October 5, 1951 in Los Angeles, California.

Clinton "Dusty" Fletcher was born July 7, 1900, in El Dorado, Arkansas. He started out playing in Vaudeville and later toured the Burly circuit in what was than known as the Chitlin' Circuit. He also worked in Burlesque Black and Tan Revues. Dusty clowned around in Mamie Smith's *Revue of 1926,* and in 1927, he toured with his own girlie revue called *The Harlem Strutters.*

Starting in 1929, Dusty was in many independently made movie-shorts that were created to entertain and appeal to Black audiences. The real reason Black films were rare was that Hollywood hadn't quite gotten with the program yet, and there were very few roles available to Black Artists. Fletcher worked with the best-of-the-best Black Comics such as John "Spider Bruce" Mason, Jackie "Moms" Mabley, Dewey "Pigmeat" Markham, Mantan Moreland, and Tinnie Rogers. In the 1947 short *Killer Diller*, Dusty worked with Butterfly McQueen who played in the film *Gone with the Wind.* He also worked with Singer/Dancer/Actress/Author Ethel Waters and a seven-year-old talented Sammy Davis Jr., who starred in his first film appearance, a short called *Rufus Jones for President.*

For over twenty years Fletcher performed the sketch that he was famous for, *Open the Door, Richard!* It was a hilarious drunk scene made even funnier by his trademark, crumpled Flapper-shoes, which he was continually tripping over. Dusty plays a very inebriated man who has

Dusty Fletcher on a Touring Burlesque bill for The Globe Theatre in Atlantic City (1940s). Photo courtesy of Authors Collection.

lost his keys and wants to get back into his apartment, but he can't wake up his roommate named Richard. After beating on the door and shouting "Open the door, Richard!" over and over, and saying, "Richard, why don't you open that door?" just as many times; he brings a ladder onstage and proceeds to climb up to an invisible apartment window. The ladder weaves back and forth while he climbs it in mid-air, and each time he falls down, he shouts at Richard to open the door. Every time he hits the floor, he drunkenly climbs back up the ladder. The whole sketch is a visual that has the audience rolling in the aisles. Fletcher eventually did a film short of his *Open the Door, Richard!* It was so popular that in 1946, Bandleader Jack McVie turned it into a novelty song. Later, in 1947, Dusty Fletcher recorded his own version; it was number one on the Billboards for five weeks. Up until his death in New York City, March 15, 1954 at age fifty-three, Dusty frequently performed his *Open the Door, Richard!* at Harlem's Apollo Theatre.

Little Eddie Collins was born in 1883, in Atlantic City, New Jersey, as Edward Bernard Collins. He was about 5' 2" small. He began his career in Vaudeville around 1905, and went into the Burly Biz around 1925. In 1935, while working as a Burlesque comic at The Follies Theatre on Main Street in Los Angeles, Collins was more or less discovered by the Walt Disney Studios. *Well, in a roundabout way, he was.* It seemed that while Disney's animation team was drawing the Seven Dwarfs for their movie *Snow White and the Seven Dwarfs,* they couldn't seem to figure out a prototype for little Dopey. One of the team thought Dopey should look like a caricature of a Burlesque comic. Disney himself suggested someone go to the nearby Follies Theatre and watch the comics perform. Someone did go to The Follies and when he saw little Eddie Collins in action; he knew he had found the characteristics for Dopey. The next day, the entire animation team went back to The Follies and seconded the motion.

Eddie was brought to the Disney Studio where they tested him and did some live-action footage of him performing, which referenced some of the Dopey scenes. Even Eddie's voice was recorded for Dopey. Well, since Dopey didn't really talk, Eddie was the voice for all the little noises made by Dopey.

Comic Eddie Collins (1943). Photo courtesy of Authors Collection.

Abbott and Costello performing their famous *Who's On First* skit.
Photo courtesy of Authors Collection.

Another Burlesque alumni Billy Gilbert, was hired as the voice of the Dwarf Sneezy. Eddie went on to work in twenty-four more films. He died of a heart attack in Arcadia, California, September 2, 1940, at age fifty-seven.

The team of Bud Abbott and Lou Costello has its roots in the Burly Biz. Both men were born in New Jersey, Abbott in 1899, and Costello in 1906. Abbott was born into a show business family and as a kid he worked in Coney Island. He toured with Carnivals, performed in Vaudeville, and did an act with his wife, the former Betty Smith. He later partnered with well-known Burly Comics Harry Steppe and Harry Evanson at both The Globe and Minsky's Theatres.

Ad wanting persons to distribute Abbott and Costello *Who's On First* Records (1940).
Photo courtesy of Authors Collection.

As a teenager, the acting bug bit Costello and he headed for Hollywood to make his mark. The only jobs he found were as a studio carpenter
and stuntman for both M.G.M. and Warner Brothers. Discouraged, Lou
frequented Vaudeville and Burlesque shows, gathering ideas for his own
act. He went into Burlesque in 1930, and in 1935, while playing The Eltinge Burlesque Theatre, Bud and Lou worked together for the first time.
Lou's wife, the former Anne Battler, was a showgirl in Burlesque, and af-

ter seeing Lou and Bud working together, both she and Bud's wife Betty encouraged the boys to form a permanent act. The duo became a comic team working in Burly houses and perfecting their famous *Who's On First* routine that became their trademark. In February of 1938, the boys made an appearance on the Kate Smith Hour radio show where they became regulars for two years. They went on to do the Broadway musical revue *The Streets of Paris,* which turned out to be a riotous smash hit of mayhem, and ran for a year.

In 1940, Universal Studios signed them to do one film, and their appearance in *One Night in the Tropics* led them to a long-term contract. Their second film *Buck Privates,* gave them star status and they went on to make thirty-seven more films for Universal. In 1952, they had their own half-hour television series called *The Abbott and Costello Show.*

Bud and Lou had their ups and downs over the years, and sometime in 1945 they had a fall-out that led Costello to refuse to speak to Abbott unless they were working together. The issue ended when, in 1947, Abbott volunteered to aid in Costello's charity project; a foundation for underprivileged children in the Boyle Heights area of California, which

Candid shot of Bud and Lou during a film break (1944). Photo courtesy of Authors Collection.

still exists today. Each of the men had reoccurring health issues; Bud had Epilepsy and Lou had bouts of Rheumatic Fever. Both were habitual gamblers and Bud had some drinking issues.

In 1947, Abbott had his own bar in Sherman Oaks called Abbotts Backstage, which was confiscated by the I.R.S. for back taxes in 1951. Both men went bankrupt from gambling and poor money management. The team ended their partnership in 1957.

After Lou died of a heart attack March 3, 1959, days before his fifty-third birthday, Bud tried to reinvent his career. He teamed up with Comic Candy Candido and they tried to recreate some of his and Lou's old routines, but in the end Bud admitted, "No one could ever live up to Lou." Bud worked as a solo in other show-biz venues, but it was never the same.

By 1970, Bud was in ill health and living off $180 a month from his social security, and his wife Betty was working to help support them. It was a terribly tragic ending for someone who brought so much laughter into the world. Bud died of cancer April 24, 1974. He was seventy-eight years old.

Candy Candido was born Jonathan Joseph Candido on December 25, 1913, in Louisiana. He was gifted with a voice that could change from high soprano to a bass that was lower than the lowest key on the piano.

Candy performed on many radio programs, and in movies during the late 1930s and early 1940s. During the same time period he performed Burlesque-type skits at the Florentine Gardens. He also worked for Walt Disney doing voice-overs for cartoon characters. He was the voice of *Peter Pan* and the voice for the barking dogs in *101 Dalmatians*.

Candy's wife Anita was the voice of the singing harp in Disney's *Jack and the Beanstalk*. Candy also made several entertaining children's story recordings. He died in his sleep in 1999, in Burbank, California. He was a very young eighty-five years old.

Hear ye! Hear ye! Here comes the Judge! *Well, not really*. It's Pigmeat Markham wearing a graduation cap and gown and wielding a gavel. Pigmeat was born Dewey Markham on April 18, 1904, in Durham, North Carolina. Later, when Pigmeat became famous, the town of Durham named the street where he grew-up "Markham Street". As a teenager, Markham left home to join a traveling carnival. In the 1920s, he was a member of Blues Singer Bessie Smith's traveling revue, where he sang and danced. In the late 1920s, Pigmeat claimed to have created the popular dance craze called Truckin'. Whether it's true or not, the dance definitely originated in Harlem and was popular well into the 1930s.

By the 1930's, Pigmeat developed a scandalously funny flair for comedy. Working alone or with other Black comics like Monte Hawley and Johnny Taylor, Markham made a name for himself as an original talent. In the 1950s, he was on the Ed Sullivan show multiple times. He created the sketch called "Have You Seen My Wife?" and the saying, "Look that up in your Funk and Wagnall," along with the "Here Comes the Judge" skit; which landed him a spot on Rowen and Martin's *Laugh-In*.

Markham starred in and directed four films with an all-Black cast including the 1947 movie *Burlesque in Harlem*, which was redistributed in 1954 and is, by all standards, an historical account of Black Burlesque. Not only does the film have sexy strippers, but hilariously funny comics doing outrageous skits.

Pigmeat cut eighteen record albums, including his version of his friend Dusty Fletcher's "Open the Door, Richard!" and one with Jackie "Moms" Mabley. He was a huge draw at The Apollo Theatre in Harlem, making more appearances than any other artist.

Dewey Markham died of a stroke in New York City on December 13, 1981, at age seventy-seven. He left behind his wife Bernice and their two children.

Billy Watson was born in 1876. He started out in Vaudeville and made a big name for himself in 1908's Burlesque Revue *Girl from Happiness*, which also starred comedian Fanny Brice. Billy got his tag-name "Sliding Billy" from his sliding banana-peel pratfall, which he invented, perfected, and performed as part of his entry onto the stage. He used talcum powder on the bottom of his shoes so he could slide all the way across the stage. According to some references, the first time he tried the trick he slid into the orchestra pit and nearly broke his neck.

In 1914, Billy appeared in a movie with Oliver Hardy before Oliver teamed up with Stan Laurel. That same year, Billy was earning $5,000 a month. He was one of the wealthiest Burly comics in the Biz and known as "everybody's favorite". In the 1920s, Billy was teamed with Tommy "Bozo" Snyder. In 1926, Billy's second wife Nellie was shot to death at her roadside nightspot in Long Island. Sliding Billy was in Burlesque most of his life, and worked until his death in the early 1940s.

Sliding Billy Watson is not to be confused with Billy "Beef-Trust" Watson, who worked during the same time period and displayed 200-pound cuties on the Mutual Burlesque Wheels. *Pardon the pun, but Billy "Beef-Trust" Watson's big revues were a huge success.* Billy "Beef-Trust" Watson was born in 1866, and died in 1945.

Joey Faye playing the role of "Banjo" in the Broadway production of *The Man Who Came to Dinner,* which ran for two years (1939). Photo courtesy of Joey Faye.

Originally, Beef Trust was the name of a conglomerate of beef produc-ers. It was later adopted by U.S. Carnival Showman W.B. 'Billy' Watson, who used it as the name for his sideshow of over-weight women.

In February 1995, I interviewed Joey Faye over the phone in his Stat-en Island home. He was sharp as a tack and awesome to talk with. It is one of my many treasured memories. Joey was born with a stutter, but while doing his skits, he used his impediment to make the skits sound funnier. In all honesty, I barely detected any stuttering from Joey during my interview with him. On the other hand, I was so nervous I started stuttering. Joey laughed and asked me, "Do you stutter, too?" I answered, "Only when I'm talking to you!" Joey told me he wasn't the only comic who stuttered, and some were worse; like Red Marshall, little Burly Comic Charles "Peanuts" Bohn, and Pinky Lee, who talked with a lisp. In every case, the audience thought it was part of their routine and even if the joke bombed; they laughed at the stuttering.

Joey was born Joseph Antony Palladino in New York City, New York, on July 12, 1902. As a teenager, Joey started out entering Amateur Contests in movie houses. He won over two hundred contests, taking home as much as $5 a night. He repeatedly skipped high school classes to hang out at The Palace Theatre and memorize the comic's lines. It caused him to be kicked out of high school several times. While finally graduating from Textile High, Joey asked a school chum what he was going to do next, and was told, "I have a job at a resort in the Catskills." Well, right away Joey wanted to know if they needed a comic. Joey told me, "When we got there, I met the owner of the resort at his home, and he introduced me to all his friends, who were sitting on his porch smoking big cigars. It went like this; Mr. Goldberg, Mr. Finkelstein, Mr..Lipchitz, Mr.Smukler, Mr. Bagelstein and his two sons, Hymie and Abbie. Then, the guy says to me, 'I didn't catch your name.'" Joey continued, "I'm not Jewish, so I got nervous and stuttered fa-fa- Faye, and that's how I got my name and a job working as a Social Director."

Faye worked with Abbott and Costello, Rags Ragland, and Phil Silvers at Minsky's Republic and Minsky's Apollo in New York. Joey stayed in Burlesque for eight years. Since most of the Burly theaters closed for the summer due to lack of air-conditioning; Joey would work the Catskills until fall, when Burlesque theaters would reopen. He made his Broadway debut in George Abbott's 1937 *Room Service,* and went on to do sixteen more Broadway shows. He was best-known for his part in the musicals *High Button Shoes* and *Top Banana,* both with Phil Silvers. Joey had replaced Phil in the later version of *High Button Shoes.*

Joey guest-starred on Burly buddies Jackie Gleason, Red Skelton, and Joey Bishop's television shows and was on dozens of others from 1949 till the 1980s.Between 1963 and 1964, Joey and Burly Comic Mickey Deems co-starred in two hundred, twelve-minute comedy shorts called *Mack and Myer for Hire.*

Joey told me that in the 1970s and 1980s, it was the television commercials that paid his bills. In 1981, Joey could be seen fondly unwrapping the foil of a Hershey Kiss and expounding on its melt-in-your-mouth pleasures. Afterward, he worked as a cowboy in a commercial called *The Fastest Sneeze in the West* for Marcal Paper Products, and as a Raisin for

Kellogg's Cereal. In the 1980s, after being second banana all of his career, Joey became a Top-Grape, and not one in the bunch was sour. Joey danced around for most of the 1980s dressed like a bunch of grapes in the "Fruit of the Loom" underwear commercials. He joked that on Halloween, trick-or-treating kids dressed like grapes, often greeted him at his door.

Very rare shot of young Billy "Cheese and Crackers" Hagan, his wife Anna and Sliding Billy Watson. Photo courtesy of Authors Collection.

On April 26, 1997, just two years after I interviewed Joey Faye, he died of a heart attack at The Actor's Home in Englewood, New Jersey, at age eighty-seven.

Micky Deems was born in Englewood, New Jersey on April 22, 1925. He started out in the 1940s as a Drummer and Musical Arranger, but like a lot of musicians, he liked to clown around onstage. Around 1945, Mickey began taking comedy seriously and started writing his own skits. He was in the 1984 Broadway hit *Sugar Babies* with Mickey Rooney and dancer Ann Miller. He has thirty-one acting credits. His last credit was in the film documentary about Burlesque, *The Last Comic*, featuring Irving Benson. Mickey Deems died of cancer April 14, 2014, at his home in Sherman Oaks, California.

German-Dutch Billy Hagen was born William Hagedorn in San Francisco in 1888. In his teens Billy was a lightweight boxer. He began his Vaudeville career alongside his brother in 1907. Billy played the Straight Man to his older brother, who already had his own shows in New York. Their act, called the Hagan Brothers, later reversed itself when they realized the Straight Man was funnier than the Comic. Hagan developed his own act while working with his wife Anna Toebe, who was one of Burlesque's first strippers and straight women. He did all his routines with an exaggerated Dutch dialect, and wore large, baggy pants that he rigged to go up and down. On the stage, Billy Hagan dressed like a clown, but off the stage he had the reputation of being a very dapper dresser. Hagan was one of Burly's most popular comics in the 1920s and 1930s.

It was a well-known fact around the theaters that Hagan was adept in the socially unacceptable use of cursing and reciting unabashedly, naughty little ditties. One day while onstage, something unusual happened and Billy almost said one of the forbidden words. Instead, he caught himself and shouted, "Cheese and Crackers!" It became his substitute for profanity and his tag line for the duration of his time in Burlesque; which was close to seventy years. Every winter for nearly fifty of those years, Billy played at The Trocadero Theatre in Philadelphia. Summers, he liked playing The Globe in Atlantic City. He was also one of the regular comics at The Gayety and The Bijou.

You can catch a glimpse of Hagan in action in the Burlesque Film *Scanty Panties*, along with Comics Murray Briscoe, "Slapsie" Maxie Furman and his wife Alma Maiben, Irving Benson, and popular Stripper Virginia "Ding Dong" Bell. The film was shot at The Globe Theatre in Atlantic City, New Jersey, in 1961.

Hagan and his wife of fifty-five years, Anna made their home in Rochester, New York. After Anna died in 1968, Billy retired and moved to Carmichael, California, where his only son Billy lived. Hagan died in Carmichael in June of 1986. He was ninety-seven years old.

One of the longest living Burlesque Comics Irving Benson was born in Brooklyn, New York on January 14, 1914. He turned one hundred years old in 2014, and at the time of this writing he's still kicking. Irving worked the East Coast American Burlesque Circuit during the 1930s and 1940s. Benson's original Straight Man was Harry Ryan, and in July 1945, due to contractual issues, both Ryan and Benson were granted a ninety-day deferment from going into the service. In early 1947, Benson was in a revue called *Fun for Your Money* with Joey Faye. Later in 1947, Irving paired up with Straight Man Jack Mann, who he remained with off-and-on the rest

Older Billy Hagan. Photo courtesy of Authors Collection.

of his career. Benson has been married to his wife Lillian since 1936, and they have two children. His daughter writes a gossip column in Las Vegas called "Claire Voyant".

In 1961, Irving was part of a comedy group in the Burlesque film *Scanty Panties*. Around that time, Irving went to work in Las Vegas in several Follies revues and he started showing up on the Johnny Carson show. Carson loved the old Burlesque skits and brought Benson back several

Ann Jillian and Mickey Rooney in *Sugar Babies*. Photo courtesy of Authors Collection.

times to perform sketches with him. The same applied to Milton Berle, who often hired Benson to sit in a small balcony box and heckle him with Burlesque barbs.

Both Berle and Carson were fascinated by Benson's Burlesque history. Benson is the Headliner for a cast of veteran Burlesque alumni in the 2011 award-winning documentary *The Last Comic*. I highly recommend this film, which also show-cases Betty Rowland and Dixie Evans. Together with a team of historians, they visually take you inside the Wonderful World of Burlesque.

Claude Mathis, with Helen Levett on his left and Vickie Daigle on his right in *This Was Burlesque* Revue. Photo courtesy of Authors Collection.

Chapter 10

Burly Ads: A Peek at the Previews

EARLY LEGITIMATE THEATER, Vaudeville, and Burlesque newspaper advertisements are an important art form. The popular Burlesque ads of the 1910s and 1920s are rare and most are hidden away in some obscure archives. Even those enticing 1930s and 1940s ads are almost impossible to find.

In the late 1980s, I acquired two very large albums containing about four hundred newspaper ads for Burlesque shows, including candid photos and personal correspondence of Bob and Vanessa Cartwright, who were long-time Owners of The Capital Burlesque Theatre in Toledo, Ohio. It is the same theater that was originally named The People's, and housed some of the finest theatrical productions of its day. It then became The Lyceum Theatre. A following incarnation was The New Empire Theatre.

After the Cartwright's sold The Capital, it became The Town Hall and was owned by the fabulous and fondly remembered Stripper, Rose La Rose. Rose always employed the best-of-the-best comics, chorus girls, and strippers, and Rose herself was quite often the show's Headliner.

SELECTION OF VARIOUS NEWSPAPER ADS PROMOTING BURLY SHOWS (1940S – 1950S)

The Town Hall Theatre, showing "Brown Skin Scandals" with Comics Billy Hitt and Jockey Grey. Photo courtesy of Authors Collection.

The Capital Theatre, showing the "South American Can Can Revue" with Chiquita Garcia and Comic Bozo Snyder (1941). Photo courtesy of Authors Collection.

The Town Hall Theatre; starring Francine, and Zola with her 14' Python. Photo courtesy of Authors Collection.

The Gaiety Theatre, starring Mitzi and Comic Benny "Wop" Moore. Photo courtesy of Authors Collection.

The Gaiety Theatre, starring Suzanne Day and Comic Charlie Robinson (1951). Photo courtesy of Authors Collection.

The Town Hall, showing Amy Fong with Comics Tommy "Scurvy" Miller and Bob Winkler (1953). Photo courtesy of Authors Collection.

The Town Hall Theatre, featuring a "Black and White Revue" produced by Comic Dusty Freeman, and starring Beverly Arlyenne (1953). Photo courtesy of Authors Collection.

The Town Hall Theatre, starring Rusty Lane, with Comics Irving Harmon and Liffty Lewis. Photo Courtesy of Authors Collection.

The Town Hall Coming Attraction, featuring Sirena doing her underwater strip. Photo courtesy of Authors Collection.

The Capital Theatre, showing Renee in "Follies Brassiere," with Comic Joe DeRita and the "Beefy Babies." Photo courtesy of Authors Collection.

The Town Hall Theatre showing Sunny Dare with Comics Bimbo Davis and Phil Sand. Photo courtesy of Authors Collection.

The Town Hall Theatre, featuring Theatre Owner Rose LaRose. Photo courtesy of Authors Collection.

The Capital Theatre closed for the summer (1942). Photo courtesy of Authors Collection.

The Capital Theatre's House Orchestra group: left to right, Clarke Mast leader and pianist, Red Langendeffer sax, Eddie Kallie drummer, Bud Hall and Irv Flynn trumpets (1940). Photo courtesy of Authors Collection.

GALLERY OF BURLESQUE THEATRES

Burlesk Theatre in Atlantic City (early 1940s).
Photo courtesy of Authors Collection.

Star Theatre a.k.a. The Embassy, in Cleveland, Ohio (1923).
Photo courtesy of Authors Collection.

Gayety Burlesque Theatre, Kansas City, Missouri, corner of Twelfth and Wyandotte Streets (1923). Photo courtesy of Authors Collection.

Dicks Greater Traveling Carnival Burlesque Shows (Pennsylvania, June 1949). Photo courtesy of Authors Collection.

Carnival Theatre showing a girlie show (1943). Photo courtesy of Authors Collection.

Burlesk Carnival at the Orange Show in San Bernardino, California (1941). All servicemen were admitted free. Photo courtesy of Authors Collection.

The Gayety Theatre in Detroit, Michigan (1917). Photo courtesy of Authors Collection.

Irving Place Theatre (1930). Photo courtesy of Authors Collection.

The Grand Follies in St. Louis, Missouri. Photo courtesy of Authors Collection.

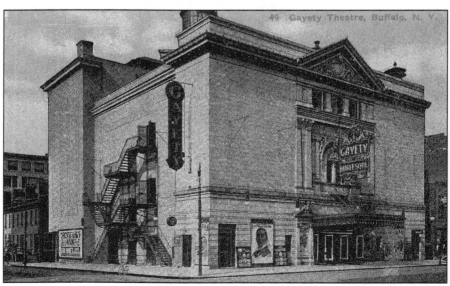

Gayety Theatre in Buffalo, New York (1920). Photo courtesy of Authors Collection.

Unknown Burlesque theater sidewalk Marquee (1946).
Photo courtesy of Authors Collection.

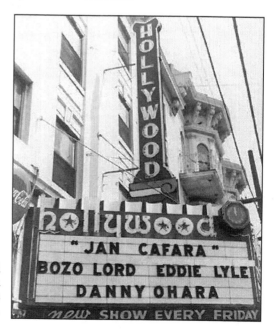

Marquee for The Hollywood
Theatre in San Diego, California
(1940s). Photo courtesy of Authors
Collection.

Rialto Burlesque Theatre (1950s). Photo courtesy of Authors Collection.

Burlesque Follies in Chicago (1950s). Photo courtesy of Authors Collection.

Chorus girls and Emcee onstage at The Hollywood Theatre (1940).
Photo courtesy of Authors Collection.

Star Stripper Inez Clare onstage at The Hollywood Theatre (1940).
Photo courtesy of Authors Collection.

Star Stripper Hillary Dawn onstage at The Hollywood Theatre (1940).
Photo courtesy of Authors Collection.

Chorus girls onstage at The
Hollywood Theatre in San
Diego, California (1943).
Photo courtesy of Authors
Collection.

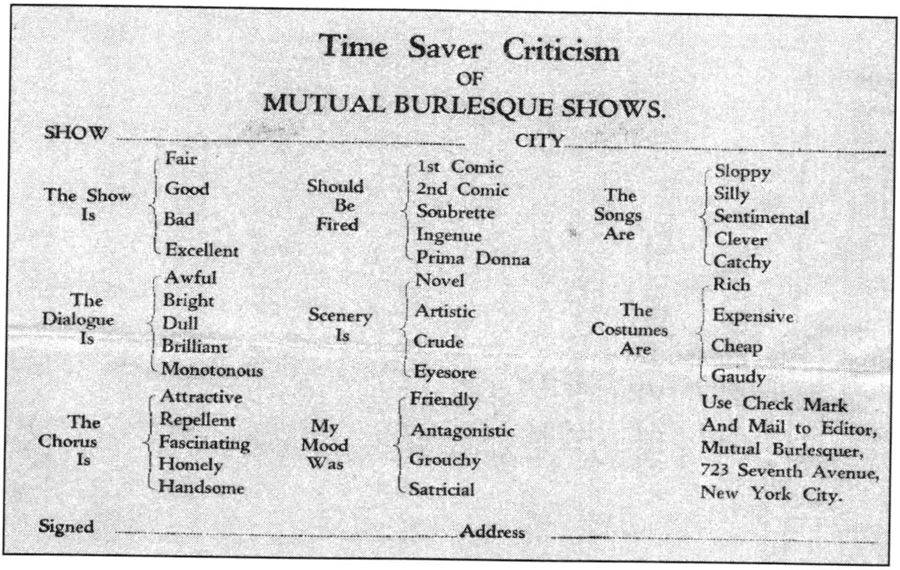

Time Saver Criticism
OF
MUTUAL BURLESQUE SHOWS.

SHOW .... CITY ....

The Show Is	Fair Good Bad Excellent	Should Be Fired	1st Comic 2nd Comic Soubrette Ingenue Prima Donna	The Songs Are	Sloppy Silly Sentimental Clever Catchy
The Dialogue Is	Awful Bright Dull Brilliant Monotonous	Scenery Is	Novel Artistic Crude Eyesore	The Costumes Are	Rich Expensive Cheap Gaudy
The Chorus Is	Attractive Repellent Fascinating Homely Handsome	My Mood Was	Friendly Antagonistic Grouchy Satricial		Use Check Mark And Mail to Editor, Mutual Burlesquer, 723 Seventh Avenue, New York City.

Signed .... Address ....

Extremely rare theater questionnaire handed out to Burlesque show patrons in the 1920s and 1930s. Photo courtesy of Authors Collection.

BOX OFFICE STATEMENT

FOLLY THEATRE
Gross– CHICAGO, ILL. 1565 45

THE EMPIRE CIRCUIT CO., Directors

ATTRACTION Century Girls Co.

~~Matinee~~
Evening Mar. 6 1906

216	Gallery	@ 15	32	40
	Balcony Reserved	@		
199	Orchestra Circle	@ 25	49	75
69	Parquet	@ 50	34	50
49	Loges	@ 75	36	75
	Boxes (Upper)	@		
17	Boxes (Lower)	@ 75	12	75
		@		
	TOTAL		166	15
50	% Share for House		83	07
50	% Share for Company		83	08

House Manager

Company Manager

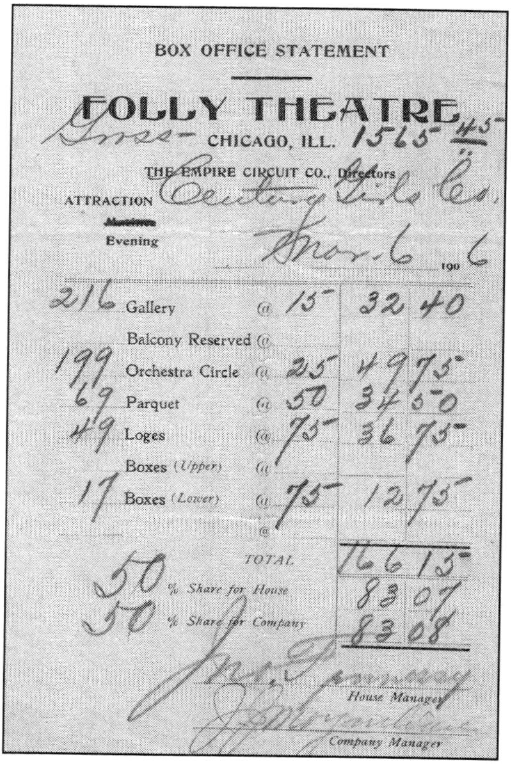

Possibly one-of-a-kind Folly Theatre box office statement for $100.15 (March 6,1906). Photo courtesy of Authors Collection.

THEATRE DRESSING ROOMS

Dressing rooms were an integral part of Burlesque theaters. It was where the powder puffs were busy concealing flaws, and the smell of stale cigarettes and sweet perfume hung heavily in the air. Chorus girls borrowed cake-mascara and traded gossip and a giggle. Sometimes they played cards while anxiously awaiting their next performance. It was more often than not, a stuffy room that was shared by six or seven girls; while the Star Strippers (like Gypsy Rose Lee), had the luxury of languishing in the privacy of their own dressing rooms.

Some theaters, like The Folly in Kansas City, Missouri, had as many as ten dressing rooms. Others had two or three, divided by a curtain with one sink that everyone shared, along with a toilet down the hall. The better theaters had a room for the wardrobe ladies to work on costumes for the chorus girls. Most chorus girls were provided costumes, which were often reworked for the following week's new routine. The star of the show and the featured strippers had to provide their own gowns and wardrobe out of their much larger paychecks. If they needed an adjustment, they paid the wardrobe woman extra.

Five unknown strippers chitchatting in their dressing room while waiting to go onstage (1940s). Photo courtesy of Authors Collection.

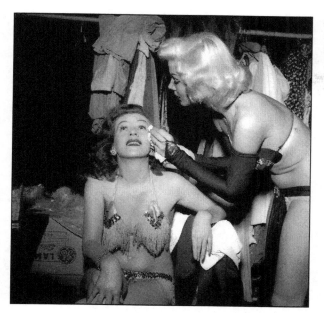

Strippers helping apply their make-up in the dressing room (1950). Photo courtesy of Authors Collection.

Jeanine France in her dressing room. Photo courtesy of Jeanine France.

Lili St. Cyr in her dressing room. Photo courtesy of Authors Collection.

Dixie Evans in her dressing room. Photo courtesy of Dixie Evans.

Chorus girl in the wardrobe room for an adjustment. Photo courtesy of Authors Collection.

Stripper Evelyn West having an adjustment by the wardrobe woman (1950). Photo courtesy of Authors Collection.

Virginia "Ding Dong" Bell being measured by her wardrobe lady. Photo courtesy of Authors Collection.

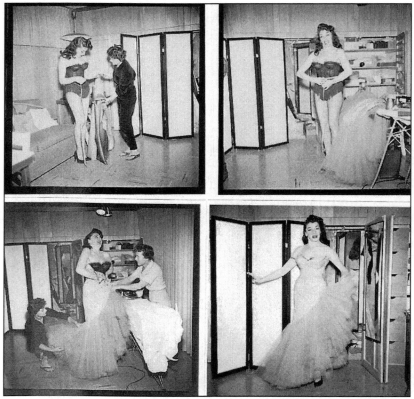

Contact sheet of Rusty Lane with Costume Designer Gussie Gross, in Gussie's studio at her home in Torrance, California (1950s). Photo courtesy of Gussie Gross.

In the late 1940s and the 1950s, small movie producers leased Burlesque theaters for the time between the Matinee and the Evening Show. Strippers often performed in those films to make some extra money. Luckily for us, these movies preserved an important part of Burlesque history. A few of these films provide complete Burly shows that include many well-known comics.

Wrestling was popular on television in the 1950s, and there are even some films of strippers wrestling in the late 1950s as well. Distributors placing ads in men's magazines sold most of these films. Some ads sold their films under the guise of Gentlemen's Movie Clubs, where you could join by buying five films in advance and also receive a small movie projector for free.

Dee Milo advertising strip movies (1950s). Photo courtesy of Authors Collection.

Betty "Blue Eyes" Howard onstage displaying her dynamite body (1950).
Photo courtesy of Authors Collection.

Chapter 11

Exotic World's Grand Finale
with
Added Attractions
Jennie Lee and Dixie Evans

JENNIE LEE

If it hadn't been for the voluptuous Jennie Lee, there never would have been an Exotic World. Jennie was born Virginia Lee Hicks on October 23, 1928, in Kansas City, Missouri. After graduating Wyandotte High School at age eighteen, Jennie began her Burlesque career at The Folly Theatre in her own hometown. Because she didn't know how to strip and had never taken any dance lessons, she began as a showgirl parading back and forth across the stage. Everyone, including the prop-men, repeatedly told Jennie that with her body, she should become a stripper. One month later, after being fired for something frivolous, Jennie's Dance Director and new friend Jack convinced her she was wasting her time as a showgirl. Jack found an ad for a stripper at a small theater in nearby Joplin. He helped Jennie prepare for her next audition and taught her to act like a pro. The Manager took one look at Jennie and gave her the job; no audition needed. It took guts to do her first actual strip, but after the first few times, she was encouraged by the audience's response and the recognition her talents received from the other dancers. The Theater Manager gave Jennie her first title, "The Bazoom Girl." She later acquired the nickname "Miss 44 and Plenty More."

Not long after, Jennie found herself an agent in Chicago, who signed her up and helped her locate a gown-maker whose specialty was Strippers. Then, it was on to well-known Photographer Maurice Seymour for publicity shots. After only a few months experience onstage, and watch-

Jennie Lee at age fourteen.
Photo courtesy of Jennie Lee.

One of Jennie Lee's
first publicity photos
(Chicago 1945). Photo
courtesy of Jennie Lee.

ing other strippers do their thing, Jennie was a hit! She had found her niche, and the rest is history.

Jennie had always been athletic. In high school she was on the swim team. She loved to swim and always had a pool in all the homes she owned. Jennie used to joke about what the breaststrokes did for her figure. Even though she was more often than not the center of attention, she never acted like a star to her friends. She easily formed friendships and held them close; so much so that most of the girls considered Jennie to be their best friend. In her prime, Jennie Lee was one of the top strippers and one of the most well-remembered names in Burlesque history.

Surf-Singers Jan and Dean immortalized Jennie in their song "Jennie Lee." It seems these two guys were together in an earlier group known as "The Barons." One day in 1958, out of boredom, curiosity, and raging hormones, the whole group sneaked into The New Follies Burlesk Theatre in Los Angeles. Jennie Lee, the star performer, was onstage twirling her tassels to the beat of a lone drummer. As she bounced up and down the audience, which was filled with regular patrons, chanted their usual boom-

Strippers get-together at Jennie's home in Palos Verde. Sitting on side of pool, Jennie Lee and Jeanine France. Left to right in the pool are Stacy Farrell, Flame, and Maggie Rose (1974). Photo courtesy of Authors Collection.

da-de-boom ditty that referred to her bouncing boobies. The entire band was inspired by the biggest bosoms they had ever seen! The group agreed Jennie was poetry-in-motion and something to write about. Shortly after, Dean Torrance was drafted into the service and Jan Berry, along with another Barons group member Arnie Ginsberg, wrote the words to the song "Jennie Lee." It was first recorded by Jan and Arnie. You can hear the group chanting, "Boom da de boom, da de boom, boom, boom, boom," in the background throughout the recording. Later, when Dean returned from the service, he teamed up with Jan and they re-recorded their version of "Jennie Lee" on a different label. The original record cut was donated to Jennie by Jan and Dean, and was on display at The Exotic World Museum in Helendale.

At one point, Dixie Evans, the Museum's Curator, was worried about the one-of-a-kind record being stolen, so she packed it away and replaced it with one from my record collection.

Maybe this is the time to explain part of Jennie's famous tassel routine. Unlike Carrie Finnell's muscle control, Jennie Lee's bosom bonnet's had long tassels attached by fishhook swivels. When she bounced up and down it made her tassels twirl. She often combined her back-bends with her muscle control. Leaning backwards, Jennie would roll her shoulders from side to side, causing the tassels to spin. Jennie was a strong dancer and her breasts really had been strengthened from years of swimming.

On May 30, 1949, Jennie married Daniel Lewis Wanick in a little Methodist church in Jackson, Missouri. Danny was born in Connecticut, but grew up in Kansas City where Jennie went to high school with his sister and a cousin. Jennie was two years older than Danny, who graduated from Westport High, a private military school. His parents were Russian-born Lithuanians; his father was a chef at a restaurant specializing in Russian cuisine.

Danny was devoted to Jennie Lee. When Jennie worked in Europe, the Orient, Hawaii, Mexico, Canada, and Cuba, Danny usually traveled with her and attended to her every need. With Jennie's encouragement, Danny tried his hand at working as a Stand-up Comedian in several nightclubs where Jennie was performing, but his act never caught-on and he ended up working as an announcer for a radio station in Santa Monica; which he also managed.

Jennie and Danny were married for almost twenty years, but were separated for the last six of those years. Although he and Jennie remained close friends, Danny lived in hopes that they would one-day get back to-

Jennie's publicity picture (1947). Photo courtesy of Jennie Lee.

Jennie Lee (1948). Photo courtesy of Jennie Lee.

gether again. Finally, after realizing Jennie wasn't returning, and according to court records, Danny and Jennie started divorce proceedings. They filed in September of 1967, but Danny died in November making Jennie a widow and the benefactor of his life insurance policy. Danny had always been thin and on the frail side, but Jennie wasn't aware that Danny was ill; she was crushed.

Jennie's work gradually brought her closer to the West Coast Burlesque scene and by 1950, she was working off-and-on at all the Burlesque theaters in Los Angeles, in addition to The Hollywood Theatre in San Diego and The President Follies Theatre in San Francisco.

With Jennie's out-going personality other strippers gravitated to her. Even more appealing, Jennie didn't have a pretentious or jealous bone in her body. What you saw was what you got. When problems surfaced at work, Jennie was first to offer solutions. For years, the strippers had complained about the poor working conditions in the theaters, and the lower

Photo of Jennie Lee offered by The Bazoomers Fan Club, the official Jennie Lee Fan Club located in Hollywood, California. Louis Marks was the Club's President. Photo courtesy of Authors Collection.

Baseball skit onstage at The Burbank Theatre; left to right, unknown female comic with a rubber nose, Beetle-Puss Lewis, Pat Flannery, unknown comic, and Jennie Lee (1950s). Photo courtesy of Jennie Lee.

pay scales for strippers on the West Coast. Jennie suggested they form a group to protect the rights of strippers and possibly protest in front of the press.

On July 19, 1955, a group of nine prominent strippers had a meeting to pool their resources, make suggestions, and see what collectively

First meeting and formation of Exotic Dancer's League of America. Left to right, sitting; Champagne, Peggy Stuart, Jennie Lee, Novita, Rusty Lane with her dog Tina, and Betty Rowland. Standing are; Denise Dunbar, Virginia Valentine, and Daurene Dare (1955). Photo courtesy of Jennie Lee.

they could accomplish. Jennie took notes, all the girls contributed ideas, and the concept for an "Exotic Dancers League of America" (E.D.L.) was born. Jennie was voted Founder and President, and Novita was voted Vice President. The organization was founded to help strippers fight for better pay and working conditions, and to promote more public acceptance of their art form.

Although the Exotic Dancers League of America was formed in 1955, it wasn't formerly documented or legally registered with the State of California until November of 1963. Originally, Jennie filed the legal papers as "Exotique" Dancers League of America. The good news was announced at the Sixth Annual Convention of the E.D.L., which was held at the swanky Bel-Air Hotel in Los Angeles. Thirty-two strippers and over one hundred newspaper reporters and photographers were present. There was an Exotic Fashion show revealing what the well-dressed stripper wears, and was demonstrated by Strippers Lavender Hill, Crazylegs Griffin, Nona Carver, Jeannie Lafayette, Linda Doll, and Jennie Lee. Later, Linda Doll had a bit too much of the bubbly and gave an impromptu strip

Author's E.D.L. Membership Pin. Photo courtesy of Authors Collection.

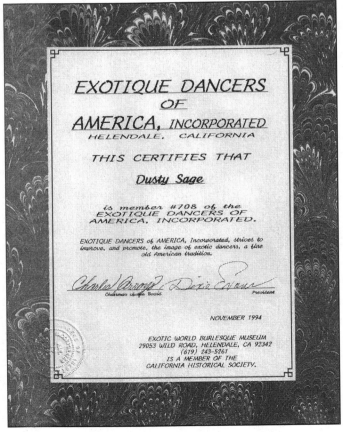

Author's E.D.L. Membership Certificate (1994).
Photo courtesy of Authors Collection.

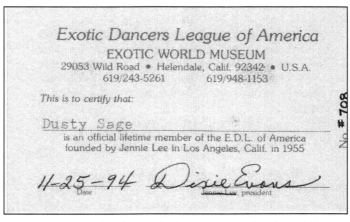

Author's E.D.L. Membership Card. Photo courtesy of Authors Collection.

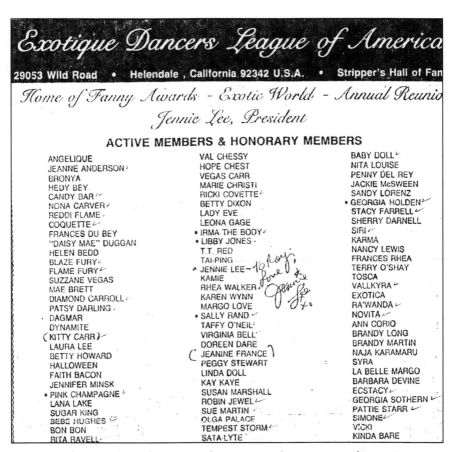

Jennie's personal list of E.D.L. members in 1989. Photo courtesy of Jennie Lee.

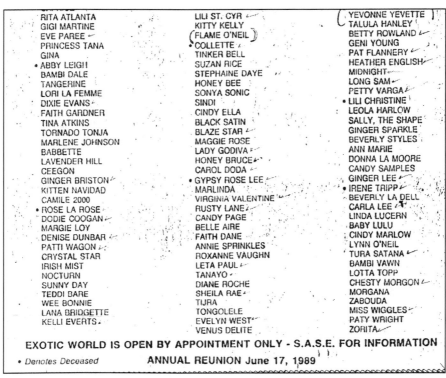

RITA ATLANTA	LILI ST. CYR	YEVONNE YEVETTE
GIGI MARTINE	KITTY KELLY	TALULA HANLEY
EVE PAREE	FLAME O'NEIL	BETTY ROWLAND
PRINCESS TANA	COLLETTE	GENI YOUNG
GINA	TINKER BELL	PAT FLANNERY
• ABBY LEIGH	SUZAN RICE	HEATHER ENGLISH
BAMBI DALE	STEPHAINE DAYE	MIDNIGHT
TANGERINE	HONEY BEE	LONG SAM
LORI LA FEMME	SONYA SONIC	PETTY VARGA
DIXIE EVANS	SINDI	• LILI CHRISTINE
FAITH GARDNER	CINDY ELLA	LEOLA HARLOW
TINA ATKINS	BLACK SATIN	SALLY, THE SHAPE
TORNADO TONJA	BLAZE STAR	GINGER SPARKLE
MARLENE JOHNSON	MAGGIE ROSE	BEVERLY STYLES
BABBETTE	LADY GODIVA	ANN MARIE
LAVENDER HILL	HONEY BRUCE	DONNA LA MOORE
CEEGON	CAROL DODA	CANDY SAMPLES
GINGER BRISTON	• GYPSY ROSE LEE	GINGER LEE
KITTEN NAVIDAD	MARLINDA	• IRENE TRIPP
CAMILE 2000	VIRGINIA VALENTINE	BEVERLY LA DELL
• ROSE LA ROSE	RUSTY LANE	CARLA LEE
DODIE COOGAN	CANDY PAGE	LINDA LUCERN
MARGIE LOY	BELLE AIRE	BABY LULU
DENISE DUNBAR	FAITH DANE	CINDY MARLOW
PATTI WAGON	ANNIE SPRINKLES	LYNN O'NEIL
CRYSTAL STAR	ROXANNE VAUGHN	TURA SATANA
IRISH MIST	LETA PAUL	BAMBI VAWN
NOCTURN	TANAYO	LOTTA TOPP
SUNNY DAY	DIANE ROCHE	CHESTY MORGON
TEDDI BARE	SHEILA RAE	MORGANA
WEE BONNIE	TIJRA	ZABOUDA
LANA BRIDGETTE	TONGOLELE	MISS WIGGLES
KELLI EVERTS	EVELYN WEST	PATY WRIGHT
	VENUS DELITE	ZORITA

EXOTIC WORLD IS OPEN BY APPOINTMENT ONLY - S.A.S.E. FOR INFORMATION

• *Denotes Deceased*　　　**ANNUAL REUNION June 17, 1989**

Second-half of Jennie's membership lists, showing date of her last annual reunion before her death. Photo courtesy of Jennie Lee.

to the salacious surprise of the photogs who formed a circle around her, whistling and clapping in appreciation. Also at the convention was the luscious Actress Mamie Van Doren, who starred in a film with Jennie Lee. She was made an Honorary Member of the E.D.L. Jennie wrote everything that happened that day in her column *Who's Who in Bur-Le-Q*, which she penned for a tabloid magazine called the *Confidential Flash*.

Thanks to Jennie, the E.D.L. became a reason to keep in touch socially. The E.D.L. formed a softball team and a bowling team, both cleverly called the "Barecats," and these gals could really score big. The Barecats played at the Griffith Park Baseball Field in Los Angeles. Their team efforts were written up in both *Life* and *Sports Illustrated* magazines. Jennie told me, "The Barecats played softball on the field, and hard-to-get everywhere else."

Not to be outdone by the famous annual "Blackwell's Top Ten Best-Dressed List," Jennie sent out yearly forms to the members of the E.D.L, allowing the girls to pick winners for Jennie's "Top Ten Best UN-Dressed

Jennie Lee holding her life-sized cardboard publicity picture.
Photo courtesy of Authors Collection.

List." In 1962, the winners were: Lili St.Cyr, Ann Corio, Tempest Storm, Jennie Lee, Blaze Starr, Faith Dane, Evelyn West, Virginia Bell, Libby Jones, and Taffy O'Neil.

Jennie, always the entrepreneur par excellence, was resourceful in finding ways to promote her business ventures. In 1958, during the time when exercise gyms were popping up all over the country and Jack LaL-anne became the first exercise guru on his long-running television show, Jennie came up with her own get-fit method. She designed a signature Slant-Board and recorded her own exercise tape to accompany it. It was

Jennie Lee's write-up in her column. Jennie holding the document that legally incorporated the E.D.L. Nona Carver on left, legal council Leland Zeman standing behind, and unknown county clerk on right (December 14, 1963). Photo courtesy of Charlie Arroyo.

E.D.L. bowling team, left to right; Marlene, Kaye Kay, Jennie Lee, Rita Revell, and Nona Carver. Photo courtesy of Charlie Arroyo.

Sassy Lassy dancer and Comedian Tangerine Sublett, unknown, Jennie Lee, and unknown, outside of courtroom waiting to plead not guilty to minor infractions. Note: Jennie holds paper reading "Register for E.D.L. Barecats bowling team." Photo courtesy of Authors Collection.

aptly named "The Jennie Lee Better-Built Slant-Board." *I'm sorry I don't know how she marketed it or if it was successful.*

Jennie was featured in several stripfilms in the 1950s. She was active in the Screen Actors Guild of Variety Artists and in The American Federation of Television and Radio Artists. She was in several off-Broadway plays in the early 1960s, where she played Daisy Mae in *She Dood It In Dixie, Will Success Spoil Rock Hunter*, and a small production of *Gypsy* where she played the role of Electra. Throughout her career she posed for innumerable magazine covers and centerfolds. During the 1970s, Jennie gave private or small group lessons at her School for Strippers in San Pedro. At the peak of her career, Jennie was earning $1,500 a week stripping. That was big money in the 1950s and 1960s.

Jennie retired in 1964, and in late 1968, she used some of Danny's insurance money to buy the Sassy Lassy Club in San Pedro, California. Many of her retired stripper friends worked at the Sassy Lassy part-time, or sometimes they would just drop in for a drink with Jennie and end up on the stage for old-times sake. It was the location of several of E.D.L.'s

JENNIE LEE

BAZOOMERS FAN
CLUB SPECIAL No. 26
For Reorders Write:
3830 Clayton
Hollywood 27, Calif.

Ad for Jennie Lee's photos for sale. Photo courtesy of Authors Collection.

Annual Reunions. Jennie also owned a small beer bar called The Blue Viking in San Pedro, which was frequented by nearby dockworkers.

Jennie had always been an avid collector of Burlesque memorabilia; not only her own, but photos, programs, costumes, and other collectables belonging to her Burlesque buddies. Her home in Rancho Palos Verdes had two rooms full of memorabilia that she deemed her "museum," fond-

Jennie Lee featured in two souvenir booklets. Photo courtesy of Jennie Lee.

Jennie playing pool at her Sassy Lassy Club. Photo courtesy of Authors Collection.

ly calling those rooms Exotic World. She promoted the art of stripping by inviting reporters to tour the small museum at her home and listen to her speak about Burlesque's grand history. This was actually the seed that grew into the world famous Exotic World in Helendale, California.

On July 29, 1979, Jennie opened up a two-room museum near her clubs in San Pedro, which was open to the public by appointment only, for a fee of $5. It was called the Stripper's Hall of Fame and Museum, and was located at 2317 S. Pacific Ave. At the grand opening were nine of Jennie's close stripper friends. Among them were Stacy Farrell, Jeanine France, Petti Varga, Nona Carver, and Karla. The celebration party was held at Jennie's Blue Viking bar and lasted late into the night with a few of the gals putting on surprise performances. Congratulation notes arrived from strippers all over the states.

Very young Jennie Lee pasting photos and reviews in her scrapbook (early 1950s). Photo courtesy of Charlie Arroyo.

Jennie at her first Exotic World Museum in San Pedro, California.
Photo courtesy of Jennie Lee.

In 1968, Exotic Belly Dancer Denise Dunbar took Jennie for a drink at the Hollywood Roosevelt Hotel where Charlie Arroyo was bartender. Charlie had been a singing/guitarist in New York nightclubs where he was known as "Puerto Rico's Singing Cowboy." Jennie and Charlie hit it off, and although they were only married for the last few years of Jennie's life, they lived together twenty-two years.

In the late 1980s, after nine years of profit making, The Sassy Lassy Club was starting to lose money, mostly due to the move of a nearby military base. Jennie sold both The Sassy Lassy and The Blue Viking, and invested her profits in three rental properties located in the High Dessert near Victorville, California. One was on Sultana Street in Hesperia, and four rentals were on a property on the outskirts of Victorville. Her main interest was the forty-acre property she purchased in Helendale. She planned to live there and develop part of it into a larger, more accessible museum that would be available to the general public. The place was to be known as Jennie Lee's Exotic World and Strippers Hall of Fame Museum.

Jennie was in her fifties and tired of managing dancers and clubs. She had always had one of those zaftig figures that men find so appealing, but after retirement from performing she gained a lot of weight and was close to two hundred pounds. It was starting to affect her health. Her husband

Carlos (Charlie) Arroyo in New York (1948). Photo courtesy of the Arroyo Family.

Charlie told me she went to several diet doctors but none of it worked; plus, she loved to go out and eat. By now, Jennie was ready for a change and looking forward to taking her family of three horses, four cats, and two dogs to live on her big ranch in Helendale.

The ranch was a former goat farm that had been abandoned and seized for back-taxes. It was close to old Route 66 and had the potential to fulfill Jennie's dreams for a Burlesque museum, small bed and breakfast, strip school, and a small theater with dressing rooms. There was already a large farm house that had been built in 1938, a smaller house the farm-hands had lived in, and a long building that had been used to milk the goats and house their baby kids. This goat shed would eventually become the Exotic World and Stripper's Hall of Fame Museum.

Jennie and Charlie brought Ziggy along when they moved to the desert. Ziggy was their long-time, loyal friend and caretaker who was devoted to Jennie, and loved all of her animals. Charlie, Ziggy, and another hired hand began putting the ranch back in shape. Their first project was remodeling the main house and having a large pool built so Jennie could swim; a place where her stripper friends could cool off in the desert heat. Next came the costly and laborious work of renovating the goat shed and turning it into seven rooms, including a bathroom. This was followed by installing large wrought-iron gates at the entrance with the words "Exotic World" over the top, and large statues of Lions poised on each side.

In the next few years, Jennie filled the main house with memorabilia, and she covered every wall with photos of herself with her famous and non-famous stripping friends. I remember using the bathroom in the main house and looking up to see an autographed photo of Actor Ed Asner, smiling down on me. When questioned about it, Jennie laughed and said "Ed and I went to high school together in Kansas. We both made it big, but Ed kept his clothes on."

Jennie kept up with her correspondence and personally answered all of her fan mail. Now and then, someone would make an appointment to view the photos displayed in the Museum during its early stages.

Jennie became an active member of the Chamber of Commerce in Hesperia, Victorville, and Helendale; was a member of the High Desert Republican Woman's Club, and sometime- advisor to Liz Mauk, the advertising consultant for Calico Ghost Town near Helendale.

Jennie finished decorating two of the Museum's rooms with photos, but by 1984, she had begun to feel tired all the time. Thinking she was simply overworked, Jennie did not receive any medical advice. Instead, she told Ann, her fellow club member and friend that her energy level was low and something felt wrong with one of her breasts. Apparently, a mole on Jennie's breast had changed and grown larger over the past few years. Ann, who was also a Registered Nurse, was shocked by Jennie's revelation and insisted Jennie go to a doctor as soon as possible. Ann even offered to accompany her.

Sadly, Jennie was diagnosed with a malignant tumor in one breast, which required immediate removal of most of that breast and all of the connecting lymph nodes. Amazingly Jennie, who had been famous for her beautiful, bountiful bosoms, gracefully accepted the loss. She continued to think positive and carry on with her dream for an Exotic World Museum that would visually and historically show the beauty and bliss connected with Burlesque entertainment. By the first part of 1989, how-ever, Jennie's cancer had returned with a vengeance, and she was again having a series of daily chemo treatments. Through it all, including the side effects and loss of hair, nothing could discourage Jennie in her dream for an Exotic World. With Jennie's undaunted courage and zest for life, a blonde wig and her brightest smile, she continued to have write-ups in local newspapers and talk on local radio shows. One very sick club owner back east offered Jennie $1000 to perform for fifteen minutes and expose her one breast. Sadly, she considered it momentarily because her chemo treatments were so expensive, and she had very little cash left.

Jennie was courageous to the end and kept fanning the proverbial flame that would eventually ignite, and shed light on Burlesque's past glo-ries for future historians. Although Jennie gradually became aware that she was starting to lose her battle with cancer, she was still part of several more annual reunions. She had her last reunion at the Exotic World Ranch on June 17, 1989. Three of Jennie's loyal, older photographer friends, who had captured most of the reunions for her, were on hand to record the last reunion and lend Jennie some well-needed encouragement. One pho-tographer friend, in ill health himself, became so distraught over Jennie's condition that he succumbed to a heart attack later that evening and died the following day.

Ann Corio, Bambi Vawn, Leola Harlow, Jennie Lee, Yvette Paris, and Annie Sprinkles (1989).
Photo courtesy of Yvette Paris. Photo by David March.

Candid of Kellie Everts (who stripped for God), Leola Harlow, and Jennie Lee.
Photo courtesy of Leola Harlow.

The small group of strippers who came to show their support and love for Jennie Lee were Dixie Evans, Stacy Farrell, Jeanine France, Barbara Bliss a.k.a. Flame O'Neill, Jeannie Anderson, Jennie Lee's neighbor—who wanted more than anything to become a stripper—and myself, Dusty Sage.

In August of 1989, along with several other guest strippers, Jennie Lee was featured on the Sally Jessie Raphael television show. After the show, all of Sally's guests and some of the press were invited to a small stripper reunion to be held at the Edison Hotel in Manhattan. During the festivities, Jennie Lee presented Yvette Paris with the coveted Fanny Award and later that day the girls, along with a smiling Jennie Lee, playfully took to the streets in Times Square to strut-their-stuff for the press.

In October 1989, I received an invitation to come to The Ranch and help celebrate Jennie, Charlie, and Ziggy's "October Birthday Blast". Ziggy had recently received a small accident settlement and paid for everything. The remaining money he gave to Jennie to help with her medical expenses. All the gals from the June 1989 Reunion, plus Nona Carver and Maggie Rose, a.k.a. Scarlet Rose (real name Janet Baker) were on hand, and each did their best to keep up a cheerful appearance for Jennie's sake.

Exotic Dancers League of America
Jennie Lee Pres. & Founder
Exotic Museum & Strippers Hall of Fame
S.A.S.E. For Information
29053 Wild Road Helendale, Ca. 92342

Fanny Awards
NyC · AUG 10 89
Strippers Annual Reunion

Mr. Victor Valley Pagent
Victor Valley B.P.W. Emcee, Jennie Lee
Holiday Inn Victorville Cal.
JUNJ Z 1989

Design by Wes Koehler *JENNIES BIRTHDAY BLAST*
Oct. 21 1989

Dear Dusty; Hope you can make it! Love Jennie Lee

Jennie's Invitation with a drawing of Jennie, her Fanny Award, Exotic World gates,
and her elegant Rolls Royce. Photo courtesy of Authors Collection.

Several times, one by one, each girl excused herself to step out for a short cry and, now and then, I noticed a tear or two being brushed aside. Jennie put on a brave face too, and hugged each of the girls a little tighter than usual. As fate would have it, it turned out to be Jennie's farewell birthday party. *I felt honored and fortunate to have witnessed such a remarkable group of women, whose honest respect and genuine love shown for Jennie Lee is something I'll never forget.*

By February 1990, ex-Stripper Nona Carver was spending most of her time at the Exotic World Ranch helping Charlie look after Jennie. Dixie Evans was working during the week as a caretaker for a wealthy elderly woman in Los Angeles, and spending her weekends helping with Jennie. Jennie and Charlie discussed plans for the future of Exotic World. Together they made the final decision that Dixie Evans would become Jennie's successor and complete the plans for Exotic World that had already been set in motion. Dixie met all the requirements needed to sell herself and Exotic World to the press; she was well-known, resourceful, ambitious, single, and available. Knowing Jennie's demise was imminent; plans for E.W.s changing-of-the-guard began to take place immediately.

The phone rang continually with calls from Jennie's friends, wanting updates on Jennie's condition. Two of Jennie's close friends, Roy Rogers and Dale Evans, who lived nearby in Apple Valley, stopped by several times a week to comfort and pray with Jennie. Then on Saturday evening

Jennie Lee's ashes displayed directly under her portrait. Photo courtesy of Charlie Arroyo.

near midnight of March 24, 1990, at age sixty-one, Jennie died peacefully in her sleep. Jennie Lee was gone, but for Dixie Evans, the "Marilyn Monroe of Burlesque," the task of completing Jennie's vision of an Exotic World Museum in the middle of the Mohave Desert, was just beginning.

DIXIE AND EXOTIC WORLD

By early May of 1990, Dixie was completely moved into Exotic World's main house. Shortly after, she was privy to a peek preview of Charlie's new role as Chairman of the Board and sole Owner of E.W. During Jennie and Charlie's time together, Jennie had been Queen and Charlie had been handyman and court-jester. When Jennie became ill, she married Charlie to reward his loyalty, but mainly for legal purposes. *Over my many years at E.W., I had often heard Jennie's long-time friends bandy-about the term 'gopher' in reference to Charlie's previous role at E.W.* Now Charlie intended to establish boundaries; if Jennie had been Queen, Charlie would be King and Supreme Ruler of Exotic World's forty-acre kingdom.

Dixie was totally overwhelmed for the first few years and especially the first few months. She had to answer an enormous amount of incoming calls, make plans for the upcoming Reunion, and tackle the difficult undertaking of cataloging, framing and hanging the hundreds of photos still stored in boxes. Plus, she was expected to cook the evening meals. In fact, to say that Dixie was overwhelmed is an understatement. The final blow was struck when Charlie announced that he expected Dixie to pay part of the household bills. Dixie was sixty-four years old and about seven months from collecting full Social Security payments. She ranted, raved, and cried, but in the end she filed for early Social Security and paid Charlie $200 a month.

During Dixie's first year on-board, she was in constant fear of Charlie finding another stripping legend to replace her. Several of them openly tried to work their way into Charlie's good graces, but as time passed it became apparent that Dixie was irreplaceable. It was then that Charlie and Dixie developed a deep respect for each other, and each other's positions at Exotic World. It was a respect that lasted until Charlie's death after a series of small strokes, February 8, 2006, at age seventy-six.

Dixie began her publicity campaign within a few months of Jennie's passing. Since I lived nearby, I helped her give many of the bigger tours, including those to the Route 66 Historical Museum Society, the local Corvette Club, and even a vintage Harley Davidson motorcycle club, where I

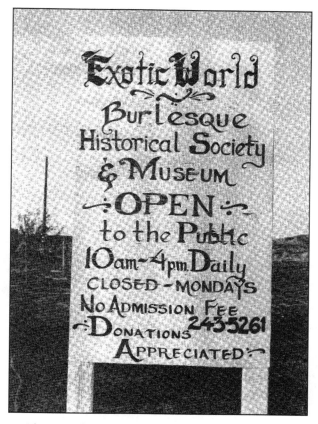

The original Exotic World Burlesque Historical Society
and Museum sign, showing hours open and closed.
Photo courtesy of Dixie Evans.

had fun showing myself on the cover and centerfold of *Easyriders* while telling inside stories about my twelve-year association with the magazine. Later on, my buddy Barb Burrows began helping us manage the bigger tours. For Dixie, it didn't matter if it was only one visitor or a group of twenty; she was always a gracious and entertaining hostess. She often prepared snacks for the producers and camera crew filming documentaries. She was over-worked and under-paid.

In 1990, after the first Reunion without Jennie Lee, the Los Angeles, Orange County, and San Bernardino newspapers printed full-page layouts of Exotic World. By the next year's Reunion, Dixie had shared the stage with several other well-known strippers on the Sally Jessie Raphael, Phil Donahue, Montel Williams, Jenny Jones, and Joan Rivers television

Dixie Evans, Bambi Sr., and Jeanine France on the *Just Between Us* T.V. talk show in Las Vegas (May 1991). Photo courtesy of Jeanine France.

Sheila Rae in the 1950s. Photo courtesy of Sheila Rae.

talk shows. Needless to say, Dixie plugged the Exotic World Museum on each and every show.

Sheila was a great gal who called me often and never failed to send me a card on Christmas and my birthday. She had been very attractive in her youth, but never was the least bit conceited, just a fun person. Sheila told me how, when she worked on the East Coast, she dated a big-time mobster who bought her a Jaguar and a pet monkey. She got a bit too tipsy one night and driving home after her show, she rolled her Jag over and over in the snow. Sheila wasn't badly hurt but she had her poor little mon-

Another lovely shot of Sheila Rae. Photo courtesy of Authors Collection.

key in the car with her. Somehow he was uninjured and managed to get out of the car and run away. When the police arrived, Sheila was wandering aimlessly, looking for her monkey. Sometime later, local zookeepers found the monkey hiding in a tree at a nearby park.

Dixie came up with the idea of incorporating a Miss Exotic World Pageant with the yearly Exotic World Reunion. It was a concept that would catch fire and bring journalists and photographers from around the world to this small desert town and stripper's competition. It was an event that would forever be Dixie Evans legacy.

Charlie spent months building a large outdoor stage behind the pool. The pool itself would serve as a focal point and runway, leading up the stairs to the stage. Later on, Charlie added a runway coming from the center of the stage. Above and behind the stage, the words Exotic World were spelled out in wrought iron and highlighted with a row of stars. Dixie sent out press releases to newspapers, television hosts, and radio stations. The press releases named all the famous strippers who received invitations to attend the First Miss Exotic World Pageant. On the list were Tempest Storm, Lili St.Cyr, Betty "The Ball of Fire" Rowlands, Candy Barr, Blaze Starr, Margie Hart, and Zorita. On the day of the Pageant there was more press than participants! The photographers were set up on the roof,

Good Morning, America talk show hosts on the left, with Dixie & Tanayo sitting, Stacy standing (1991). Photo courtesy of Authors Collection.

Stacy proudly displays her trophy at age thirty-nine. Photo courtesy of Stacy Farrell.

and so many were positioned in front of the stage that the paying guests couldn't see the show. All the stripping "Icons" were no-shows. Clever Dixie defended her press releases by saying, "Well hell, they were all invited. They just couldn't make it!"

Stacy's first trophy win, was First Prize for Most Beautiful Stripper in a Strip-A-Thon Contest held at North Hollywood's Zomba Club in 1958. She also won a Legend trophy at Exotic World.

At age seventeen, Stacy danced at The Los Angeles Follies Theatre. She performed in Dance Director Howard Montgomery's *Chorus Line* for several years. Stacy told me she had a huge crush on Howard Montgomery. She loved dancing in the chorus and retained many of her friendships from her Follies days. One in particular was Betty Briggs, who later became a stripper known as The Zebra Girl.

Cute little Betty Briggs early promo picture. Photo courtesy of Betty Briggs.

One of Stacy's few regrets was at age seventy-seven when she was turned down for the popular Palm Springs Follies. Especially since Tempest Storm had performed there the previous season. I went with Stacy for her audition; she still remembered all her time-steps and was very excited about dancing in The Follies. I watched Stacy audition and she was really great, but because of her age related macular degeneration, she couldn't see well enough to hit her mark. She called the following day to tell me she didn't get the job and I could tell she was crying. We talked about it for months; it was the only time she sounded down, in spite of be-

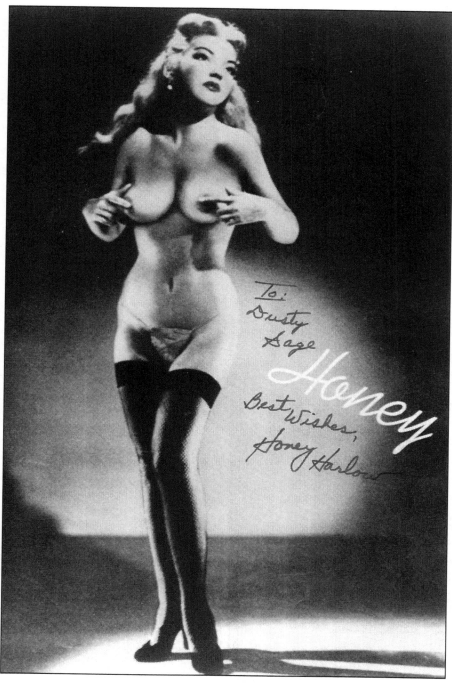

Honey Harlow. Photo courtesy of Honey Harlow.

ing the most positive person I've ever known. She owned her own night-club in Long Beach, California, and for several years she did an act called the Country Hypnotist. It was a take-off on glamorous Pat Collins' Hip Hypnotist show.

Stacy worked with Lenny Bruce at several clubs and acted in his 1954 movie *Dream Follies*. She was a close friend with Lenny's mother Sally Marr and Lenny's wife Honey Harlow, who Stacy also stripped with at The Colony Club in Gardena.

Howard Montgomery was from a family of well-known dancers, show producers, and choreographers. His brother Jack was a Dance Director/Agent/Producer, and their sister Betty was a Specialty Dancer. Howard performed solo on the Jackie Gleason T.V. Show in the 1950s. His chorus line, called The Montgomery Girls, danced background at the Los Angeles Follies Theatre in the 1930s and 1940s.

In 1991, adorable 5' 1" pocket pin-up Toni Alessandrini became the first Miss Exotic World. She was also the first child model for Mattel Toys; winner of Tucson, Arizona's 1980 Miss Bare-Bottom, and she was the stripper in the Tom Hanks movie *Bachelor Party*. Toni was forty-one years old when she was crowned Miss Exotic World, and was chosen over

Betty Briggs, Howard Montgomery, and Stacy Farrell dancing at Betty Rowland's get-together in Santa Monica. (1995). Photo courtesy of Authors Collection.

Toni with her trophy for Miss Exotic World 1991. Photo courtesy of Authors Collection.

The two 1991 Miss Exotic World Runners-Up; unknown, and Christina. Photo courtesy of Authors Collection.

girls half her age. She and Dixie became very close friends, and Toni was part of Exotic World's inner circle.

During the first Miss Exotic World Pageant there was some confusion over the gender of several of the 1991 contestants. It was apparent to not only the press, but Charlie as well, who kept saying, "We almost had a Mr. Exotic World." Dixie commented about including "strip-search may be required" on next years Miss Exotic World Application.

Many of Burlesque's past legends began donating their timeless treasures to the Museum. In exchange, Dixie promised to always keep them on display. She spent hours each day adding, arranging, and rearranging photos and gowns. *Dixie loved being in the Museum and I often called it "Dixie's Playhouse."* The small donations received from the daily tours went right back into the Museum. There were glass cases, manikins, beaded curtains, and hundreds of picture frames to buy. Plus, Dixie was always on call. Should a car arrive unexpectedly and begin honking in the driveway asking to see the Museum, Dixie, bless her big heart, never disappointed any visitor. When asked, she could and would go into her Marilyn Monroe routine at a moment's notice. She loved doing it and once jokingly said in her very best Marilyn Monroe voice, "Oh, it makes me forget that I just scrubbed the Museum's toilet bowl without my underwear." Dixie had a witty sense of humor.

Amid all the preparation for the next years Pageant, Dixie put herself on her favorite 1930's Hollywood Diet of boiled eggs and grapefruit. She lost over twenty pounds and then proceeded to make a deal with a plastic surgeon in Apple Valley. In exchange for a mini-lift, he could come to the next Pageant, show off his work, and pass out his business cards. Dixie looked great, but as I remember, most of the older gals were a bit put-off by his efforts. *Imagine sitting in the Stripper's Hall of Fame and being handed a card from a cosmetic surgeon; bad scene.* We all giggled while commenting on the clever and ingenious ruse Dixie had just pulled off. Hooray! Here's one for the Stripper!

After the first two Miss Exotic World Pageants, the older, more intimate Reunions like Jennie Lee used to put together, became a thing of the past. No longer could the older strippers meet as they had done for the previous Exotic Dancers League Reunions. The regulars missed letting their hair down, sharing a glass of wine, comparing wrinkles and wondering where the hell the Wonderful World of Burlesque had gone. Some of Jennie's loyal, older strip-sisters still showed up at the Pageants for old time's sake, and some even secretly shared more than a glass of

Dixie, looking beautiful in yellow, performing at Exotic World.
Photo courtesy of Authors Collection.

Geritol. However, Exotic World had become congested with youthful hopefuls and Neo-Burlesque acts like, the "Cantankerous Lollies" from San Francisco, and Roobie Breastnut. *Both, by the way, were always a big hit!* Roobie—real name Christina Turek—was one of Dixie's favorite performers and person.

For over fifteen years, Dixie and Charlie worked hard to make a go of Exotic World. It really was a labor of love since the Pageants barely earned enough money to pay back their cost. Many of the girls who were close to Dixie knew there were times when Dixie and Charlie could barely pay their utility bills. At one point Charlie had to sell Jennie's Rolls Royce just to keep Exotic World afloat. Sometime later, Charlie borrowed $30,000

Roobie Breastnut in her signature attire. Photo courtesy of Roobie Breastnut.

Roobie, diva-diving in the deep-end. Photo courtesy of Roobie Breastnut.

on one of his properties to build a small theater with a dressing room. He also built a snack bar that sold hamburgers, hot-dogs, soft drinks, and bottled water. During the earlier years, Charlie used Jennie's fabulous Rolls Royce to bring legends like Mitzi and Tempest from the L.A. airport to The Exotic World Ranch. The car itself was so classy looking that visiting photographers often paid extra to use it in their shoots. The girls were filmed sitting on the hot top of the Rolls in 100-degree desert heat, wearing little more than a smile and burnt buns!

There was never any shortage of journalists wanting a story, or strippers hoping to be the next Miss Exotic World. I personally did at least seven documentaries and four television shows. I know a lot of the girls did just as many or more; but I think Dixie may easily have given over a hundred interviews.

Exotic World was so popular that during one Pageant a couple got married in its new theater. The couple drove a hundred miles up to the desert from Los Angeles in a rented bus, bringing along a minister and a busload of wedding guests. Our half-naked contestants in the Theater's dressing room were surprised to see a preacher pop in, change into his clergy robes, and pop back out. *Poor man; he must have secretly broken at least two of the Ten Commandments for that ceremony!* It was the oddest

The Exotic World snack bar with two of Jennie Lee's cats, snacking.
Photo courtesy of Authors Collection.

type of wedding ceremony I ever saw. As I recall, the Bridesmaids were asked to perform somersaults and the Best Man had to give the Bride a piggyback ride. I wish I could remember what the Bride and Groom was asked to do, but when they started removing their clothes I went into a fog. The last thing I remember was seeing Dixie dodge the bridal bouquet and say something that began with an S and ended with T.

Exotic World was really a wonderful place to visit, but finding it could be a real desert safari; people were always getting lost. During the Pageants, the office phone rang off-the-wall with people asking for directions. It happened so many times, Dixie had to ask for phone volunteers with map reading skills to guide the guests in. Since the office phone was next to a dressing room full of Strippers; we had more volunteers than we needed.

Everyone who ever had the good fortune to visit The Exotic World in Helendale can consider themselves not only lucky, but a part of its past history. During the Pageants, Exotic World was an experience similar to the Glamourcon Conventions; there were strippers being interviewed every few feet, and most were delighted to have pictures taken with the many visitors. The atmosphere is hard to describe; it was both laid-back and exciting, but it was mostly Fantasy Island with pasties!

Before and during the contest, guests could wander thru the Museum and view the thousands of photos, or purchase Burly items from the Museum Gift Shop. There were always several volunteers walking around in the rooms to answer questions and to be sure nothing was stolen. Sadly, and very early on, Dixie was showing the Museum to a large group and someone stole the display of her ex-husband, middleweight boxer Harry Braelow, fighting in the ring. After that incident, Dixie recruited Barb Burrows, Liz Mauk, and your Author, to act as Dixie's Pixies and monitor the Museum during the Pageants. We often dressed alike so Dixie could describe us and say, "If you need help, find one of my Pixies."

Exotic World itself covered much of the forty-acre grounds. After arriving at the huge entry gates and dodging a few tumble weeds, visitors drove down a long dirt road lined with trees and rows of statues of half-dressed, Grecian Goddesses standing on each side. Halfway down the road, visitors were greeted by star-covered wooden monuments dedicated to past and present Burlesque Icons. Then the whole of Exotic World would come into panoramic view. There was a white guesthouse on the right-hand side where Jane Briggeman spent several months beginning research for her book *Burlesque: Legendary Stars of the Stage,* which won her the 2005 Gold Ippy Award in the Performing Arts category. Both

Left to right; Author, Barb Burrows, Liz Mauk, Dixie Evans, and Karla at the Patton Museum in Indio, California, where we performed in a 1940's World War II Revue. For the opening number, an Army soldier drove us up a ramp and onto the stage in a jeep where we sang "Six Jerks in a Jeep." Photo courtesy of Authors Collection.

Tempest Storm and the infamous Stripper Candy Barr lived there for a short time. Behind the guesthouse stood the two story main house where Jennie Lee and her husband Charles Arroyo had lived, later occupied by Dixie and Jennie's widower.

Towards the back, the stables could be seen in the distance. Looking closer, you might see all three of Jennie Lee's spirited horses tossing their manes and holding their tails high as they greeted you at the corrals edge. The oldest of the horses was named Sassy, after Jennie Lee's nightclub the Sassy Lassy. Some of the handyman's small dogs might greet you, and one or two of Jennie Lee's cats could be found napping in the shade of some desert greasewood bushes. There were even more Grecian and lion statues located around the grounds.

To the right was the long, seven room Museum packed with floor to ceiling photos, gowns, glass cases of pasties donated by the strippers who wore them, Sally Rand's Ostrich fans, Gypsy Rose Lee's steamer-trunk, Jennie Lee's big brass bed, sparkling rhinestone- covered gowns from well-known Burlesque divas, and rare memorabilia. In front of the Museum were inviting concrete tables and benches waiting in the outdoor patio. Behind

Dixie with Clydesdales during an E.W. event.
Photo courtesy of Authors Collection.

Jeanine France during the E.W. wagon rides.
Photo courtesy of Authors Collection.

the Museum was the Theater, which seated an audience of ninety to a hundred people. The walls behind the stage, and the Theater walls themselves, were covered with photos and memorabilia. There was an outside bathroom conveniently located near the main house carport. Directly across from the Theater and next to the main house was Jennie's pool, where many a contestant cooled her tootsies in the inviting crystal blue water. Often times, following the long days Pageant, there were private pool parties where, with or without their, shall we say rubber duckys, everyone went for a swim.

Dixie rarely knew for sure who would be participating in any of the Pageants until they showed up. Then she would frantically put together her line of flag holders for the opening ceremony, and give last minute rules to the Judges sitting in the shade of a small cabana near the stage. Somehow, at the last chaotic second, Dixie would grab her American Flag and say, "It's Showtime!" and off she went, working her way around the pool followed by a group of flag-waving strippers.

Dancer Bob "Rubberlegs" Tanenbaum, who for years owned his own Carnival Girlie Shows, would usually drive in from Las Vegas to act as Emcee. He was our Mr. Dependable. He also had the not-so-pleasant task of making a list to see who was naughty or nice, and place the contestants in some sort of sequence. Among Bob's many accomplishments, he was an Eccentric Dancer working with Lionel Hampton and his or-

Dixie at the entrance to the Museum. Photo courtesy of Dixie Evans.

Dixie inside the Museum posing by the donation box. Photo courtesy of Dixie Evans.

Jennie Lee's big brass bed in the Museum. Photo courtesy of Authors Collection.

Exotic World Limousine. Photo courtesy of Ben Urish.

Sadie Burnett and Tempest Storm in the Theater's dressing room. Photo courtesy of Authors Collection.

Display of Blaze Starr's costumes. Photo courtesy of Ben Urish.

Tempest Storms silver gown and her photos on the wall. Photo courtesy of Ben Urish.

Display of Sherry Champagne's costumes and Jane Mansfield's heart-shaped love seat. Located at far right are Sheri Champagne's ashes in a golden urn. Photo courtesy of Ben Urish.

Signs in Exotic World. Photo courtesy of Ben Urish.

Long, tree-lined drive in Exotic World. Photo courtesy of Ben Urish.

Museums glass showcases filled with memorabilia. Photo courtesy of Ben Urish.

Fun view of entry to Museum and main house. Photo courtesy of Ben Urish.

Display of Exotic World Trophies. Photo courtesy of Ben Urish.

Part of E.W. Museum entry.
Photo courtesy of Authors
Collection.

Dixie inside the Museum giving a tour. Note Sally Rand's fan in far showcase. Man in plaid is Bill, long-time E.W. handy man. Photo courtesy of Authors Collection.

chestra when they entertained President Nixon at his Inaugural Ball in 1968.

Exotic World wasn't just exotic; it was patriotic as well. Dixie had everyone, including the audience, stand up and sing the National Anthem during our 1991 Pageant when we gave tribute to the returning Desert Storm troops.

The Pageants brought in some very talented and gorgeous younger girls. We had Mermaids, Egyptian Priestesses, Strippers twirling around in Champagne glasses, Sea Nymphs with baby Sea Serpents, bodybuilding beauties, Sci-fi Sirens with ray-guns, dancers with Amazon and Cockatoo parrots. We even had a tall, thin Elvis impersonator who used his limo to escort guests back and forth to their hotel, and a heavier Elvis who entertained for our other special events. One year we had both Elvis's at the same time. It was like having the before and after Elvis. *No wonder we were all-shook-up!*

I have to comment on Rio Savant's performance because I couldn't get close enough to photograph it. Photographers were practically knocking each other down to get a shot. Her whole act was simply mesmerizing! I've never seen so much body control, particularly her fanny, which rippled! She lay on the runway and her butt seemed to have a mind of

Rubberlegs interviewing some of the dancers at the Pageant.
Photo courtesy of Authors Collection.

Dixie strutting around the pool
with the flag. Note Dixie's star in
the cement in front of her. Photo
courtesy of Authors Collection.

Pageants opening ceremony, left to right; Trina Lynn's sister, *whose name I've forgotten*, Dixie Evans, Sadie Burnett, Trina Lynn, Tanayo, and your chubby Author. Photo courtesy of Authors Collection.

Jeannie Anderson onstage thanking our troops for their service. Photo courtesy of Authors Collection.

Dixie Evans and Elvis, before the fried-peanut-butter-and-banana-sandwiches; Catherine D'Lish, receiving one of her two Miss Exotic World Trophies; Sadie Burnett with her Third Place Trophy, and Tanayo. Photo courtesy of Authors Collection.

Catherine D'Lish, who is a Classic Burlesque performer, getting ready to climb into her water-filled Champagne glass. Note: as you can see by the flag blowing behind, it was windy and cold that day, yet she smiled as she swirled around in the icy water. Photo courtesy of Authors Collection.

Charlie Arroyo and Dixie Evans presenting Catherine D'Lish with a gold ring. Julie Uto with her Second Place Trophy and winning prize money. Photo courtesy of Authors Collection.

Barb Burrows, famous Elvis impersonator David Prezley acting as Entertainer/Emcee at E.W.s Car Show and Oldies Dance, along with your platter-playing D.J. for the event, Dusty Sage. Photo courtesy of Author's Collection.

Barb Burrows in antique racing car at E.W.s car show, and Author, in front of our newly built Exotic World Theater. Photo courtesy of Authors Collection.

Dixie, Cindy Kaye and Author filming a documentary in the new E.W. Theater. Photo courtesy of Authors Collection.

Tall, Daisy Delight onstage performing. Daisy was Miss Exotic World Runner-up in 1995 and 1996. Photo courtesy of Authors Collection.

Jeannie Anderson with her trained Macaw and Cockatoo, headed for the stage. Courtesy of Authors Collection.

The marvelous Mermaid who wouldn't go in the water. Photo courtesy of Authors Collection.

Our Mermaid grew legs. Photo courtesy of Authors Collection.

Rio Savant carrying her royal Egyptian Ankh and wearing a Lapis lazuli-colored gown with matching Egyptian headdress adorned with a golden serpent. Beside her walks her near-nude slave, who fans her with Ostrich feathers. Photo courtesy of Authors Collection.

Rio stripped-down; ready to do her breath-taking Belly Dance. Photo courtesy of Authors Collection.

its own. *The movement reminded me of ocean waves going back and forth towards the shore. The motion almost made me seasick.* The whole crowd stared in utter fascination. Rio's unique talents and creativity won her the 1996 title of Miss Exotic World.

Flame O'Neill started her career as a talented torch singer. Her real name is Barbara Adele Rose Bliss; she was known as Barbara "Heavenly" Bliss. She was a beautiful girl with a sultry voice, who developed a drinking problem early in her life. Barbara had a sad and somewhat lonely life. Her parents, Adolf and Marie, were both Austrian immigrants who divorced

Our adorable little Spanish Stripper with her purple boa and headdress. Photo courtesy of Authors Collection.

Stripping Legend Tanayo, the Puerto Rican Bombshell. Photo courtesy of Authors Collection.

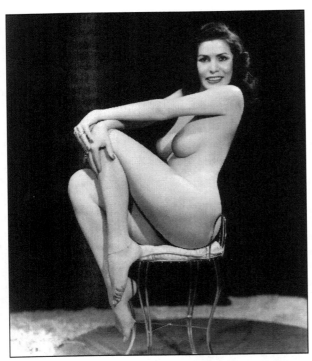

Publicity photo of Tanayo in the 1950s. Photo courtesy of Tanayo.

Publicity photo of Flame O'Neill in gown. Photo courtesy of Flame O'Neill.

Flame wearing same gown forty years later at Exotic World. Photo courtesy of Flame O'Neill.

Barbara "Heavenly" Bliss Stylist of song and dance (late 1940s). Photo courtesy of Authors Collection.

when Barbara and her sister were very young. Her mother was a music teacher who worked for the school district and gave singing and piano lessons to Barbara when she was a child. After Barbara's sister died at age 20, her mother didn't want to be alone. So, although Barbara was often on the road singing in clubs, she lived in Long Beach with her mother until her mother's death at age eighty-six. Because of her drinking, Barbara lost her lovely voice. In the early 1950s, Barbara began stripping under the name Flame. She was also a talented Artist and Seamstress. Barbara was best friends with Stripper Jeanine France; they were neighbors in Long Beach and in Clearlake, California, where they spent the last years of their lives. Both gals liked a good battle and life in the bottle. Barbara died of a liver disease in June of 2004.

Jeanine France was 6' 2" of leggy loveliness. She was a merry mixture of innocence and street smarts, daffy, darling, and so darned delightful to be around. In her prime, Jeanine was elegant and charming; her stage presence was naturally unique. She began her career around age seventeen and stripped in Mexico, Hawaii, Canada, and across the United States.

Long-limbed Jeanine France (1950s). Photo courtesy of Jeanine France.

Lovely Jeanine France, the "Eyeful Tower Girl" (1950s). Photo courtesy of Jeanine France.

Jeanine France at Exotic World. Photo courtesy of Authors Collection.

Jeanine France was very close to Jennie Lee. Jennie used to write to a lot of male pen pals, but when her cancer was in its final stages, one of them asked Jennie to please find him another famous stripper to correspond with. So Jennie Lee gave her pen pal to Jeanine France. Years later, when the man died, he left Jeanine over $100,000 and she never even licked the stamps!

Jeanine was quite religious, yet she used to write me the funniest letters that would begin with "Hello, you old douche-bag," then go on about the latest drunken squabble she had with best friend Barbara Bliss; and end with something like "Love, Your old broken-down Burlesque buddy, Jeanine France." After all that wild writing, she would include a cloth Catholic Scapular. Sometimes, she would call me late at night obviously half in the bag, and yak about the good old days for hours. *I just loved her to pieces.* After Barbara died, Jeanine was like a lost soul. She passed away on January 22, 2008. *I have this picture in my head of Jeanine France and Barbara Bliss somewhere floating on a cloud. They're both about three-sheets-to-the-wind, having a great ol' spat, and laughing their Heinekens off.*

Dee Milo and I did an H.B.O. Documentary together. She looks as good without her make-up as she does with it, and is a very intelligent woman.

Author and Stripper Cindy Kay in the Museum. Photo courtesy of Authors Collection.

Author and Stripper Dee Milo in front of the Theater, Kitten De Ville by the door. Photo courtesy of Authors Collection.

Pillow was a popular body builder and stripper from Alaska. She performed at many of the Pageants, always wearing incredibly creative costumes. Pillow became close to Dixie and Charlie, and was part of their inner circle. In 1995, she won Miss Exotic World and in 1996, Pillow received The Special Honorary Award for Extraordinary Service to Exotic World and Burlesque. It was well deserved.

One of the gals Dixie knew and trusted was related to an attorney. She offered to help Dixie and Charlie make Exotic World a non-profit status organization. After waiting for several years, I could see it was going to be a no-go. So, since my own lawyer was also my close friend, I begged, beguiled, and boo-hooed until he agreed to agree and file the non-profit forms as a donation. Sometime in 1998, my Attorney Le Roy Labarre met with Charlie and Dixie to fill out the paper work. They both put their

Author Dusty Sage and Author Holly Knox, who wrote the book *Sally Rand, From Film to Fans.* Holly has been a Las Vegas performer, Actress, and Song Stylist.
Photo courtesy of Authors Collection.

Toni Alessandrini and Author in the main house. Notice photo of Ed Asner in the foyer.
Photo courtesy of Authors Collection.

Pillow, Miss Exotic World winner, (notice trailer behind stage serving as extra dressing room). Photo courtesy of Authors Collection.

names on the forms but Labarre told them there had to be three names or more on the Board of Directors, or it wouldn't be accepted. That's how I became the first non-owner on the Board. After the meeting, Dixie teasingly told Mr. Labarre, "With a name like yours, you should have been a stripper."

When I met Linda Doll, I was drawn first to her personality; she was so genuine and sweet. When she smiled, she sparkled. As a young dancer, she really was a little redheaded doll. Linda's real name is Virginia Opel Byrd. She was Miss Tulsa Oklahoma, long before she started dancing. In 1964, she danced in the movie *Viva Las Vegas* and befriended Elvis Presley, the film's star. Elvis gave Linda a Cadillac and she was still driving it in 1995. By then it was a classic. Linda was close friends with Mickey Rooney and had many other friends who were celebrities. Lili St Cyr gave her John the Baptist's head on a platter from her "Dance of the Seven Veils" routine. Liberace allegedly gave her a piano, and someone left her a home in Hollywood. Her home was over-flowing with mementos that were given to her by famous people. She was Broderick Crawford's girlfriend for a while, and in 1959, she was arrested for breaking into Crawford's Bel-Air home while he was filming in London. She once referred to herself as Mrs. Crawford and claimed Broderick gave her the stage name

Pillow, Dixie, and Author. Photo courtesy of Authors Collection.

Dixie and Jonathan Ross with Gloria Pall in the background, at E.W.
Photo courtesy of Authors Collection.

of Linda Doll, and helped her get into the Screen Actors Guild. *I used to talk to her over the phone and even I wanted to give her something. I offered her my husband, but she politely declined, saying, "No, I don't have room for him."*

Linda Doll passed away from cancer and Alzheimer's disease on April 26, 2015. *Strangely, she died during the time I was writing about her.*

In 2004, I too, received an award. It was The Shining Star; "Awarded To Miss Dusty Sage For Her Outstanding Dedication And Long-Time Support Of Exotic World."

I never expected to receive any trophy, so it came as a complete surprise. It just happened to be the year Barb and I decided to lock-up the Museum for an hour and perform some kind of comedic Burlesque skit. Dixie said we could do anything we wanted as long as it was funny. Well, we'd heard this hilarious song about the poor Proctologist who was "… working where the sun don't shine," and we decided to sing it. Barb

Stripper/Actress Linda Doll onstage at Exotic World.
Photo courtesy of Authors Collection.

My Trophy. Photo courtesy of Authors Collection.

dressed as Nurse Ratchit the dominatrix, and I dressed myself in a cardboard tube with Preparation H printed on the front. My head was covered to look like the cap; just my round face was showing, and my hands came out like little flippers. Barb carried an over-sized thermometer and yes, dear Readers, the dreaded enema bag.

As soon as we got on the stage, we both went blank and kept repeating "Slaving away in the heart of darkness, working where the sun don't shine." Finally, Barb remembered a line and nudged me a few times with the nozzle; loudly chanting "Lift up your hands and join us, lets all do the finger wave!" The crowd was stunned and didn't understand what we had to do with Burlesque. I felt like my tube was melting and our message was falling on deaf ears. We both started laughing; I got nervous and grabbed the bag, which we had filled with wine for the finale, and I chug-a-lugged some of it right out of the hose. My ears were immediately filled with the humming sound forty or fifty people make when they collectively say, Ewww! It was that very moment Emcee Ed Bell awarded me the "Shining Star." It felt like getting the Academy Award with my pants down!

* * * * *

DIXIE WAS BORN MARY LEE EVANS on August 3, 1928, in Long Beach, California. Her father worked for a large oil refinery; his job was supervising the many oil wells being drilled along the coast of California. Because of his skills, he worked for five years on oilrigs for the Australian government. Dixie, her mother, and her older sister Betty always had financial security. Then, after returning to the states on August 25, 1946, a few days before Dixie's thirteenth birthday, the families secure world shattered. Local newspapers reported "Prominent oil man Leroy Evans, dies near Taft, California. He was hurled over a sand-wheel-drum breaking his neck; and spent a week in the hospital, paralyzed from the neck down, before dying."

Dixie often talked about how her father's death affected her, and alleged that her mother just fell apart, wandering around the house wearing an old chenille robe and worn-out slippers, with curlers in her hair and cold cream on her face. Other times, her mother would sit for hours crying and wringing her hands in distress. After school, Dixie would pick up soda-pop bottles and cash them in for pocket change; and later on, she took a series of menial jobs to help out, including picking celery in the fields near her home in Bakersfield. At age sixteen, she quit school to work full-time at an aircraft factory.

Dixie told me she started out as a Page at The El Rey Club in Oakland, where its Manager/Director Lillian Hunt recognized Dixie's potential as a dancer. Dixie became a dancer in The El Rey chorus-line and did some modeling on the side. According to Dixie, sometime in 1950 she modeled for two of the *Fredericks of Hollywood* lingerie catalogs.

Lillian Hunt directed Dixie in several small cheesecake films including; *Sleepy Time Girl, Hula Dancer, Too Hot to Handle,* and *The Casting Couch,* also known as *The Producer.* The latter film is the most well known; it has a clever story line and shows Dixie's acting capabilities. Dixie told me that she improvised throughout most of the film.

Dixie was always more than a stripper; she was really an Actress and Writer. Like Jennie Lee, Dixie knew how to attract free publicity and keep

Dixie Evans, while attending East Bakersfield High School in California at age sixteen. Photo courtesy of Dixie Evans.

the public interested in Burlesque's role in American history. She always emphasized the effect it had on cultural standards.

After The El Rey, Dixie worked at The L.A. Follies and stripped in a couple of San Francisco's nightclubs. She then moved to Newark, New Jersey, where she found work at Harold Minsky's Adams Theatre. Minsky quickly noticed Dixie's resemblance to Marilyn Monroe and came up with a gimmick. He convinced Dixie she could be the Marilyn Monroe of Burlesque. At first, she was a bit embarrassed about the idea and didn't take Minsky seriously. That night, Dixie barely slept. Her mind was whirling with ways to creatively emulate Monroe. She practiced Marilyn's breathy speaking voice over and over, and perfected the Marilyn Monroe look with the help of make-up and hairstyle.

The following day, Harold Minsky was amazed by Dixie's enthusiasm and readiness. Minsky wasted no time in changing The Theatre's Marquee. Before the afternoon matinee it read, "Featuring Dixie Evans" in big, bold letters, and "The Marilyn Monroe of Burlesque" in smaller print.

Dixie's Marilyn act evolved over a period of time. At first, it was a routine centering on Marilyn Monroe's facial expressions, her patter, and her sensual-but-innocent movements combined with sweet-but-sexy dialog. It then became a skit about Marilyn's break-up with her ex-husband baseball star Joe DiMaggio who, according to Dixie's act, left her flat except for his bat and two balls. Dixie would do her skit and at the end, she would kiss

Dixie starring in *The Producer*. Photo courtesy of Dixie Evans.

Dixie's favorite photo of herself as Marilyn. Photo courtesy of Dixie Evans.

two baseballs and toss them into the audience. Dixie also tossed out a lot of risqué innuendos, but she always left a little to the audience's imagination.

Later on, Dixie did parodies of some of Marilyn's movies, mainly *The Prince and the Showgirl*. She had a life-size dummy made, which she dressed in an elaborate copy of Lawrence Olivier's Prince character. Her routine was built around her seduction of the Dummy-Prince. Dixie told me her boxer husband Harry was jealous of her attention to the dummy on and offstage. He accused Dixie of spending way too much money on its upkeep and clothes. When Harry got really upset with Dixie, he would say "Tell it to the Dummy." Dixie would smile and reply, "I just did."

For close to a decade, Dixie performed her imitation of Marilyn Monroe at the Place Pigalle in Miami Beach, Florida. She was quite famous in Florida, and was part of Miami's in-crowd. The hipster Comic Lord Buckley befriended Dixie and called her Lady M. She used to take long walks on the beach with Buckley and his latest group of royal followers. Buckley was always dressed to the T's in his black tie and tails. He could be seen shuffling bare-foot across the hot sand, an entourage of his newly knighted Lords and Ladies behind him, all anxious to smoke their afternoon's high-tea. *I was with Dixie when she was interviewed for a documentary regarding Lord Buckley's time in Miami.*

After Marilyn died on August 5, 1962, Dixie's career as the Marilyn Monroe of Burlesque was over. She not only saw the end of the act that brought her fame, she was overcome with grief and guilt for having exploited Marilyn, who she loved and admired. At one point in 1958, Marilyn had considered filing a lawsuit against Dixie, but after Dixie toned down her act; Marilyn let the matter go.

Dixie tried several other routines but they never caught on, partly because she had become typecast. This caused her to go through a long period of depression. For a couple of years she ran a hotel on the island of Bimini in the Bahamas. She worked some small, unmemorable jobs and in her later years, Dixie was companion and caretaker for a succession of elderly well-to-do ladies.

Because of a series of coincidences and similarities, Dixie felt a strong connection to Marilyn Monroe. Both were born in 1926 in Los Angeles, and to name just a few more coincidences; they both grew up without a father figure, both worked in an aircraft factory in their teens, both started out as models, and they were the same height. Both were married to sports figures; both wore Channel No. 5; both of them favored Dom Perignon Champagne; both were natural brunettes, and both had a friendship with James Haspiel. Both Marilyn and Dixie worried about their lack of education. At the time when Marilyn's life ended, there was a film being developed for her titled *The Stripper*. Marilyn was to play the stripper. Oddly, Dixie's career as a stripper was over, just as Marilyn was about to portray one.

I shared a very eerie coincidence with Dixie that made her, my, and Jeannie Anderson's hair stand on end. In August of 1992, Jeannie Anderson and I took Dixie to Los Angeles to supposedly have lunch at the beach, but I was giving Dixie a surprise reading by my Astrologer of close to fifteen years. Dixie seemed somewhat fidgety that day, as if her thoughts were elsewhere. When we questioned her, she simply brushed it aside. After delivering Dixie to my Astrologers' apartment (I prefer she remain anonymous), we waited outside to give them privacy. Dixie wasn't inside more than fifteen minutes when she came rushing out the front door, white as a sheet. She was shaking so badly we had to help her into the car.

On the way back to the E.W. Ranch she slowly began to tell us what happened to her. She had told my Astrologer that she used to be the Marilyn Monroe of Burlesque and it so happened, my Astrologer had co-writ-

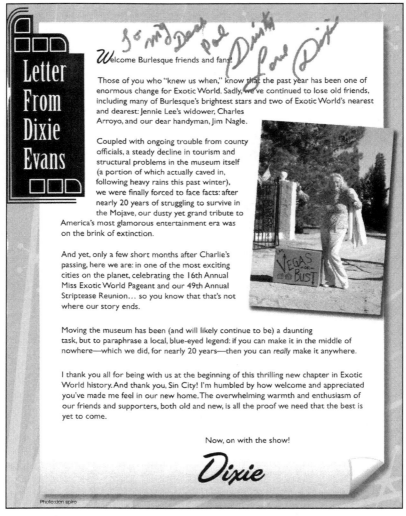

Letter From Dixie Evans

*W*elcome Burlesque friends and fans!

Those of you who "knew us when," know that the past year has been one of enormous change for Exotic World. Sadly, we've continued to lose old friends, including many of Burlesque's brightest stars and two of Exotic World's nearest and dearest: Jennie Lee's widower, Charles Arroyo, and our dear handyman, Jim Nagle.

Coupled with ongoing trouble from county officials, a steady decline in tourism and structural problems in the museum itself (a portion of which actually caved in, following heavy rains this past winter), we were finally forced to face facts: after nearly 20 years of struggling to survive in the Mojave, our dusty yet grand tribute to America's most glamorous entertainment era was on the brink of extinction.

And yet, only a few short months after Charlie's passing, here we are: in one of the most exciting cities on the planet, celebrating the 16th Annual Miss Exotic World Pageant and our 49th Annual Striptease Reunion... so you know that that's not where our story ends.

Moving the museum has been (and will likely continue to be) a daunting task, but to paraphrase a local, blue-eyed legend: if you can make it in the middle of nowhere—which we did, for nearly 20 years—then you can *really* make it anywhere.

I thank you all for being with us at the beginning of this thrilling new chapter in Exotic World history. And thank you, Sin City! I'm humbled by how welcome and appreciated you've made me feel in our new home. The overwhelming warmth and enthusiasm of our friends and supporters, both old and new, is all the proof we need that the best is yet to come.

Now, on with the show!

Dixie

Photo: don spiro

Dixie's open letter and picture of her move. Photo courtesy of Dixie Evans.

Dixie with Author, having some well-needed rest and relaxation in Stateline, Nevada (early 1990s). Photo courtesy of Authors Collection.

ten a book on Marilyn. In the conversation, Dixie learned the book was *Marilyn: The Last Months* and the other writer was the Astrologer's cousin Eunice Murray, who had been Marilyn's housekeeper when Marilyn died. It totally freaked Dixie out. *The worst part was, I knew about the Murray thing but had long forgotten it.* Dixie kept saying, "Don't you know what day this is?" We had no idea what she meant. Finally, she blurted out, "It's August 5th, the day Marilyn died."

In 2006, after nearly twenty years of tears, triumphs, and trophies, Exotic World in Helendale was coming to an end. Dixie sent me a copy of her open letter to the Press, explaining her decision to move everything to Las Vegas. I will share her letter with my readers.

Back in April of 1990, Dixie wrote me a letter just before she moved in to Exotic World. She writes of her age and the overwhelming task ahead, and her need to accomplish something. The letter ends with this statement; "Maybe some day soon. We will have something to celebrate." *Well, it's been a long, long celebration and I am very fortunate to have been a part of it.*

Until her death August 3, 2013, Dixie continued to be a part of The Las Vegas Museum and The Las Vegas Miss Exotic World Pageants. After her death, strippers all over the world donated money to have Dixie's ashes buried in Westwood Memorial Park where Marilyn Monroe is laid to rest.

I can't tell you what an honor it has been to share my experiences with all the wonderful, remarkable, and memorable people who lived in the real world of Burlesque. I hope this book will preserve the more personal part of Burly's folklore, and contribute to a better understanding of the people who were previously just a faded, jaded memory.

I'll leave you with pictures of two different generations of dancers representing a century of friendships, and one photo of me, when I was a topless and nude dancer.

Dixie's letter. Photo courtesy of Authors Collection.

I must accomplish something this time.
I havent discussed any type of arrangements with Charlie. yet.

I truley value Your friend-ship more than You can ever immagine.

Mabey some day soon We will have something to celebrate.

always

Dixie

Second part of Dixie's letter. Photo courtesy of Authors Collection.

Dixie visiting Marilyn Monroe's Crypt. Photo courtesy of Dixie Evans.

Dixie's ashes. Photo courtesy of Authors Collection.

Stacy Farrell and Betty Briggs, almost sixty years of friendship (Betty Rowlands Club 1995).
Photo courtesy of Betty Briggs.

Author and best dancing buddy Jan Grainger, almost fifty years of friendship (Exotic World). Jan died in 2012. I miss her everyday. Photo courtesy of Authors Collection.

Author with Cameraman shooting documentary at Exotic World Museum (2004). Photo courtesy of Authors Collection.

Chapter 12

EXTRA Added Attractions

NOEL TOY

The lovely and delicate Noel was born Ngun Yee on December 27, 1918, in San Francisco, California. She began dancing lessons at a young age, and later performed in San Francisco's Forbidden City nightclub for many years. It was there she became scandalously infamous for being the first Asian to bare her breasts in her version of the Fan Dance. She was fully nude in her Bubble Dance.

Her work at Forbidden City, which by the way, featured only the crème de la crème of Chinese performers, brought her to the attention of Hollywood's film makers. She not only exhibited her exquisite choreo-

Noel onstage. Photo courtesy of Authors Collection.

graphic agility, but her acting skills shined in many 1940 and 1950 movies. She went on to perform small roles in numerous television series including several episodes of *Mash*. In 1989, Noel was reunited with many of her fellow Forbidden performers in a PBS Documentary titled *Forbidden City, USA.*

Noel died at age eighty-four on December 27, 2003, in Hollywood, California. She was married for fifty years to prolific Actor Carleton Young, who saw her dance and instantly fell in love with her.

Noel and husband Carlton Young. Photo courtesy of Authors Collection.

A few other famous Asian ecdysiasts:

Jadine Wong. Photo courtesy of Authors Collection.

Barbara Yung. Photo courtesy of Authors Collection.

Ming Toi. Photo courtesy of Authors Collection.

ANN CORIO

And Her

"GIRLS IN BLUE"

With

CLYDE BATES

Theater program for Ann Corio's *Girls in Blue* Revue (1928).
Photo courtesy of Authors Collection.

Ann Corio at the movie studio where she filmed *Jungle Siren* and *Sarong Girl*. Photo courtesy of Authors Collection.

Ann Corio along with two service men in 1942. Photo courtesy of Authors Collection.

Lili St. Cyr and two Comedians at the El Rey Club with guest, First Lady Eleanor Roosevelt. Photo courtesy of Authors Collection.

Lili St. Cyr with Attorney Jerry Giesler at court hearing after her acquittal on charges of indecent exposure (1951). Photo courtesy of Authors Collection.

Lovely Jeannie Thompson who worked with both Sammy Davis Jr. and Black Comic Rozelle Gayle. Photo courtesy of Authors Collection.

Strippers arrested at the Jungle Club in Miami, Florida (1949).
Photo courtesy of Authors Collection.

Tina Martin. Photo courtesy of
Authors Collection.

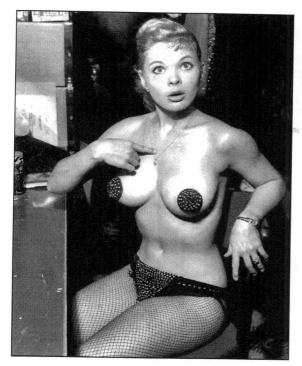

Adorable Candy Barr who shot her first husband, made an infamous porn film while still in her teens, dated mobster Mickey Cohn, befriended Jack Ruby, and went to prison for possession of Marijuana. Photo courtesy of Candy Barr.

Trudy Wayne. Photo courtesy of Dixie Evans.

Ad poster for the stripfilm *International Burlesque*. Photo courtesy of Authors Collection.

Gorgeous unknown stripper (1942). Photo courtesy of Authors Collection.

Lily Christine, was born Martha Theresa Pompender on December 17, 1923 in Dunkirk, New York. Her father was Italian and her mother was polish. She began dancing in 1948 and was featured for many years at Prima's 500 Club in New Orleans, Louisiana. Her stunning looks were shown on covers and in centerfolds of more than fifty Men's magazines. She had small uncredited parts in four different movies and tried out for the title role in the *Sheena* T.V. series, but the part went to Irish McCalla. Lilly lectured on physical fitness for several Universities. Lilly died of peritonitis on January 9,1965 in Broward County, Florida. She was only 41 years old and was still performing.

Stunning Lilly the Cat Girl, who was a yoga enthusiast and everyone's favorite fitness fanatic.
Photo courtesy of Authors Collection.

There were many famous Specialty Acts in Burlesque shows in the 1920s, 1930s, and 1940s. Among them were Revere and Roche with their elaborate costumes and creative routines. Here are photos of just three of their acts.

Revere and Roche in their playful Donkey Routine. Photo courtesy of Authors Collection.

Rare picture of naughty Hindu Wassau whose strap broke while performing, making her the first gal to strip onstage. Photo courtesy of Authors Collection.

Adorable Tai Ping. Photo courtesy of Authors Collection.

MARGIE HART

Margie Hart was born September 28, 1913, in Edgerton, Missouri. Her father was a farmer and she had six sisters and one brother, all living in a small farmhouse. At age sixteen, Margie, whose real name is Edna Margaret Bridget Cox, ran off to dance in a chorus line in Chicago, Illinois. It was then she began using her mother's maiden name, Hart.

Margie had beautiful titan-colored hair, and she was charming, competitive, and daring. She was a natural in the world of Burlesque and quickly became a featured dancer in the chorus line. She went on to become one of the most famous Burlesque Queens. Margie was also noted for being the first gal to remove her G-string and flash the audience. This

Margie Hart arrives on the Chief for her first look at Hollywood.
Photo courtesy of Authors Collection.

caused her arrest during Minsky's revue of *Wine, Women, and Song,* along with the entire cast, including Comic Jimmy Savo. At her arraignment, she performed that particular part of the play and the Judge dropped all charges.

Margie tried her hand at acting and starred in the 1942 film *Lure of the Islands;* and she was in a traveling production of *Cry Havoc.* She also tried her hand at writing, and for a short time wrote a small show-biz column called "My Night."

In 1942, Margie married prolific New York Screenwriter Semon Block Jacobs. He wrote for Red Skelton, Lucille Ball, and George Burns among many others, and too many television series to mention. They had one son. They later moved to Los Angeles and went through a messy divorce where Margie received a large settlement, which she invested in real estate and made a ton of money.

Margie's second husband was ex-football player and politician John Ferrara. They were married in 1982 and remained together until her death from a stroke in June 26, 2000.

Burlesque star Valerie Parks (1940s). Photo courtesy of Dixie Evans.

Burlesque star Joan Mavis (1940s).
Photo courtesy of Dixie Evans.

Burlesque star Carole Le Clair
(1940s). Photo courtesy of
Dixie Evans.

Burlesque star Nadine (1940s).
Photo courtesy of Dixie Evans.

Margie Kelly (1935). Photo
courtesy of Dixie Evans.

Myrna Dean (1940). Photo courtesy of Dixie Evans.

Collage of Burlesque ads from 1920s and 1930s. Photo courtesy of Authors Collection.

Betty Briggs, Stacy Farrell, Author, and sweet little Tai Ping at Betty Rowland's club (1995).
Photo courtesy of Authors Collection.

Carmela, the Sophia Loren
of Burlesque.
Photo courtesy of Carmela.

Rita Atlanta, "Miss International," who was also a Booking Agent for strippers. Photo courtesy of Dixie Evans.

Gorgeous Taffy O'Neill (1956). Photo courtesy of Tanayo.

Poster from *Kiss Me Baby* starring Taffy O'Neill (1957). Photo courtesy of Authors Collection.

Patty LaBelle and strippers Sheila Rae, Tanayo, Taffy O'Neill, and Stacy Farrell at Betty Rowland's club in Santa Monica, California (1996). Photo courtesy of Authors Collection.

Gloria Pall and Taffy O'Neill at Betty Rowland's club. Photo courtesy Authors Collection.

Burly dancer Cynthiana and Author at Betty Rowland's club.
Photo courtesy of Authors Collection.

Chorus girl in 1950. Photo courtesy of Dixie Evans.

Unknown chorus girls and M.C. at the Los Angeles Follies Theatre (1957).
Photo courtesy of Authors Collection.

Unknown stripper at the Los Angeles Follies Theatre (1957). Photo courtesy of Dixie Evans.

Star Markee, the "Cherokee Flash." Photo courtesy of Jennie Lee.

Stripper Do May on her horse at her ranch. Photo courtesy of Jennie Lee.

Gail Winds, the "Original Twister." Photo courtesy of Authors Collection.

Promotional headshot of Yvette Dare (1944). Photo courtesy of Authors Collection.

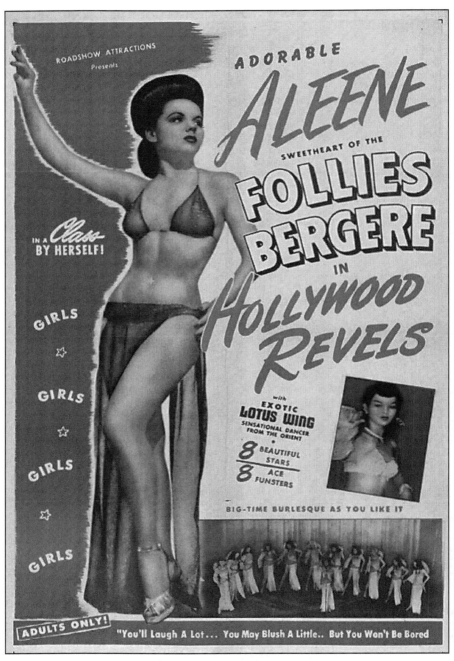

Poster ad starring Aleene in the Burly film *Hollywood Revels* (1948).
Photo courtesy of Authors Collection.

Lilly Christine the "Cat Girl" on cover of *Cabaret* (1955). Photo courtesy of Authors Collection.

Unknown 1930s stripper. Photo courtesy of Jennie Lee.

Bambi Vawn. Photo courtesy
of Yvette Paris.

Unknown Half-and-Half act.
Photo courtesy of Dixie Evans.

Gorgeous Lily St. Cyr. Photo Courtesy of Jennie Lee.

Rose La Rose's headstone. Photo courtesy of Ben Urish.

Comic Billy "Bumps" Mack's headstone. Photo courtesy of Authors Collection.

Las Vegas Revue *The Best in Burlesque* (1949). Photo courtesy of Jennie Lee.

More of 1949 Las Vegas Revue. Photo courtesy of Jennie Lee.

Final photo of 1949 Las Vegas Revue. Photo courtesy of Jennie Lee.

Ever-popular Hudson Theatre in
Union City, New Jersey (1952).
Photo courtesy of Jennie Lee.

The vivacious Dee Milo (1950s).
Photo courtesy of Dee Milo.

Jennie Lee doing a publicity stunt with whip expert Dave Kishman. The trick was to remove Jennie's clothes with his whip. Photo courtesy of Jennie Lee.

Pat Darling, who received Jennie Lee's Fanny Award. Photo courtesy of Jennie Lee.

Copy of Tempest Storm's El Rey Fan Club card. Photo courtesy of Authors Collection.

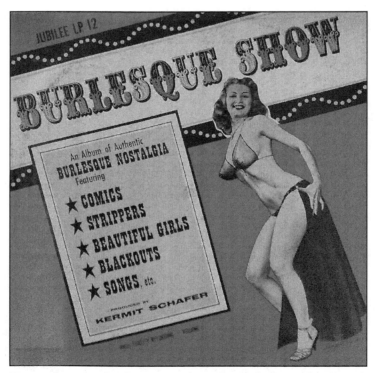

Tempest Storm on the album cover of a Burlesque show recording (1950s).
Photo courtesy of Authors Collection.

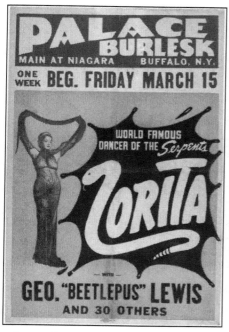

Poster of Zorita (1940). Photo courtesy of Authors Collection.

Program for the Old Howard Theatre starring Zorita (1939). Photo courtesy of Authors Collection.

Neo-Burlesque Star Dirty Martini in a tribute to Zorita. Martini won the 2004 Miss Exotic World Contest. (Photo by Neil Nez Kendall.) Photo courtesy of Dirty Martini.

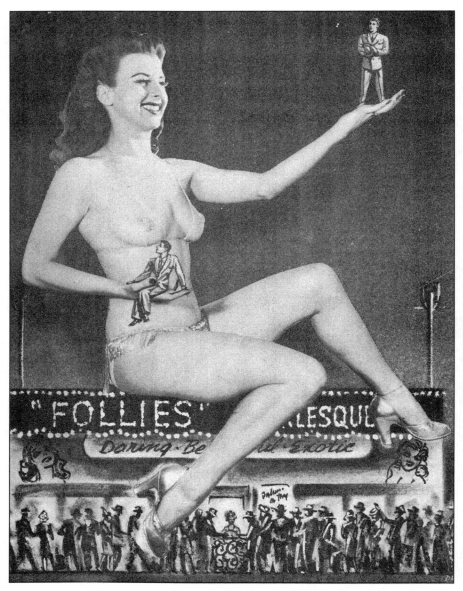

Cover of 1941 Los Angeles Follies Program. Cover girl is Scarlet Knight.
Photo courtesy of Authors Collection.

MORE MEMORABLE MENTIONS

Burlesque Comics often shared professions and billing with their siblings. A few comics were even father and son, the father usually coming into Burlesque straight out of Vaudeville. Similar situations have ap-

Joe "Rubber Face" Gallagher holding a picture of his Comic father, the "Bum" (1928). Photo courtesy of Authors Collection.

The Vaudeville "Bum" (1888). Photo courtesy of Authors Collection.

Dolly "Legs" O'Day in 1955.
Photo courtesy of Misty Knyte.

Misty Knyte, daughter of
Dolly O'Day. Misty worked
with snakes and danced
on broken glass. Photo
courtesy of Misty Knyte.

Stuttering Joe Frisco, Specialty Dancer and Burly Comic (1936). Photo courtesy of Authors Collection.

PROGRAM

Opening—Legs and Laughter	Denny Lyons and Ensemble
Ladies Love Brutes	Harry (Hello Jake), Fields, Lyons,
	Dorothy Wahl, Marian Wakefield
Good Old Swing	The Garden Girls
A Sparkling Flower	Dorothy Windsor
Ballet—Wysteria Time	Dorothy Wahl, Denny Lyons and Ensemble
Three Loose Nuts	Al Rio, Bob Alda, Denny Lyons
Saucy	Marion Wakefield
Beautiful Babies	Baby Dotty and Our Kindergarten
Who's Crazy	Hank Henry, Marion Wakefield and Bob Alda
Sirens of Paris	Billy Branch and Company
A Little Temptress	Pat Paree
Fresh from College	Harry Fields and Denny Lyons
In the Garden of Eden	Daughters of Eve
Seqno—The Maiden and The Serpent	Zorita
Headed for Hollywood	Bob Alda and the Two Stooges
Moanin' Low	Hank Henry, Al Rio, Bob Alda, Marian Wakefield
Venus with Charms	Maxine Deshone
Finale—With Memories	The Gay 90's Quartette and Entire Co.
Perfect Balance	Goodrich and Nelson
Opening—Beauty and the Beast	Our Circus Maids
Sweet and Pert	Marion Wakefield
The Argument	Al Rio, Dorothy Wahl, Denny Lyons
Don't I Know?	Pat Paree
The Model Beautiful	Hank Henry, Al Rio, Bob Alda, Denny Lyons
Ballet—Reflections	Maxine Deshone
Along the Volga	Dorothy Wahl, Drake, Lyons and Ensemble
Daring and Howl	Harry Fields, Alda, Wahl, Lyons, Wakefield
Finale—Out of the Night	Zorita
	The Entire Company

ON THE SCREEN

THREE CHEERS FOR THE IRISH	Priscilla Lane, Tom Mitchell
THE QUARTERBACK	Wayne Morris
Comedy — News	

★ ★ COMING ATTRACTIONS ★ ★

BILLY AINSLEY	Week of Mar. 24
GEORGIA SOTHERN	Week of Mar. 24
CHAS. KEMPER	Week of Mar. 31
DICK RICHARDS	Week of Mar. 31
MARIAN MILLER	Week of Mar. 31
MARY LANE	Week of April 7
VALERIE PARKS	Week of April 14
JEAN MODE	Week of April 21

Old Howard Theatre program with Comic Hank Henry and Straight Man/Singer Robert Alda (1940). Photo courtesy of Authors Collection.

Straight Man/Singer/Actor Robert Alda, wife Joan, and their son Alan Alda at an amusement park. Photo courtesy of Authors Collection.

Jack Carson and Comic Hank Henry acting as Best Man for Robert Alda's second marriage to Italian Actress Flora Marino (Las Vegas 1957). Photo courtesy of Authors Collection.

Comic Mike Sachs and his wife and Straight Woman Alice Kennedy. Photo courtesy of Authors Collection.

Hollywood Playhouse ad for Minsky's Revue (1936). Photo courtesy of Authors Collection.

plied to the strippers and talking women. Mothers and daughters have been known to share the same stage.

When members of Billy Minsky's troupe arrived in Los Angeles on August 12, 1936, they were given a police escort to The Hollywood Playhouse. Ten days later, after a raid on the Playhouse resulted in the arrest of nine

Three members of Billy Minsky's Troupe being booked in Los Angeles, California (1936). Left to right: Marie Voe, Alice Kennedy, and Dagmar. Photo courtesy of Authors Collection.

Program for Pittsburgh, Pennsylvania's Variety Theatre, featuring Comic Attractions Steve Mills, Herbie Faye, Murray Lewis, and Sid Stone. Coming Comic Attractions are: Shorty McAllister, Harry "Katz" Fields, Charles "Red" Marshall, and Murray Leonard (1935). Photo courtesy of Authors Collection.

Program for The Kansas City Missouri Gayety Theatre's Twenty-Five Years of Columbia Burlesque (1925). Photo courtesy of Authors Collection.

GAYETY
THEATRE
KANSAS CITY, MISSOURI

M. T. MIDDLETON
Manager

FRED. WALDMAN
Treasurer

ANNIVERSARY
25th YEAR OF
COLUMBIA
BURLESQUE

Week of Feb 8, 1925

OUR HONOR ROLL

OUR ROLL OF HONOR

Al Jolson, Leon Errol, Gallagher and Shean, Sam Bernard, Weber and Fields, Grace LaRue, Dorothy Jardon, Belle Baker, Emma Carus, Will Rogers, George Beban, Harry von Tilzer, Charlotte Greenwood, Mack Sennett, Eddie Cantor, Billy Van, Fanny Brice, Sophie Tucker, Howard Brothers, Fred Stone, Alex Carr, George Sidney, Clark and McCullough, Doyle and Dixon, Watson Sisters, Rosco Ails, Bert Baker, Lester Allen, Jim Barton.

————o————

Have we not reason to be proud of our accomplishments of the past quarter of a century? Some of the original promoters are dead. Others have acquired a sheen of silvery locks, while others have retired to make way for the younger generation of producers and managers, though the same old wheel will turn and others of our present list of performers will win stellar honors and take their places with the great array of Broadway stars listed above.

Inside of 1925 Gayety Program, listing the appearance of it's famous past Burlesque stars. Photo courtesy of Authors Collection.

dancers and four Comics on charges of participating in an indecent show, the police again escorted the troupe. This time it was to the outskirts of town.

Starting in the early 1940s, many lavish Burlesque revues endeavored to capture the flavor of true Burlesque. Producer Mike Todd had a finger on its pulse with his extravagant Revue, *Star and Garter*, which began June 24, 1942.

During it's first few years, *Star and Garter* starred Comic Bobby Clark sharing yucks with old-time Comic Joe Lyons. By 1944, vintage Comedian Willie Howard replaced Clark who went into Todd's' *Mexican Hayride* Revue; and seasoned Comic Jack Coyle stood in for Joe Lyons. During the shows complete run, it featured Gypsy Rose Lee, Georgia Sothern,

Bobby Clark on 1944 program cover for *Mexican Hayride*.
Photo courtesy of Authors Collection.

Cover of 1944 *Star and Garter* Program.
Photo courtesy of Authors Collection.

Comic Willie Howard and two
showgirls in the 1944 *Star and
Garter* Revue. Photo courtesy
of Authors Collection.

Carrie Finnell, and Rosita Royce. It was a smash hit, playing nightly to a packed theater that ran for 609 performances.

Beginning in 1963, Danny Thomas dug up his Burlesque roots for a television special, which was comprised of four editions and was called *The Wonderful World of Burlesque*. The show was chock-full of guest stars who all wanted to get-in-the-act. The farcical skits, fabulous chorines, and watching well-known stars poke fun at themselves made this show a hit at a time when Burlesque was on the wane.

Some of the shows participants were: ladies first; Shirley Jones, Lee Remick, Edie Adams, Cyd Charisse, Nanette Fabray, and Carol Channing. Lucille Balls outrageously funny butterfly dance was a hilarious show-stopper. Some of the funny men were: Mickey Rooney, Phil Silvers, Jack Benny, Carl Reiner, Jerry Lewis, Don Knotts and Andy Griffith, Jim Na-

Danny Thomas and Jerry Lewis in the *Wonderful World of Burlesque*.
Photo courtesy of Authors Collection.

bors, Dean Martin, Frank Sinatra, and Sheldon Leonard. Even Tennessee Ernie Ford and Wayne Newton jumped on-board for a riotous ride.

Then there was the unforgettable *Sugar Babies*, the Burlesque musical that ran from October 9, 1979 to August 28, 1982 with 1,208 performances. The show had it all; it was fast, feisty, fun, and starred long-limbed Ann Miller with short-limbed Mickey Rooney at his show-biz best. Other comics were Sid Stone, Jimmy Mathews, Tom Boyd and Jack

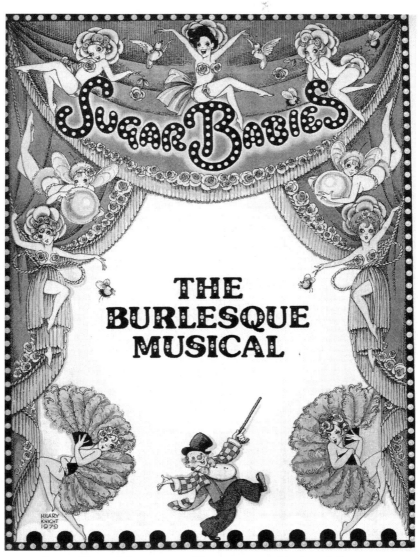

Cover of *Sugar Babies* program. Photo courtesy of Authors Collection.

Cover of *This Was Burlesque*. Photo courtesy of Authors Collection.

Fletcher. Dancer/Straight Woman Ann Jillian was a standout. Later in the shows run, leggy and lovely Juliet Prowse took Ann Millers role.

Ann Corio's *This Was Burlesque* was really the quintessential nostalgic Burlesque show. It was true to its source in every way. Its stars were the real-deal. Some had been in The Biz since Burlesques beginnings. Corio's show brought Burlesque back to basics and gave us a last look at Burlys long-lost laugh factory. It revisited the innocence of an era and the impact it left on the history of a really bare, bawdy-naughty Burlesque. It was, in essence, like stepping back into the Burly theaters of the 1920s, 1930s, and the 1940s.

Ann's lovable revue began sometime in 1961, and ran in varied versions for close to thirty years. Her last performance was in Florida in 1991. It was a theatrical phenomenon. Corio's 1968 book *This Was Burlesque*, is a pictorial history of not only her revue, but the history of Burlesque itself, and is a real collectors item. Ann also made two record albums called *How To Strip For Your Husband*.

I tried to interview Ann Corio in 1995, and Ann's husband Michael Iannucci answered the phone. He was cordial to me and explained that Ann's condition was one of constant change in the midst of having Alzheimer's disease, and it wouldn't be fair to subject her to an interview. He talked to me for a while and wished me luck with my book. Ann Corio was ill for several years and left us on March 1, 1999. She was in her eighties.

In 2015, I made contact with relatives of two Burlesque dancers who were roommates and best friends of Ann Corio in the 1920s. Through this

Ann Corio around 1926. Photo courtesy of Leslie Redpath.

Ann Corio's autographed photo to Ethel and Jennette with letter on back (1928). Photo courtesy of Leslie Redpath.

Letter on back of Corio's 1928 picture. Photo courtesy of Leslie Redpath.

Ethel McGregor, Burlesque dancer in the 1930s. Photo courtesy of Leslie Redpath.

Ethel McGregor's husband, Burlesque Comic Charlie Harris (1930). Photo courtesy of Leslie Redpath.

Publicity photo of Jennette in the 1920s. Photo courtesy of Leslie Redpath.

Burlesque dancer named Irene, who worked with Corio in the 1930s. Photo courtesy of Leslie Redpath.

Ann Corio starting to make films (1939).
Photo courtesy of Leslie Redpath.

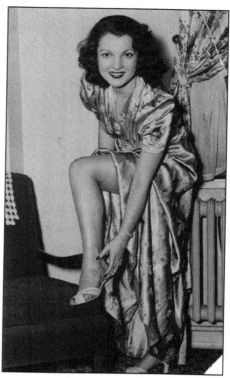

Ann Corio and all-time Top
Banana since 1924, Steve Mills.
Photo courtesy of Jennie Lee.

contact I acquired some extremely rare photos of Corio along with her Burly buddies Ethel and Jennette McGregor, when they first began working in Burlesque chorus-lines.

Harry Ryan, who was Irving Bensons Straight Man for over a decade; Helen Levitt; and the Comic's favorite Comic, Claude Mathis. Photo courtesy of Jennie Lee.

Harry Conley one of the greatest, and the Burly Cuties. Photo courtesy of Jennie Lee.

Seasoned Comic Maxie Furman and the Burly Cuties. Photo courtesy of Jennie Lee.

Ann Corio and Actor/Comic Jerry Lester in a promotional photo. Photo courtesy of Authors Collection.

Cover of rare 1934 program for Minsky's New York Apollo Theatre. Top left is Georgia Sothern, top right is Gypsy Rose Lee before she wore her hair pulled back, and lower right is pretty June St.Clair, who committed suicide at age thirty-five. Photo courtesy of Authors Collection.

Inside of Apollo Program listing the players and acts; including Jess Mack, Mike Sachs, Alice Kennedy, and Steve Mills. Photo courtesy of Authors Collection.

1946 poster advertising Georgia Sothern. Photo courtesy of Authors Collection.

Comic Jack "Check" Hayes who began his Burly career in 1932.
Photo courtesy of Authors Collection.

I was lucky to learn that Ann had generously given Jennie Lee some promotional pictures of her revue, and Jennie shared them with me for this book. I am now sharing them with all of you readers.

Looking at this program gives some insight into the length of time some of the really big Burlesque Queens spent in the spotlight. It also highlights the endurance required of the Burly Comics to remain on the theaters marquee. The Apollo Theatre opened at nine-thirty in the morning and showed continuous performances up until eleven in the evening; plus, a midnight show on Saturday. All that work onstage and waiting to go on in-between must have been grueling. Not only that, there was a new show starting every Friday, which meant that the chorus girls who preferred to wear more, and make less, had to find time to rehearse and be fitted for the next weeks show. The admission price was 25-cents, 35-cents, and the front row seats went for a whopping 50-cent ticket.

In the 1934 Apollo Program, Gypsy and Georgia were working together for the first time. They had both already established themselves as Headliners. There was never any type of competitiveness with these two; their routines and styles were totally different. After all, there is only one Gypsy Rose Lee and only one Georgia Sothern. They remained close gal-pals, and a decade later they were both featured in 1944s long-running *Star and Garter*.

The lights have flickered and faded on the stages of Minsky's and other marvelous theaters where the thundering applause can no longer be heard. Forever may its memories linger, reminding us of the grand old days when Burlesque still meant "Girls, Gimmicks and Gags," and the label read "Made in the U.S.A."

Let's all raise our glasses and tip a toast to Burlesque—Bottoms Up!

It's Curtain Call ~ that's all she wrote, Folks! Photo courtesy of Authors Collection.

Made in the USA
Charleston, SC
20 June 2016